Dr. Michael S. Gerber received his BA degr
York and MA and PhD degrees from New
has worked in some of the poorest countrie
1998 as Director General of AMREF
Foundation) and its well-known Flying D
received a Fulbright award to study in India, then served, with his family, as a
U.S. Peace Corps volunteer on the faculty of Bicol University in the
Philippines. He has held voluntary positions on numerous non-governmental
and international organization Boards and is currently Chairman of IIRR
(International Institute of Rural Reconstruction) with its headquarters in
Silang, Philippines. He lives with his wife in Portimao, Portugal.

SWEET TEETH AND LOOSE BOWELS

THE ADVENTURES OF AN INTERNATIONAL AID WORKER

Michael S. Gerber

*t*₂

Troubador Publishing Ltd
9 De Montfort Mews
Leicester LE1 7FW, UK
Tel: (+44) 116 255 9311
Email: books@troubador.co.uk
Web: www.troubador.co.uk

ISBN 978-1905886-463

Cover photo courtesy of the African Medical and Research Foundation (AMREF)

Typeset in 11pt Times New Roman by Troubador Publishing Ltd, Leicester, UK
Printed by The Cromwell Press Ltd, Trowbridge, Wilts

t² is an imprint of Troubador Publishing Ltd

For Ina

CONTENTS

Author's Note   ix
Preface   xi

BOOK ONE
YOUTHFUL IDEALISM: THE PEACE CORPS YEARS

1   The Chicken Expert   3
2   Peace Corps – The Beginning   9
3   The Invitation   13
4   Training – San Jose, California   17
5   Training – In Country   19
6   The Philippines   27
7   A Peace Corps Family Copes   31
8   Transportation And Travel   37
9   Doggie, Doggie... Where Are Ye?   41
10   Religion Number One   45
11   Religion Number Two   49
12   Our Old Friends – The Peace Corps Organization   53
13   Research And Politics   57
14   The End Game – A Death In The Family
        And Getting Out   63
15   The Long Way Home   69

BOOK TWO
MAKING OF A SKEPTIC: THE AFRICAN YEARS

16   The Next Life: First Stop India   77
17   Who Turned Out The Lights?   85
18   Hello Africa   87
19   Welcome To The NGO World   91

20	Transportation And Travel – Act II	95
21	The Sudan – Never A Dull Moment	99
22	How the Other Half of 1/10th of 1% Lives	105
23	What Are Those Big Birds Doing? Africa Through A Youngster's Eyes	117
24	Was *Catch 22* A Novel About Somalia?	121
25	A Country That Is Not A Country	127
26	Travel – Act III	137
27	Kenya And Tea Money: Corruption Small And Large	143
28	Airplanes Big and Not So Big	151
29	The Flying Doctors – Emergency Evacuations	159
30	A Value Structure For African Management	165
31	The Burdens Of A Chief	171
32	Sabotage	179
33	Management And Time	185
34	Sweet Teeth And Loose Bowels	189
35	Dealing With Government	193
36	Through Whose Eyes?	201
37	Making A Difference	211
38	A Violent And Sad Goodbye	223

BOOK THREE
THE "BUSINESS" OF DEVELOPMENT: THE ACTORS AND THE ISSUES

39	The Cast Of Characters	237
40	God Will Provide Or If Not, Then Marie Antoinette	245
41	The Vulture Culture	251
42	The Development Business	255
43	Working Oneself Out Of Existence	259
44	Mr. Bono and Mr. Geldof – Good Try But. …	267
45	The End	273
46	Postscript	277

AUTHOR'S NOTE

Authors frequently begin their acknowledgments by expressing thanks to many individuals who had an impact on their lives and writing. I want to begin by recognizing three organizations that in essence, made what you will read in all of the following pages possible. First, there was the United States Peace Corps, whose professionalism could often be questioned during the time of our association, but it nevertheless gave my family an opportunity for three years of total immersion in a country we came to love – the Philippines. Secondly, AMREF or the African Medical and Research Foundation, provided the chance to really know and appreciate a continent whose fascination can only be matched by its great needs. And lastly, IIRR, the International Institute of Rural Reconstruction, whose Board of Trustees in a moment of madness, elected me Chairman, which has allowed my continued involvement with both Asia and Africa.

In reading, you will find that not everything was completely rosy during the time of my involvement with the above-mentioned groups, especially Peace Corps. There were definite ups and downs, and as in marriage we were joined for periods of time, as the saying goes, "For Better Or For Worse." At least it wasn't "Until Death Do Us Part." I am still writing.

Over the past thirty-nine years of living and working in Africa, Asia, Europe, and the United States, many people influenced my work and directly or indirectly, contributed to the production of this book. Without them, there could not have been the stories you will read about in the following pages. Though in numerous cases, while their names have been altered, hopefully they will be able to recognize who they are. In some other instances, with a bit of good fortune on my part, they will not be able to do so.

One can be considered lucky if in a lifetime, there is one extra special person who shares the same values, the longing for adventure, the ability not to take oneself too seriously, and the perseverance to put up with me. That singular person is my wife Ina who for the past forty-four years has been able to bear the burden of my wanderlust and was almost always willing to share many of the "adventures" described in this book. Without her love and companionship, patience, sharp eyes, and critical judgment, this enterprise would not have been possible. To Ina I can only say: Salamat Po; Mabalos; Asante Sana; Obrigado; Thank You.

Portimao, Portugal
January 2007

PREFACE

One day, some twenty-five years ago, my youngest son who was eleven at the time, asked me, "Dad, what do you do?"

I responded with, "What do you mean by that question?"

"Like when my friends ask me what does your father do, what should I tell them? What is your job?"

I then went into a rather lengthy explanation of what it entailed to be the head of a Non-Governmental Organization (NGO) that works with and tries to help poor people in Africa.

"Where does the money come to pay you?" he wanted to know.

"One of the most important parts of my job is to help raise all the money we need to do the work in Africa and also to pay me and other people who are employed by the organization. I spend a great deal of my time trying to raise money."

"Now I understand your job. I can just tell my friends you are a 'professional beggar.' "

At that time, the boy was able to describe what his father did in simple terms that his friends could understand. Had he been born twenty years later and asked that same question, he would have answered, "My father is an 'Aid Worker,' whatever that means." I, however, preferred to characterize my job somewhat less simply.

For nearly forty years, my professional life has taken me to some of the world's poorest nations, from India and the Philippines in Asia, to Kenya, Somalia, Sudan, Ethiopia, Rwanda, and other countries in Africa. I have worked extensively as a salaried employee and as a volunteer on both continents. While great physical beauty, fascinating history, wonderful people, and interesting cultures can be found in each country mentioned in this book, most of them would probably not be voted as top choices to live in by the average westerner.

I have had a truly fortunate and peripatetic life, which has been shared with my wife of forty-four years and with our three sons while they were growing up. There are strong memories of adventures and experiences from both Asia and Africa. Some of these one wants never to forget. Others I have tried to wipe from the conscious part of the mind, usually without success.

My job, at times, involved meeting with Presidents, Kings, Queens, Princes (Royal and of the corporate world), Princesses, Prime Ministers, Maharajas and Maharanis, and prominent world leaders. This book, however, is not about any of these famous people. It is about the average and the exceptional, about some enormously rich and some extremely poor, about many who have crossed my path and either enriched my life or made it more difficult. The individuals described, whether Asian, African, European, or North American, are for the most part, not household names.

Although witnessing a number of horrific disasters, some brought about by natural causes and others instigated by man doing harm to his fellow man, I have also observed great courage, dignity, and generosity by people who struggled to survive day after day. Early on, I realized that balance, perspective, and humour were the keys to maintaining a calm state of mind. One must be able to balance great tragedies and human cruelty with wonderful success stories and maintain compassion without becoming emotionally wiped out. One must be able to come face to face with the extreme poverty of many in Asia, with hardships in refugee camps of Africa, with genocide in Rwanda, and continue to work with people so their lives and those of their children will become better.

Realizing that a balance was needed happened on my first trip to India in 1969. Arriving in Calcutta at about five o'clock in the morning, I was too excited to sleep and went out for a walk at first light. The streets were already teeming with people. On the Howrah Bridge, which crossed the Hooghly River, a group of people were gathered in a circle. A woman was sitting on the pavement with a straw mat in front of her. On the mat was a dead infant. People were tossing coins onto the mat. The baby was too young to be cremated in the Hindu tradition so money was being collected for its burial.

That was my introduction to Calcutta. It had an immediate and profound effect. As the years went by, such sights became all too familiar. By the second, third, or fourth time, the shock wears off. Because similar scenes are all too common, as time passed it became too easy to keep on walking without stopping to pause. And that is the danger, taking so much for granted that one's compassion moves into a subconscious level. The true test for maintaining balance is never allowing for a loss of compassion while recognizing that it is not possible to change the whole world at once.

Looking at the humorous side of things is also a wonderful tool for maintaining perspective. And life fortunately allows such opportunities. My career began with the situation of the dead infant in Calcutta and its emotional toll. As it was about to end with retirement towards the end of 1998, a less stressful incident allowed for a different kind of memory. The NGO I headed was sponsoring an important conference on Health Issues in Africa. It was being held in one of Europe's major capitals. A prominent member of that country's royal family was the Patron of the NGO. This royal person agreed to make an appearance at our conference to greet the participants, many who had come from Africa.

The venue of the meeting was in a former palace, an elaborate and ornate building. We were told that the royal would come for exactly one hour, arriving at 1:00 pm and departing sharply at 2:00. Lunch was scheduled for that time and it was to be served in the main reception hall. It was not a sit down lunch. Waiters would bring around finger food on trays and the conference participants would stand around chatting informally. The royal wanted to walk around the room greeting and speaking with small groups of people.

We made sure the morning's session ended promptly at 12:45 pm so the participants could be ushered into the reception hall and be ready for the royal's entrance. One o'clock came with the guest of honour not appearing. By ten past one, the Chairman of our NGO was becoming panicky and quietly asked me to call people to attention and address the group in order to kill time. This was done by introducing remarks with the comment that I was the opening act for royalty that was to follow. Then about five minutes into this ad-libbed speech, we heard a loud noise outside, sounding like an explosion. Everyone froze, I stopped speaking, and we were all wondering what had happened. Almost immediately after the noise, in came the royal person as if nothing had happened and very gracefully began making the rounds in the room, greeting each participant. The luncheon proved most pleasant and the royal thanked us for the invitation, leaving promptly at two for another engagement.

It was only after the guest left that we discovered what had happened. It seemed that the royal's security detail came to the palace thirty minutes prior to the scheduled arrival time. They did a security check of the area outside the building in order to account for all vehicles that were parked nearby. They were able to establish the ownership of each with the exception of one motorbike. It turned out that determining who owned the motorbike was just not possible. So rather than take any chances with security, the royal's bodyguards cordoned off the area to keep away the public and then blew up the motorbike, hence the noise of the explosion we heard inside the reception hall. As soon as the bike was destroyed, the royal was given the all-clear signal, and in he came. It didn't take a lot of imagination to picture the look on some poor messenger's face when after delivering whatever package he had been entrusted with, he discovered that his bike had been blown to bits by the royal's security detail. The exploding bike became one of my last working memories.

To function in environments where there is great need, keeping a balance is easier when one follows a course of "pragmatic idealism." A sense of doing well in one's job must be measured in finite ways. There is a tendency to initially set large, often unrealistic goals. But as experience is gained, targets often become more reasonable. My first teaching job proved this to be the case. At the start of the school year I was determined to have an impact on 100 per cent of my students. By the second year, the realization quickly set in that the first goal was unachievable. So the goal was lowered. By the fourth year, I was hoping for a serious influence on 10 per cent. Eventually, one became aware that as a teacher, if you could positively impact the lives of one or two young people each year, then your job was worth doing. When committing to a professional career of working with those who were seriously underprivileged, a sense of pragmatism is absolutely necessary.

A wise man, or perhaps it was a wise woman, once said: "Take everyone whom you meet very seriously. Take yourself less so." I have always placed great store in being able to laugh at myself and to laugh with others, not at them. This book is meant to share an observer's and participant's viewpoint and personal insights with those curious about a life spent overseas in poor but interesting countries. It is often anecdotal. And it endeavours to look not only at the serious but at the humorous sides of such a life as well. For without humour, it becomes impossible to cope with the emotional roller coaster one is constantly exposed to. All the included tales should provide evidence of my transition from an energetic and idealistic volunteer with a young family living on practically a pittance in the Philippines to the Chief Executive of a large, well respected African NGO – a transition that also encompassed a shift from youthful "do gooder" to mature "development veteran."

While impossible to completely steer clear of dealing with history and politics, I have tried to avoid lengthy discussions of these subjects. There has been little attempt to provide an academic or analytical treatise about foreign aid and international events, except when necessary as background information to understand a situation being described.

The United States Peace Corps figures prominently in the book's first part. While a number of comments will appear highly critical of Peace Corps as an organization, they were, in my opinion, applicable during the time of our involvement in a special family volunteer programme, from 1969 through 1973. Having little contact with the Peace Corps since our service as volunteers ended, I would hope that the policies criticised in these pages have either been eliminated or changed for the better.

Numerous people are referred to in this book. In certain circumstances and stories, actual names have been used. In others, names have been changed to avoid embarrassment, embarrassment for either the person being mentioned or for me.

BOOK ONE

YOUTHFUL IDEALISM: THE PEACE CORPS YEARS

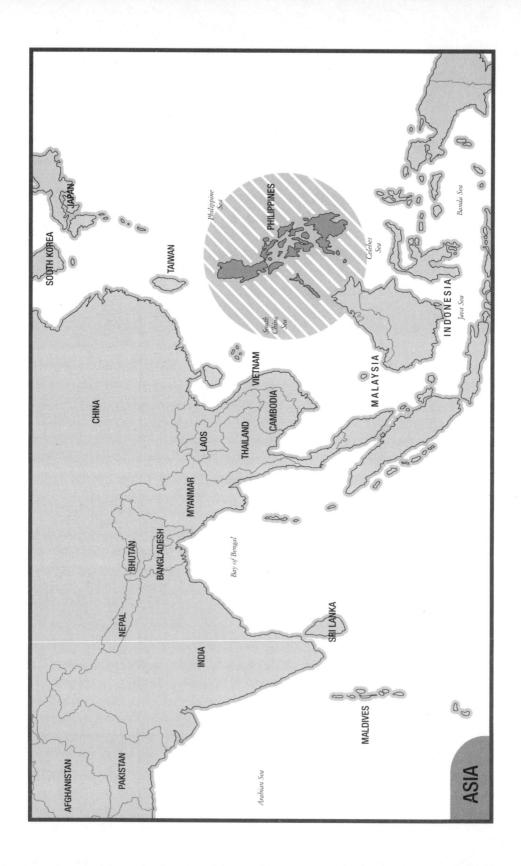

CHAPTER 1

THE CHICKEN EXPERT

One morning, at the offices of the Food and Agricultural Organization (FAO) in Addis Ababa, the capital of Ethiopia, staff received a request from Ethiopia's Ministry of Agriculture. The FAO is a United Nations agency. With headquarters in Rome, Italy, it has offices in many African and Asian countries. In its request to FAO, the Ethiopian Ministry of Agriculture wrote:

> "We have an important income-earning project in the Sidamo region of southern Ethiopia. Our Ministry is helping a large farmers' group to develop a profit-making poultry project. In recent weeks, a number of hens have died and egg production has severely decreased. Unfortunately, neither the farmers nor we have the type of technical expertise needed to solve the problem. Since FAO is the U.N. organ skilled in agricultural development, we are requesting your agency to provide a knowledgeable specialist who would be able to advise the farmers and help increase production."

The FAO office in Addis Ababa did not have anyone on staff who could immediately help the farmers' group. They therefore made a request to headquarters in Rome, urging that a poultry expert be dispatched to Ethiopia immediately.

A highly placed senior chap, who had spent many years within the FAO system in Rome, was asked to take up the assignment. Upon hearing that the request had come from Ethiopia, he reluctantly agreed and only after much persuasion. Taking everything into account, Addis Ababa was not particularly appealing when compared with Rome.

The expert flew to Ethiopia and was met at the airport by an FAO driver.

3

Showing much deference to this senior specialist from Rome, the driver took him to the new Addis Sheraton Hotel, where room rates started at over £130 a day. Following a good night's sleep in splendid luxury, the expert was picked up in the morning and brought to the FAO office. By now his spirits had lifted considerably. After all, spending ten days to two weeks in the comfort of the five star Addis Sheraton Hotel wouldn't cause undue hardship.

Upon reaching the FAO office, to the expert's great surprise, he was informed that the assignment was not in Addis Ababa but in the Sidamo region to the south.

"Well then, book me on a flight tomorrow," commanded the expert.

"Sorry, but there are no flights to that area," replied the FAO Addis boss.

"Then how do I get there?"

"We will provide a driver and an air-conditioned vehicle."

The expert nodded. "And how long by road to the project site?"

"Oh, about twelve hours."

"Twelve hours!" exclaimed the expert. "Twelve hours in a car?"

"Yes, and sadly, the road is quite rough for the second half of the trip."

Returning to the Sheraton, the FAO Rome expert spent a fitful night, unable to sleep, even in the comfort of five star luxury. All he could think of was the anticipated discomfort during the trip ahead.

At seven o'clock the following morning, bright and sharp, the FAO driver picked up the expert and they headed south. By about four that afternoon, they had travelled over many miles of rough roads, and still they appeared to be literally in the middle of nowhere. The expert was irritable and weary from his sleepless night, and was about to complain when smoke began rising from the vehicle's engine. The driver pulled over, opened the hood, and stuck his head underneath for an inspection.

"Sorry sir, but the vehicle has a serious problem. I can fix it, but we will not be able to continue until tomorrow morning."

"Tomorrow morning?" shouted the expert. "What will I do until then? Where will I sleep tonight?"

"Sorry sir, I am not exactly sure."

"Okay, then tell me how I get to the nearest Sheraton Hotel."

"Sorry sir, no Sheraton."

"The Hilton then."

"Sorry sir, no Hilton."

"A Holiday Inn?"

"Sorry, no hotels within fifty kilometres."

"You don't expect me to sleep out here in the bush, do you?"

Thinking the situation over at great length, the driver finally responded,

"No sir. Down the road, about one kilometre, there is an especially nice house. It is owned by a wealthy widow. Her husband died five years ago and now she lives alone. The house will be comfortable for you and the widow will surely give you lodging for the night."

With little alternative, the FAO expert started walking down the road. Sure enough, after about one kilometre, he came to a solid cement house, which stood out in marked contrast to the local mud and thatched huts of the general population. Up to the door he went and knocked. The door opened and he was greeted by a quite attractive woman who appeared to be in her early forties.

"Good afternoon, ma'am. I am an expert from the Food and Agricultural Organization's headquarters in Rome. We are on a mission to a project further south and our vehicle just broke down. The driver will not be able to repair it until tomorrow morning. I need a place to sleep tonight and if you will be so kind to accommodate me, I can pay for my room and board."

The widow, having lived alone for the past five years, eyed this foreign gentleman with great interest and anticipation. Having a male guest seemed quite appealing after being without company for so long. She invited him in gladly, insisting that he was a guest in Ethiopia and needn't pay her anything.

"My dear man, you must be so thirsty after such a long drive and walk. Please sit down and I'll bring you a nice cold drink."

Bringing her guest a tall, icy drink, she then excused herself for a few minutes. She returned dressed in her finest attire, with hair beautifully combed.

"I imagine you must be very hungry after that long journey from Addis. Let me prepare you some food."

"Some" food turned out to be a sumptuous Ethiopian feast with meat, vegetables, and potatoes served over Injera, the pancake-like staple food made from the grain Tef. The FAO expert, famished from the trip, tore into the food as though it were his last meal.

After dinner, the widow told the expert to follow her. She opened the door to a bedroom in which there was a large double bed.

"I have only one bedroom in this house and only one bed. But as you can see, the bed is very large. It can easily accommodate two people. I don't mind sharing my bed with you and I promise, you'll have a pleasantly comfortable and enjoyable night."

A more direct offer to the FAO expert was impossible. Eagerly awaiting his response, the widow was astonished to hear,

"Your bedroom is really nice and your bed looks accommodating, but I would prefer to sleep in the living room on the couch."

Disbelieving her ears, the widow looked at the FAO expert as if he were from Mars. "What kind of man is this?" she thought. Without another word, she angrily slammed her bedroom door shut, leaving him standing alone in the living room.

The next morning, a car pulled up to the widow's house. The FAO driver, having repaired the vehicle, was there to pick up his charge.

"Ready to go, sir?" called the driver.

"I'll be right out."

As he was leaving the house, the FAO expert tried to thank the widow for her hospitality. She returned his words with only silence and an icy stare. Moving toward the car, he noticed a number of cocks and hens off to one side of the house. His interest piqued.

"Ma'am, I am an FAO poultry expert. Do you mind if I look at your poultry farm?"

Without waiting for an answer, he marched over to the chickens. The widow followed right behind.

The expert stood for a few minutes counting all the poultry. After noting precisely one hundred cocks and exactly the same number of hens, he turned to the widow and said,

"What you are doing here is not correct. I am the FAO expert. We strongly recommend that for each ten hens, you should only have one cock to cover them. For your one hundred hens, you only need ten cocks. But you have one hundred hens and one hundred cocks. That's ninety cocks too many."

The widow listened with an expressionless face. After a moment of silence, she said,

"Mr. Big FAO expert, I actually have only ten cocks. What you don't know Mr. Expert is that the other ninety cocks are FAO experts just like you – just like you, they cannot perform."

*　　*　　*

A good Ethiopian friend related this story to me. Whether true or not, it nicely illustrates attitudes that many Africans have toward "so-called" experts.

For the better part of thirty years, my professional career was spent first in Asia, and then in Africa. During that time, I was fortunate enough to collaborate with many wonderful (and some not so wonderful) people. My job allowed me to work in numerous countries overseas with cultures much different from my own. There is little doubt that I learned a great deal. Hopefully, there was mutuality in that others gained something from their contact with me. But looking back, I'm sometimes overtaken with the nightmarish idea that those who knew and worked with me in Asia and Africa might have viewed me in a similar vein as that FAO man, a "so-called expert." I sincerely hope not.

How does a peripatetic life begin? The following chapters will describe a life that saw a young, idealistic, and enthusiastic Peace Corps volunteer in the Philippines with a wife, three small children, and very little money become, later in life, a well-respected Director General of one of Africa's largest and best known non-governmental organizations (NGOs), and a "development skeptic" at the same time.

CHAPTER 2

PEACE CORPS:
THE BEGINNING

"Let's join the Peace Corps."[1]

"Are you nuts? We have three kids."

"No problem. We can take them with us."

"O.K. Let's go."

So went a conversation between my wife and myself in October 1969. Soon after, an application was properly filled out, signed by the both of us, and sent to Peace Corps headquarters in Washington D.C. Thus began an odyssey that would take us from Ridgefield, New Jersey through San Jose, California and ultimately to Legaspi City in the Philippines. It was an odyssey filled with adventure, excitement, complexities, and often, a lot of fun along the way.

Why did an average couple, aged twenty-nine and twenty-eight at the time, with three young sons who were five, two, and one year old, take such action? At this point in our lives, I was on the faculty of the School of Education at Brooklyn College of the City University of New York. My wife, Ina, who had taught biology and science, was now basically a full-time mother. Besides teaching, I was also working on a doctoral degree at New York University.

Filling out a Peace Corps application was not really a spur-of-the-moment decision. A number of underlying factors contributed to what many friends and relatives started calling our "insanity." They couldn't believe we would

---

[1] The U.S. Peace Corps sends volunteers to less developed countries around the world. Other industrialized nations have similar volunteer programmes. The United Kingdom has VSO, Volunteer Service Overseas; Canada has CUSO, originally Canadian University Services Overseas; Japan has JOCV, Japanese Overseas Cooperation Volunteers; the Netherlands and United Nations also post volunteers abroad.

contemplate turning our lives upside down and drag three small boys off into the wilderness of some unheard of country. But we did contemplate it, we did do it, and here is why.

I was a person who, from childhood onwards, had never really been able to sit still in one place for more than five minutes (inherited from my mother). There is a wanderlust that has always driven me. The urge to keep moving was there at a young age and is still with me at the age of sixty-six. It keeps popping up all the time, as the following example will illustrate.

A few years back, after many years of working and living in Africa, Ina and I were considering several options for retirement. Having lived in Nairobi, Kenya, we were spoiled by its perfect climate. In thinking about retirement, we narrowed down the list to a few countries, which had comparable weather patterns. These eventually included South Africa, New Zealand, and Portugal. Different friends tried to sell us on the merits of each, although I was quite familiar with South Africa, having worked there for some time. Since we did not know New Zealand at all, during a business trip to the United States it was decided to make a stopover. After exploring both the North and South Islands in two weeks, we were able to get some feel of what the country was like.

It turned out to be one of the most beautiful places we have ever visited but just not right for our retirement. During the two weeks, we saw a great deal of both islands. Ina's assessment was that if we moved to New Zealand, we would spend the rest of our lives in a car continuously driving in circles around the two islands. There is this need to always keep moving.

While teaching world history at a New York City high school in 1968, I had the good fortune of winning a National Defence Education Act (NDEA) fellowship to study about India and Pakistan. The programme was offered at Brooklyn College during the two summer months when students were normally enjoying their holidays. We were a group of twenty from all over the East Coast of the U.S. and spent eight weeks in intensive study. With a long-standing interest in Asia, that summer programme greatly heightened my desire to know even more.

Participation in the NDEA programme resulted in a job offer to join the faculty at Brooklyn College and the winning of a summer Fulbright grant in 1969 to visit and study in India. At the same time, a senior professor colleague offered me the opportunity to lead a comparative education graduate seminar to Norway, Sweden, and Finland that summer. A choice had to be made. I chose the Fulbright programme, went off to India, and never looked back. Those few months in India, probably more than anything else, had the greatest impact on filling out the Peace Corps application.

At the same time my own opportunities were being broadened, in 1969 the

United States Peace Corps started rethinking its original policies. From its inception under President John F. Kennedy in 1961, Peace Corps basically recruited fresh college graduates and sent them to developing countries in Asia, Africa, and Latin America. Most volunteers were young, in their early twenties, with little or no previous job experience. Almost all were single with a few married couples (no children) thrown in. On rare occasions, a few older, more experienced volunteers were sent abroad on special assignments.

With the election of Richard Nixon as President, his administration reviewed the first eight years of the Peace Corps' performance. Many of the host countries by now were requesting more experienced Americans to serve overseas as volunteers. However, it was quickly realized that more qualified people would be older than fresh university graduates, mostly married, often having children. Then the Peace Corps initiated a new experimental programme in 1969, advertising for experienced volunteers and willing to accept families with children. That provided the impetus for us to submit an application.

CHAPTER 3

THE INVITATION

"DO NOT CONTACT MY CURRENT EMPLOYER"

These six clear words highlighted on the Peace Corps application turned out to be a real eye opener. They taught us a hard-won lesson about the organization we were soon to join. As a second year instructor, without tenure, struggling to make an impression upon my Dean and department chairman, it was with great pleasure that I found the above clearly stated on the Peace Corps application. It was preferable not to have one's superiors catch a hint that I might be contemplating departing their esteemed university. I not only checked off the box next to these six wonderful words but also placed three checks into the box, having felt secure that an organization as efficient as the U.S. Government (ha, ha) would assess the application without my employers knowing what was being planned.

What happened next was like a bad act out of the old vaudeville theatre. If a performer was really terrible and the audience was beyond hissing and ready to revolt, the stage manager would stick out a long cane with a hooked end (like a big version of the Christmas candy cane), grab the performer by the neck, and yank him or her off the stage.

Well, vaudeville was about to come to Brooklyn College. About two months after submitting the Peace Corps application, and only silence coming out of Washington, we just assumed that it was going to come to nothing. One morning, while walking down the hallway past the Dean's office, I was sort of yanked by the neck and dragged into his office.

"Gerber, what's this I hear about you going off to Timbuktu or someplace like that?"

"Excuse me Dean, what do you mean?"

"Some secret service or FBI spook was just in here checking on you and telling us they are about to send you off to someplace in Africa. Are you an ingrate? We just brought you here to the university and now you want to leave."

Well, so much for the famous six little words – **Do Not Contact My Current Employer**. Without informing us that we were being considered for acceptance, the first place Peace Corps checked was with my current employer. Now, if we were not sent to Timbuktu or someplace as far, surely I was not destined for future greatness at Brooklyn College. This was our welcome to the efficient and professional world of the Peace Corps organization.

To our surprise, in April or May of 1970, an invitation was received requesting Ina and myself to serve as volunteers in the Philippines. We were asked to come to San Jose State University in California at the end of June for one week of briefing before flying to Manila. Oh yes, the letter also said we could bring our kids along. Since the original Peace Corps application asked where we would prefer to serve and since we again placed three checks in the box marked Africa, I ran to my atlas to find out if someone had actually moved the Philippines to Africa. Fortunately, my atlas also had a map of Asia. It was now quite obvious that three checks in a box just did not work with the Peace Corps.

For its new programme, Peace Corps had recruited a small group of families, which they sent to Korea as volunteers in 1969. We were now among the second set of families chosen – six in all –to be sent to the Philippines. We were to be part of an education group which was to include experienced teachers and administrators, as well as university instructors, school administrators, and principals.

In any case, we now had all of two months to get our act together which included saying goodbye to disbelieving family and friends, selling off all of our worldly possessions (one car and some furniture) and notifying my employer that while we were not going to Timbuktu, we were leaving. The five of us were going off to the Philippines with everything we owned packed into two large army surplus duffle bags. While uncertain about what would happen in the long-term (no job to come home to, no possessions), we were all excited about the opportunity that was about to unfold.

Just prior to departing for California, an invitation was received from NBC's Today Show for us to appear on the programme for an interview with Barbara Walters. Our assumption was that they wanted the two of us to turn up and speak about the new Peace Corps family initiative.

"No" they said, "not just you and your wife, we also want the kids."

 Our response was,

"Since your programme is done live, how do we handle an interview while three energetic and rambunctious young boys are running all over the place? Remember, they are only six, three, and one and a half years old and your programme is done live, not taped."

"Not to worry," responded NBC. "We will organize a set with a lot of toys and the children can play while the two of you are interviewed by Barbara Walters."

"OK, if that is the way you want it."

For two days before this TV appearance, we tried all we could to convince the boys that they had to behave better than they ever did in their young lives. They were told there might be millions of people watching them on television. Of course, they were not very impressed, especially the three and the one year old.

The big day arrived. Living in Ridgefield, New Jersey, we got up at four in the morning in order to get to the studio by seven. Upon arrival, we were informed that we were the "last act of the day" and would appear for about twenty minutes during the 8:30 to 9:00 am time slot. There was now an hour and a half to kill with the three kids. And since there was a wait, they showed us the actual set. Some ingenious staff member bought a lot of toys for the kids to play with and these were laid out on the floor in front of the chairs where we would be sitting. It was supposed to be somewhat idyllic, the parents about to go off as Peace Corps volunteers being interviewed, while the three handsome blonde children were calmly playing in the foreground.

There were only two problems with this scenario. First, many of the toys that NBC bought were of the squeeze type variety – you squeezed them and they would make all sorts of noise. We both immediately realized that all those at home watching the show would hear nothing but a chorus of loud, honking squeeze toys. We envisioned a sort of animal farm on the Today Show. Sadly it was too late to change the toys. And secondly, our kids had never in their short lives ever sat still for twenty minutes.

The interview began and of course we were speaking over the cacophony of barnyard sounds. To Barbara Walter's credit, she was not fazed by any of it and carried on like the true professional. However, that only lasted until we heard this loud "crack," a noise that did not come from any squeeze toy. Adam, the three year old, while walking around, slipped and fell, hitting his head against a small table on the set. The cracking noise was his head against the table. All this live on national TV.

Now as parents, we had seen our children fall many a time. Parents have an innate sense of whether their child is seriously hurt or not. We could tell that Adam, while going down with a bang and appearing a little dazed, was not seriously hurt. Realizing we were being watched by many, Ina calmly left her seat, went over and picked up Adam, and sat back down with him on her lap, ready to continue with the interview. Our hostess though, had more trouble keeping as calm. She thought the boy might have been seriously hurt and was duly concerned. We assured her he was OK and we should just go on, which was done without any other serious mishaps in the final ten minutes. I suppose some producer backstage saw a lawsuit in front of his eyes when Adam went down.

With this interview out to of the way, our duffle bags packed, we were ready for the next two years in the Philippines after a brief stopover in San Jose.

CHAPTER 4

TRAINING: SAN JOSE, CALIFORNIA

The importance of separating the Peace Corps volunteer experience from Peace Corps the organization, quickly became evident. The volunteer experience proved to be enriching and exciting, the organization proved neither. We learned to make this distinction shortly after arriving for the one-week orientation in San Jose.

Here we were, two newly enrolled and enthusiastic Peace Corps volunteers, dragging along three small kids into a new adventure. To our great surprise, upon arrival in California, it was brought to our attention that we were not really Peace Corps volunteers. The Peace Corps big shots informed us that the upcoming week was just a pre-invitational period. We, along with five other families, and about thirty other individuals who already thought they were volunteers, were now going to be "evaluated" to determine who was and who was not psychologically fit to be sent to the Philippines. Upon hearing this news, the director of this so-called "pre-invitational" week was told in no uncertain terms and in rather blunt language what he could do with his pre-invitation. Did the idiots organizing this farce actually think someone would quit a job, sell all their possessions, and uproot a family on the premise that they were going to be given a one week tryout and if they didn't pass, would be shipped home? To what home? Welcome to the Peace Corps.

It turned out that this week, along with many other Peace Corps procedures and policies, were basically paper tigers and often never applied. In reality, no one was sent home from San Jose and the entire group was put on a plane for the Philippines one week later. It quickly became common knowledge that unless one was a convicted murderer or rapist, it was almost impossible to be thrown out of the Peace Corps. Much of it was a numbers game. In order for the salaried Peace Corps staff to maintain their jobs and existence, bodies were needed in the form of volunteers. The fewer the volunteers, the fewer staff members needed. We were to observe a year later that a small handful of volunteers in the Philippines spent their entire two years of service just travelling around, visiting friends, drinking San Miguel beer, and never doing any work at all. This was well known among the volunteer community but these people were not sent home – the necessity for a body count of volunteers.

The week at San Jose State University could either be described as unique, amusing, or both. The "prospective" volunteers were divided into small groups. A family constituted its own group. Each group was assigned a "counsellor," and ours was an awfully nice professor from one of the universities in San Francisco. We became well acquainted. He was employed by Peace Corps for the week to help evaluate the "fitness" of the volunteers for work in a different culture overseas. He was also to assess whether or not the families were really functional or dysfunctional. He himself was a family man. During our private chats, he revealed that he too had three children and actually showed me a photo of his wife and kids. I specifically commented that his wife and kids resembled mine, all being blonde haired and fair.

Our San Jose stay went by quickly, no one was declared unfit for volunteer duty and everyone was going off to the Philippines. Departure was to take place from the San Francisco International Airport on a Saturday evening. As a reward for good behaviour, a bus took us from San Jose to downtown San Francisco on Saturday morning and we were instructed to enjoy the day on our own. The bus would pick us up about 6:00 pm for the trip to the airport. We decided to take the boys to Fisherman's Wharf and visited an old sailing vessel docked at the harbour. It was one of San Francisco's tourist attractions.

As we were walking below decks on the ship, Matthew, our oldest, poked me and said, "Look dad, isn't that our Peace Corps counsellor." And sure enough, on the other side of the ship, was the fellow from the San Francisco university who spent a week judging our fitness as a family to go overseas. And there he was across from us, holding hands, all lovey-dovey with a woman—a young, attractive black woman. That was definitely not the wife in his picture or the mother of his kids. I called out at the top of my voice, "Hey Frank, how are you doing?" He looked across the ship, saw us, and with a horrified look on his face, grabbed his lady friend, flew up the steps to the top deck, down the gangplank and off the ship in a flash. So much for Peace Corps marriage counsellors.

CHAPTER 5

TRAINING: IN COUNTRY

Upon arrival at the Manila International Airport and disembarking from the aircraft, the new group of volunteers all stood at attention and sang the Philippine national anthem (Lupang Hinirang) in Tagalog, the most widely spoken language in the Philippines. We were taught the anthem in San Jose and some of the new volunteers practiced it on board during the long flight. We must have been a strange sight to the Filipinos nearby, listening to this group of American adults and children butchering their national anthem. Hopefully, the attempt was most likely appreciated.

A few days were spent in Manila, mostly visiting the doctors and receiving every vaccination invented by man. In two days, the yellow vaccination booklets needed for international travel were more than half filled. At the Peace Corps Philippines headquarters, a number of the Filipino training staff who would provide language and cross-cultural training were there to meet us. Some of the instructors introduced me to Balut, a Philippine delicacy. Balut is a duck egg that has been fertilized and contains a small duck embryo, about ten days old and just ready to hatch. The top of the egg is cracked and the entire raw contents including the little unhatched duck, feathers and all, are sucked down. This was actually an initiation into manhood. Because I ate and liked Balut, it was an immediate acceptance as one of the boys. This stood me in good stead during our years in the Philippines. Because I did not drink any alcohol, San Miguel, the national beer, was not part of my diet. A male not drinking San Miguel is automatically suspect. But anyone eating Balut therefore had to be "one of the guys."

Eating is usually an important part of cultural acceptance. People all over the world, no matter what their economic status, are often more than willing to share their food and drink with strangers they recently met. Not to accept an offer of food can result in serious insult and offended feelings. Born with a cast iron

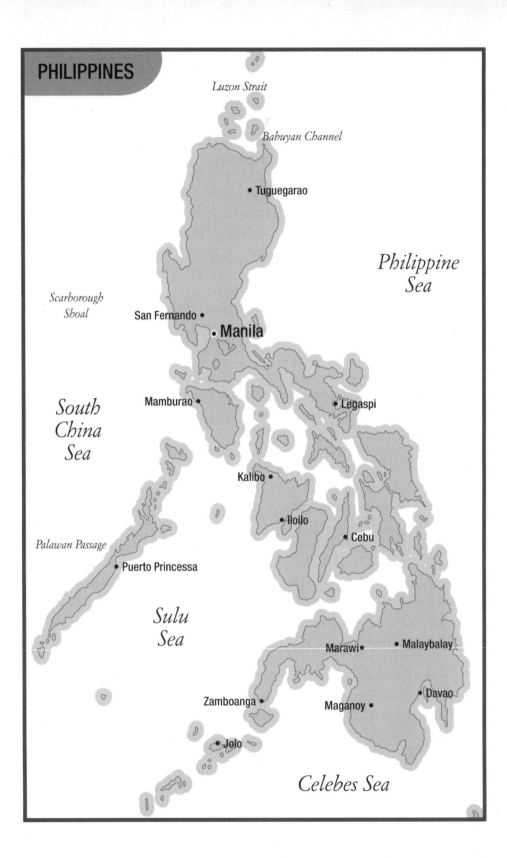

PHILIPPINES

Luzon Strait

Babuyan Channel

• Tuguegarao

Philippine
Sea

Scarborough
Shoal

San Fernando •

• Manila

South
China
Sea

Mamburao •

• Legaspi

Kalibo •

• Iloilo

• Cebu

Palawan Passage

• Puerto Princessa

Sulu
Sea

Marawi • • Malaybalay

Zamboanga •

• Davao

Maganoy •

• Jolo

Celebes Sea

stomach and the ability to eat and drink anything has been a definite advantage throughout my travels and work. Often, when travelling with other people, I acted as the "designated eater," eating what others feared to touch. Both the hosts and my travelling partners appreciated this. As you will read, experiencing food and drink has often been an adventure.

By 1970, Peace Corps had altered its training programme. Training averaged a period of three-months. It contained a number of elements of which the most important were technical, language, and cross-cultural courses. New recruits were organized into groups depending on what they would be doing. Ours, an education group, was numbered thirty-seven, meaning we were the 37th group of volunteers recruited for the Philippines since 1961. Most of the initial groups were involved in agriculture or education. Earlier, training often occurred on the mainland United States or in Puerto Rico or Hawaii. Just prior to our acceptance as volunteers, Peace Corps shifted to in-country training. The volunteers spent their three-month period in the country where they would be working. This made more sense.

For Group 37, the training site was to be in Iloilo City on the island of Panay. Panay is part of the Visayan group of islands in the central part of the Philippines. Single volunteers and married couples without children lived at the training site, St. Clements Retreat House, a nice facility that was part of the St. Clements Catholic Church complex. Separate accommodations were found for each of the six families and we were assigned a small but comfortable apartment a few kilometres from the training centre.

On our first day in Iloilo, a Filipina kindergarten teacher hired by Peace Corps took Matthew (and the other children of school-age) to be enrolled as a first grader in his new school. He was to attend an elementary school on the campus of Central Visayan State University. The school was reached by taking two jeepneys, either from the training centre or our apartment, with a transfer from one vehicle to another about mid-way. Jeepneys are the most common form of public transportation in the Philippines. Originally, they were left-over World War II U.S. army jeeps converted into public service vehicles. Today, jeepneys are specially manufactured and each one is noticeably elaborate and colourfully decorated.

In the afternoon, as we came out of a class, there was Matthew back at St. Clements Retreat House. And he was alone with no other children in sight. Wondering why he was back alone, Ina asked him how he returned and where was the kindergarten teacher. He told us he just came home on the jeepneys by himself, adding that he did not need the teacher for the return journey. After only one trip in the morning on two different jeepneys in a new country, the kid was travelling on his own. He said he knew which jeepneys to take and didn't bother waiting for the others. When Ina asked where he found the money to pay the jeepney drivers, Matt declared that he told the drivers he didn't have any pesos yet and they just let him ride for free.

When the teacher returned with the other children, she was frantic, figuring she lost a child on the very first day. Upon seeing Matthew and hearing the story, her irritation sort of changed to amazement, in awe of this six year old boy travelling alone on jeepneys his second day in Iloilo.

We started the training programme with intensive language classes. Since there are about eighty languages spoken in the Philippines and over 200 dialects, the type of language training a volunteer received was based on the area he or she would be assigned. Classes were small, usually no more than four people and one Filipino instructor. The method used was audio-lingual. No English was spoken in class from day one. In addition, each of us was assigned an informant, a college student who would practice the language with us when we were not in class.

Attempting to learn at least four languages without much success, I can attest to the fact that Peace Corps language instruction is the best Ina and I ever encountered. After training, my assignment was to be at the Bicol State University in Legaspi City. The Bicol region is on the southern tip of Luzon Island, and Legaspi is about 400 kilometres southeast of Manila by road. Bicol was the language of the region and we were in a class for three hours a day with Pat and George Gonzalez, another couple who were to be assigned to the same region. In typical Peace Corps fashion, after training Pat and George were sent to Daet in Camarines Norte, which is primarily Tagalog speaking. So much for their Bicol language exposure.

The cross-cultural course was an excellent introduction to understanding Filipino values and customs. For those who knew little about the country, this along with the language training was crucial. It helped us avoid many mistakes regarding personal relationships during our first few months in the Philippines.

Technical training was another story altogether. The Peace Corps training followed a standard format with little room for deviation. The technical component was supposed to teach new volunteers how to do their job. Now this might have made sense for volunteers freshly recruited out of college and for whom Peace Corps would be a first full-time work opportunity. Since most volunteers had been fresh college graduates, they were taught to be teachers or agriculturalists. Did it make sense for Peace Corps to train a twenty-two year old college graduate and send him out to work with farmers who had been farming their entire lives? Or to send fresh graduates to train teachers? It reminded me of the standard joke about education: "Those who can't do, teach; those who can't teach, teach teachers."

Group 37 was not made up of freshly recruited college graduates. It was supposedly representative of the new Peace Corps initiative, namely volunteers who had considerable experience in their profession before they enlisted. This Group had an Assistant Superintendent of Schools from the Detroit, Michigan school system, an assistant principal, three university instructors, and a number of PhDs. Two volunteers were going to be assigned as consultants to the National Department of Education and at least three were to be part of university faculties. Peace Corps could not figure out that it did not need a technical course to teach these people how to teach.

Peace Corps, being Peace Corps, still insisted on a technical course. Again divided into small groups, our "instructor" was Jeff, in actuality, a nice twenty-four year old "veteran" whose extensive experience in education consisted entirely of his two-year assignment as a volunteer. Interestingly enough, his two years had been spent at the same university that I was going to.

Poor Jeff. On the first day after sitting with his "trainees," he realized he was in way over his head. To Jeff's credit, he abandoned his standard syllabus and we just spent time doing other things. Jeff had married a Filipina while he was a volunteer and she was in Iliolo with him. She was particularly upset that our technical course fell apart after only one day and viewed what happened as a great insult to her young American husband. We were definitely no longer on her list of "good" Americans.

Sadly, the Peace Corps structure did not allow for much flexibility. It would have made more sense to devote all of our time during training to language and cross-cultural studies. But, we continued wasting three hours a day during the time set aside for the technical course.

At mid-point during the training, we were scheduled to visit the sites of our upcoming assignments. Our family went to Legaspi City and found a small but comfortable apartment where we would live for the next three years. It was normally standard practice for volunteers to live in Filipino households and pay rent. Given that it would not be easy for five of us to move in with anyone, policy for the new Peace Corps families was to find a separate apartment. The two eldest boys were enrolled in schools (one public, one Catholic) and I paid a visit to the Bicol University where a job was supposedly waiting for me. I say supposedly because upon arrival at the University's College of Education, a surprise was in store.

Upon learning that there was a new Peace Corps volunteer coming, my future colleagues at the university greeted me with typically warm, Filipino hospitality. After polite small talk to break the ice, the subject of my job came up for discussion. Indirectly, as was the Filipino way, I was basically asked, "What job are you talking about?" There had been no real thought given to what I was going to do. The Peace Corps staff responsible for programming jobs for volunteers had visited the university, asked if they wanted another volunteer after Jeff, was told yes out of politeness because that is also the Filipino way, and that was the extent of the planning. When I showed up, the university staff offered hospitality but had no idea of what the new person should do or was even capable of doing. It reflected poorly on Peace Corps' job placement process.

Upon further inquiry, it became obvious that my situation was not atypical. Job placement was often a hit or miss affair. To perpetuate staff positions, Peace Corps volunteers were needed. Thoughtful, carefully planned job assignments gave way to finding places that would keep the number of volunteers high. Given the nature of Filipino culture, with its priorities on smooth interpersonal relationships and keeping everything on the surface happy, it was a rare occasion that someone would say no to accepting a volunteer after being approached by Peace Corps staff.

There was a standard joke that Peace Corps procedures for placing volunteers in the Philippines was to put them in a plane, fly them over the country, drop them out by parachute, and wherever they landed, they would do their work. The lack of careful planning too often resulted in serious frustration for volunteers. Since most were young college graduates without prior job experience, they were often placed into positions with fundamentally little structure. The expectation that a clearly defined job would be waiting too often proved to be a myth.

All volunteers faced two challenges; coping with a new culture as well as a new job assignment. For young volunteers, the lack of job structure was more complicated to overcome. It was the leading factor contributing to a significant number of volunteers resigning and going home before two years were completed, much to Peace Corps chagrin. More experienced volunteers dealt with the unstructured work situation more easily and they then only had to cope with the cultural challenges.

In my case, not having a specific job proved to be a blessing in disguise. After consulting with the Dean and other senior faculty, we were able to agree on ways in which I could help. The School of Education was instituting a new graduate programme and my primary responsibility would be to help with the design of the new programme as well as teach some graduate courses. During the next few years, I was to become involved with a number of other activities as well.

Our family now felt we were well settled in Legaspi City. Ina, with her science background, explored opportunities to be involved with family planning organizations. The oldest boys were enrolled in school. We had an apartment to live in. Everyone was ready to get on with his or her new life. Having a brainstorm, we called the training director in Iloilo and told her we weren't coming back. The University was now anxious to have me start, the family was settled, and we could continue taking language training in Legaspi. There was really no reason to go back to Iloilo for another forty-five days.

Upon hearing this, the training director went ballistic. No one was allowed to leave a training programme before it finished (I imagine she felt more technical training from Jeff was needed). She called the Philiipines Peace Corp Director in Manila. Within a few hours, the phone at the regional Peace Corps office in Legaspi was ringing off the hook. Everyone was calling and either cajoling or threatening us to return to Iloilo. Finally, the Regional Peace Corps Director begged us to go back. He agreed it didn't make any sense but was under tremendous pressure from his bosses. Since we would be living and working within his jurisdiction, we returned to Iloilo for a month and a half in order to get him off the hook.

Training was not all work and no play. There were basketball games for the male volunteers and Filipino staff almost every evening. A number of social events were organized to which the whole training group was invited. One such evening was a party at the home of Fernando Lopez, who was at that time the Vice-President of the Republic of the Philippines. Vice-President Lopez had a big house in Iloilo City and this night he gave a party for a number of visiting diplomats. For some reason, our Peace Corps group was invited.

I put on my best shirt and trousers which were not really formal, but Ina wore a gold threaded Bangalore wedding sari, which I had brought back from India in 1969. Saris have historically been the traditional dress of Indian women. Ina looked quite elegant. When our group of about forty arrived at the Vice-President's house, various servants escorted us to our tables. I looked around and there was no Ina with us. Checking the huge room, there she was being escorted to the head table with the Vice-President and other dignitaries. They thought she was the wife of the Ambassador from India. When Ina politely set the record straight and explained who she was, back she came to join the rest of us plebeians.

About a week before the training period was to end, a big farewell party was organized. Besides all the volunteers and children, Peace Corps staff members, and our Filipino instructors, many of the local people from Iloilo were to be invited, including the Mayor, congressman, and other big shots. We had been learning a great deal about Filipino culture including music and dance. As a highlight of the evening, a number of volunteers were chosen to perform.

Ina and I were selected to do the "Tinakling," a traditional dance with bamboo poles. Two people sit on the floor about ten feet apart holding two bamboo poles, one in each hand. The poles are then banged together and the dancers dance in and out of the beating poles. It works on two counts and a beat – one, two and bang the poles together. The dancers dance in between the poles for two counts and then get out before having a leg chopped off at the ankle. It is continuously in and out and the beat gets quicker and quicker. I do not know why they selected me. Perhaps someone saw me moving rather swiftly on the basketball court. Ina was a natural choice, being a graceful dancer. She studied formal ballet for many years and kept up with other dance forms as an adult.

The highlight of the evening was the "Binasuhan," a remarkably complex dance performed by females. Ina was also chosen to do this. The dancer holds two glasses filled either with water or a burning candle in each hand, and for the most intricate part, also has to balance a third glass on her head. It is noted for its grace with a lot of hand movements. Of course, a glass cannot be dropped or any water spilt. The climax comes when the dancer has to get down on the floor and fully extends her body with the glass remaining atop her head and the two in her hands. She must then get up.

Ina performed this beautifully, with not a glass falling anywhere and not a drop of water spilt. She left the dance floor to a standing ovation. Needless to say, the boys and I were extremely proud of her. Our Tinakling training was never forgotten and we wound up doing it at other times later in life.

CHAPTER 6

THE PHILIPPINES

The Philippines is a country of islands, 7,107 to be exact with a total area of 300,000 square kilometres. The great majority of the islands are small and uninhabited. The largest is Luzon in the north, where the capital, Manila, is located. The second largest is Mindanao in the south. Hong Kong is about a 90-minute flight to the northwest from Manila, Taiwan is due north, Malaysia to the southwest, and Indonesia to the south. The Philippine Sea, the western-most extension of the Pacific Ocean, borders on the east, the Celebes Sea separates the Philippines from Indonesia in the South, and the South China Sea is to the west.

With its eighty languages and more than 200 dialects, many Filipinos are bilingual or even multilingual. As explained, Tagalog, the predominant language of central Luzon, is the most widely spoken. In the late 1960s and early 1970s, the Philippine Government pushed Pilipino, later changed to Filipino, as the national language. Filipino is basically Tagalog.

The inhabitants of the Philippines are about 95 per cent Malay. There has been a large influx of Chinese over the centuries, resulting in an intermixing of peoples and cultures. Over four-fifths are Catholic and about 10 per cent of the population Muslim. The Muslims are predominantly found in the south, on Mindanao and some smaller islands. In 1970, the population was about thirty-five million with Manila, the largest city, having about five to six million. Today, the population is over seventy million with Manila home to over eleven million.

From 1521 until 1946, the Philippines was a colony, first under Spanish rule and then under American. Magellan landed on Mactan Island near Cebu (he was killed there) and that marks the beginning of Spanish influence in the country. Manila became an important port for the Spanish gold trade with Mexico. The Spanish never really settled in large numbers but ruled through two groups, the priests or padres who dominated in the rural areas, and an elite group of Mestisos, those of mixed Spanish-Filipino blood, who served as intermediaries in the capital. Spanish was never widely introduced nor was mass education. The padres spoke the local languages and Spanish was reserved for the privileged. The great legacy of Spain in the Philippines is the Catholic religion.

As a result of a war between the United States and Spain which began in April 1898, the Philippines became an American possession. Known as the Spanish-American War, it started with the sinking of the battleship Maine in Havana harbour. While Cuba was the main battle theatre, the Philippines became a prize for America and by terms of the Treaty of Paris signed in December 1898, Spain ceded the Philippine archipelago to the United States for £11 million. Filipinos had actually started their own insurrection against the Spanish in 1896 but it was put down in 1897. Led by Emilio Aguinaldo, the Filipinos were not happy with being transferred from one imperialist ruler to another. In February 1899, the insurgents began fighting against U.S. troops and resorted to guerrilla war. The conflict finally came to an end in March 1901 with the capture of Aguinaldo. The Philippines was now America's first and only colony in Asia.

U.S. rule differed greatly from that of the Spanish. Education was deemed truly important and right from the beginning of the new colonial period, teachers started arriving from America. The first group of educators were called "Thomasites," named after the ship on which they arrived in the Philippines, the S.S. Thomas. A mass primary education system was initiated with the result that many Filipinos today are bi-lingual or rather tri-lingual. They will speak their local language, Filipino or Tagalog, and English. Americans came in much larger numbers than the Spanish ever did and introduced not only the English language but also American culture.

The Philippines was an important battleground in World War II, with the Japanese invasion beginning on 8 December 1941, almost immediately after the attack on Pearl Harbour. A small combined American and Filipino force resisted valiantly but was overwhelmed by the Japanese. The invasion resulted in the Bataan death march, the fall of Corregidor, and General Douglas MacArthur moving to Australia. In 1944, the American return began with a landing in Leyte and they went on to eventually retake the Philippines. After the war, on 4 July 1946, the United States granted the Philippines its independence.

Today, in every city and town, no matter how large or small, you will find two things – a Catholic Church and a basketball court – the two major legacies of the Spanish and Americans. And in almost all villages, no matter how large or small, you will find one thing – a basketball court of some kind. While a village might be too small for a church, it will have boys playing basketball, even if the court is a mere dirt patch with a pole and a ring attached to it for a basket.

I have always maintained that of all Asian countries, the Philippines is the most trying for Americans and Europeans to really understand. When you go to Thailand and land in Bangkok, you know you are in a foreign place. People are speaking a language not understood, the written script is unreadable, foods are so unrecognisable, and the religion appears strange, unless you are a Buddhist. The same is true for Japan, or South Korea, or Vietnam, Cambodia, Laos, etc. When you first visit the Philippines and land in Manila, this is not so. People are speaking English, signs and billboards are in English, the U.S. cultural influence is pervasive. While the people might be brown skinned and do speak other languages, initially all things to a westerner are comfortable.

It is easy to fall into the comfort trap. One thinks one understands it all. But this is not so because familiarity is only on the bare surface. Scratch that surface and you will find Filipinos are really very Asian, with a strong culture and value system that is different from America's. It becomes easy to draw false assumptions. "Hey, we are the same," is often a first response. But not long after the response becomes, "Hey, we are not the same." It is so much easier to come to grips with differences when everything on the surface also appears different.

Legaspi City, where we were to live for the next three years, was about 400 kilometres by road from Manila or one hour and fifteen minutes by air in a propeller driven plane (today, about fifty minutes by jet). Legaspi is in Albay Province, which along with Camarines Norte, Camarines Sur, Sorsogon, Masbate, and Catanduanes make up the Bicol Region. While not an unbiased observer, after travelling throughout much of the Philippines, I feel the Bicol region is one of the most beautiful parts of the country.

Legaspi has a small natural harbour on the Philippine Sea. From everywhere in the city, one was able to see the most outstanding feature of the region. That was Mt. Mayon, an active volcano with a history of eruptions about once in every ten years. Mayon, 7,000 feet high and shaped as a perfect cone is one of the Philippine's major tourist attractions. In 1970, the population of Legaspi was about 70,000 although most lived outside the city centre in small villages or barrios. The city centre was quite small; a few square blocks and a local market. Today, the once small city has become a mid-sized provincial metropolis with its inherent shopping malls, fast food outlets, and incessant traffic jams.

Now settled in the Philippines, our problems with the Peace Corps organization did not go away. They started with our application and continued off and on during our time as volunteers. Such problems notwithstanding, the next three years still proved to be among the best of our lives. I say three years because we extended and stayed in the Philippines for an extra twelve months. Once we were on assignment in Legaspi City, our lives revolved around the

Philippine organizations and the colleagues we worked with. My boss was the Dean and my loyalties were to the University. Although there was essentially little money, no car, or television, and few possessions, everything was done together as a family for the next thirty-six months. This included eating three meals a day in each other's presence. It was an occurrence that never happened before we were volunteers nor did it happen thereafter.

CHAPTER 7

A PEACE CORPS FAMILY COPES

"Will our kids starve to death?"

"Will we have enough for clothing?"

"Will the poor kids ever see another birthday present?"

Were we concerned about our economic position once officially assigned as volunteers? A little. Well, more than a little. But things turned out to be more than adequate. One's economic status is relative. Compared to our Filipino counterparts, the people whom we worked and associated with, we were on a par. Peace Corps' policy on maintenance was that volunteers were supposed to live at the same level as the host country nationals doing similar jobs. Ina and I were each provided with the Philippine peso equivalent of about £40 a month. The average monthly salary for professors at the university where I was assigned was £50. Peace Corps did not refer to it as salary but rather a maintenance allowance. In addition, the three boys were each allocated £10 a month. From these allowances, all costs had to be covered – rent, food, clothing, transportation, and entertainment. Peace Corps did provide separate cover for the boys' school fees, which were minimal, and for medical expenses.

The policy was that volunteers were not allowed to either own or drive cars. As if that was a concern of ours. Unless one was independently wealthy, which we were not, how do you buy and run a car on a total income of roughly £110 a month? Public transportation played a big part in our lives over the next three years.

Kids have amazing language facilities and within a few months, all three were fluent in the Bicol language. The little one, Daniel, developed a perfect accent and if you closed your eyes and listened, it would be impossible to distinguish him from a Filipino child. If the boys were part of a group that included American adults, Filipino adults, and Filipino children, it was remarkable to observe them speaking in perfect "American English" to the American adults, English with a perfect Filipino accent to the Filipino adults, and Bicol to their playmates.

The boys did not suffer at all educationally. What they might have missed in school was more than made up for by the enrichment of their lives living and travelling in Asia. The schools themselves had some excellent extracurricula activities – Adam learned to play the violin while in the Philippines. Matthew attended the laboratory elementary school at the Bicol University where I worked. It was where the university sent student teachers to practice. By our second year, both of the younger boys were enrolled at St. Agnes Academy. At both schools, they were the only non-Filipino children.

Benedictine nuns, German and Filipino, ran St. Agnes. When Adam and Daniel were enrolled, Ina explained to Sister Bertha, the headmistress, that since we were not Catholic, would she please exempt the two from religious instruction. Sister Bertha said that it would be absolutely no problem to excuse the boys from such classes. Well, two weeks after the start of school, we were having dinner one evening. Daniel got off his chair, dropped onto his knees, and uttered the words "Body of Christ." Adam then popped a potato crisp into Daniel's mouth and the two of them in unison said "Amen." Enough said for no religious instruction.

Our apartment was basic but comfortable. The kitchen had no oven, just a portable gas tank and two-burner stove atop a counter. So Ina improvised an oven. She bought a big tin can at the market which came with an opening flap in the middle. It was placed over the burners, hence an instant oven. Ina would go to the market each morning and all of our food was fresh. In addition, fish vendors came to the door daily with their catch fresh from the ocean. We would be able to buy huge prawns for just over fifty pence a kilo. Sadly, the availability of prawns did not last long. Soon they were all being shipped to Japan for appallingly high prices.

My wife was a most determined bargainer. Bargaining is essential in most countries outside of North America and Europe. After a time, the vendors hated to see her in the market because they knew they were in for a long haggle. It is a superstition in the Philippines that a vendor must make a sale to the first customer of the day. If the first customer does not buy, that vendor will have bad luck. Naturally Ina tried to get to the market by 7:00 am to be the first customer as often as possible.

Her bargaining prowess was legendary. One time in Indonesia, we were on a beach and a little boy came over trying to sell us an "ivory" carving. It was actually a cow bone carving but quite intricately done. The boy offered it to Ina as pure ivory for only £120. That poor kid didn't know what he was getting into. Negotiations started, the boy went away, came back, went away, came back. In the end, the cow bone was ours for about fifty pence. I felt sorry for the boy and would have given him more. Ina's rationale, which was really the correct one, was that no one would sell you anything unless they were making some profit. We later saw similar cow bone carvings in the market for less than fifty pence. So the kid did not do badly.

In time, Ina became expert in preparing traditional Filipino food. One day at the beginning of our stay, we all decided that for a change, southern fried chicken was our choice for dinner. Following standard procedure, she bought a live chicken, slit its throat, plucked the feathers, prepared it, and that night on the table was southern fried chicken. I took one bite and almost cracked a tooth. It seems that the chickens you bought in the market were of the "self supporting" variety. They were not bred for frying. They just roamed around the villages eating anything and everything. When the owner needed some money, off the chicken went to market. Naturally, they were as tough as nails. The secret to making them edible was that after cleaning, the chicken had to be placed in a pot of water and boiled for a few hours.

Getting completely used to local customs sometimes proved more demanding than we would have thought. Our apartment, in a block of four, backed up onto a small river, perhaps better described as a large stream. It meandered throughout the neighbourhood and was multifunctional. The stream's most frequent uses were for washing clothes and bathing humans. There was one additional use which, being naïve Americans, we thought could be changed.

Shortly after moving in, it was obvious that garbage collection was not a common occurrence in our neighbourhood. Upon further inquiry, it was just as obvious that home garbage collection was non-existent in all of Legaspi. The easiest way for people in our area to get rid of their trash was to open the windows and send the garbage flying out toward the riverbank. That was the third use for the stream.

Without doubt, we did not do as the neighbours did. For the Gerber's, there was no laundry, bathing, or garbage connected with that stream. But as the trash mounted in the apartment, we realized that something had to be done. The first move was to take the trash out near the rice field and burn it early in the evening. By doing so, it was hoped that perhaps an example would be set and trash burning would become part of the neighbourhood ritual. But to no one's great surprise, it remained very lonely out in the rice field each night with only a single fire burning.

Ina, being the most civic-minded member of our family, would not give up. She went to the town hall and met with the mayor of Legaspi City. Using her best reasoning, she tried to convince the mayor that there was a public health problem with regard to the stream near our home and probably every other stream and river for miles around. "What Legaspi needs is regular garbage collection," Ina pleaded. The Mayor listened intently and then answered, "No problem, I'll take care of it."

The next morning, a loud noise was heard outside of our apartment. To the astonishment of all the neighbours, a huge, open backed lorry was kicking up dust as it pulled into our dirt road. On the back of this monster were four guys. They jumped down, knocked on our door, and announced "Garbage collection, maam." Ina came out with one, very small brown paper bag filled with trash. The fellows took it from Ina and with great flair, tossed this small bag onto the back of their big lorry. The truck backed out of our driveway and off it went with its collection. They probably tossed the bag into the stream after turning the bend in the road. During our three years in Legaspi, that was the only bag of garbage that was ever collected. And the stream continued to serve as function number three for the community while we burned our one bag of trash each evening in a nearby field.

Filipino, and other Asian cultures, have a different sense of space and spatial relations than do westerners. With large families and limited space, people live in much closer contact than Americans often do. We learned the differences rather quickly when friends visited us. Our apartment had three small bedrooms. Ina and I shared one, Adam and Daniel the second, and Matthew, being the eldest was given the privilege of having his own room. Our Filipino friends were horrified that we would separate kids from their parents and thought it extremely cruel that poor Matthew had to sleep alone. When it was explained that even as a newborn, a child's crib was often set up in a separate room or nursery, the explanation confirmed our oddity in the eyes of our friends and neighbours. Filipinos, even if they had large houses with many bedrooms, most often slept with children and parents in the same room or at least quite a number of children in one room. No one slept alone.

I started my assignment at Bicol University and Ina worked part time for a municipal family planning organization in Legaspi City. The first few months went by quickly and by the start of December, we found it strange to hear 'Jingle Bells' and 'White Christmas' being played on the radio while the sun was shining, the average temperature being over 35 degrees Celsius and the humidity 100 per cent.

Legaspi City had two cinemas and one of them showed American films, albeit about ten years old. Each week there was a new double feature. All five of us would go but we only stayed for one of the two films. That allowed for something else to do later in the week. We could go to the cinema again, this time to see the second feature. With luck, our maintenance allowance was enough to provide for the movies twice a week.

The Philippines happens to lie in a major typhoon path in Southeast Asia as well as in an earthquake belt. Typhoons are the Pacific's equivalent to the Atlantic's hurricanes. We experienced at least one typhoon a year. They are often quite destructive, causing loss of lives and extensive property damage. Winds can be as high as 225 kilometres an hour.

The most frightening of the typhoons occurred in August 1970, shortly after our arrival in the Philippines. While still in Iloilo City for training, we decided to take the boys to the cinema after our classes ended. It was raining slightly when we entered the theatre. Upon leaving, about 8:00 in the evening, the storm had picked up in intensity. Never had we seen such gale force winds and driving rain. Should we wait it out in the theatre lobby or try to make it home, about ten kilometres away? A kindly "tricy" driver agreed to try and get us home. "Tricys" or tricycles are motorcycles with a small sidecar attached. They have three wheels and hence the name. They are a cheap and common form of transportation. How the driver kept this small vehicle from being blown off the road and how he managed to circumnavigate the flooded streets was a small miracle. We made it and the driver was rewarded handsomely.

Typhoons at home in Legaspi City were also an adventure. Windows on houses were either wooden or glass slats, one overlapping the other. When it rained, especially hard rain, it was impossible to keep the water from pouring through the slats. Doors never reached the floor. There was usually a gap of about an inch between the bottom of the door and the floor. This was another easy channel for water. When a typhoon hit, our apartment was always flooded.

Depending on the direction of the winds, water would either be coming in through the front door and windows or through the back ones. We would move whatever furniture we had to the other side of the apartment, away from the direction of the wind and water. Typhoons are interesting. When the eye or centre of the storm passes, it becomes deathly still for a few minutes. The silence is actually eerie. No wind or water, no sound at all. Then the storm shifts 180 degrees and starts all over again in the other direction with the same fierce intensity. Whenever the eye was overhead, we would be scooting around the apartment, frantically shifting all the furniture to the other side, knowing that the water would now be pouring in from the opposite direction.

Earthquakes were just as interesting. Legaspi City averaged about one a year. The first one was however, a non-event for me. I went to bed early one evening only to be awakened an hour later by Ina.

"Wake up. Wake up. Didn't you feel the whole house shaking?"

"What shaking?" I said drowsily.

"We just had an earthquake. The house shook as if it was going to collapse."

"Let me go back to sleep."

Waking in the morning, I was told that after going back to sleep, there was a second wave of shocks again shaking the house. I slept through the second one as well.

The next earthquake was not so simple. During my Peace Corps days, the university requested I serve as adviser to a number of students writing dissertations for their Masters Degrees. The process was quite formal and the student had to defend his or her dissertation before a university panel. One Saturday morning, a student I was advising was in the midst of defending her dissertation. We were in the university library. I was seated at a small table with the graduate student while the distinguished panel of inquisitors were at a table facing us. In the middle of one question, the floor started shaking under my feet. Looking up, I found myself to be the only one left in the building. Everyone had made a beeline for the door and was outside. The whole building as well as the floor was now shaking. Figuring at that point there was little that could be done to influence the situation, I just got up and walked outside. With good fortune, as my colleagues explained, the quake was "mild" by Philippine standards and there was no serious damage done. By the way, the student passed her oral exam with flying colours.

"Early to bed and early to rise" was our adopted family motto. With no television, few newspapers available, and news magazines arriving about three weeks late, there was little reason to stay up late in the evenings. Mornings began about 6:00 am with the crowing of the cocks. Everyone was up at that hour, taking care of what needed to be done before the real heat set in. To this day, I have followed the pattern started in 1970 of rising early in the morning. No matter how late to bed in the evening, the next morning sees me up about 6:00. It is like having a built-in alarm clock.

CHAPTER 8

TRANSPORTATION AND TRAVEL

Getting from one place to another with three young boys proved to be both a challenge as well as a lot of fun. As already mentioned, there were two basic forms of local transportation, the jeepney and the tricycle. Neither form was designed for tall people, given that the average size of Filipinos in 1970 was probably less than 5'8". Our heights were 6'1" and 5'8"respectively, so jeepneys and tricys both proved a test. Anyone over five and a half feet tall had to travel constantly bent in half.

Getting the five of us into a tricycle soon proved an easy puzzle to solve. Matt, the eldest, sat on the motorcycle seat behind the driver. Adam, the middle one, sat on the motorcycle seat in front of the driver. Ina and I wedged ourselves into the sidecar, usually with some part of our bodies hanging out. Daniel, the youngest, sat on my lap. And off the five of us went to wherever we had to go.

One of the best benefits of serving as Peace Corps volunteers was an opportunity to travel, both within the Philippines and to other parts of Southeast Asia. In conjunction with job related activities and meetings, we were able to see much of the Philippines. For holiday leave, Peace Corps put away a small monthly allowance for each volunteer. Leave time was accumulated as two days per month for each month of service. Most volunteers saved the days and took a twenty-four day holiday after one year. It was possible to purchase exceptionally cheap airline tickets for travel within Southeast Asia and we spent three weeks at mid-service visiting Thailand, Singapore, Indonesia, and Hong Kong.

After buying plane tickets, not much was left over for daily expenses. Plugging into the Peace Corps "grapevine," it was possible to find the cheapest ways to move around within countries and the least expensive places to stay.

Since Peace Corps never had families before, the grapevine information was collected from youthful adult volunteers. The information proved most interesting for an older couple with children.

Bangkok buses proved the greatest challenge. They never came to a complete stop. When reaching designated bus stops, the buses would merely slow down and people would jump off and get on while the bus was still moving. Now, how do you cope with the three kids and a constantly moving bus? The solution proved tricky but workable. While it was in motion, Ina jumped on the bus first. I then picked up each kid in turn and tossed him onto the bus with the hope that Ina would catch him (most of the time she did). I then jumped on last. The same system was used in getting off with me jumping down first and then catching three flying kids. Naturally, the boys loved this.

We stayed in some "quaint" and out of the ordinary places. While in Indonesia, our budget was about £3 a day. Not per person, but for all five of us. We found places such as the Three Sisters Restaurant in Denpasar, Bali where we could all eat a meal for under £1. Hotels were found that were cheap, often costing no more than £2 or £3 for the family. Some of the hotels where we stayed had never previously housed Caucasian children, even though Indonesia had been a Dutch colony prior to WWII. We surmised Dutch families never stayed in these places. On the way from Bali to Hong Kong, we had a one-night stop over in Jakarta. Never having been there before and not knowing where to stay, I asked an Indonesian stewardess on Garuda Airways, Indonesia's national airline, if she could recommend a cheap place to stay in Jakarta. She did. The result was that Ina and I sat up all night killing everything imaginable crawling over our kids while they were in bed. The boys slept through it all with no problem, but we were two tired parents arriving in Hong Kong.

*   *   *

After being requested by the university to stay beyond my two-year assignment, Peace Corps agreed to an additional one-year extension. As a result, we were given a home leave to the U.S. in June of 1972 prior to starting the third year. With our twenty-four working days of holiday accumulated, it was decided to travel back via Japan and Alaska, which did not incur any additional fare. Japan was quite expensive and proved an impossible place to stay on a £3 a day Southeast Asian budget. Rather than hotels, Japanese inns or Ryokans were our choice. With their sliding rice paper doors and walls, preventing the boys from crashing through kept us busy.

Upon arrival in Anchorage from Tokyo, it was less than zero degrees Celsius at the end of June. This compared to temperatures in the mid thirties when departing from Legaspi City. Anchorage's residents were amazed to see five crazies getting off the plane in short sleeve shirts and no coats. We didn't have any warm clothing. Some especially kind people who worked at the airport went out of their way to lend us warm sweaters and jackets for the few days we were there.

Flying at times proved eventful. Many of the most interesting flying experiences involved my work in Africa and are described in later chapters. There was one incident in the Philippines which deserves mention here. We were all returning to Legaspi from Manila after having my severely broken thumb surgically repaired. The flight back was on Air Manila, which at that time was flying Fokker 50 twin propeller planes between the two cities. Flying time was a little over an hour. Matt and Adam were sitting in front of me and I was next to Daniel. Ina was across the aisle seated alongside a young Filipino woman, about twenty years old, who was holding an infant of about two months.

The young woman was extremely nervous, both about flying and about caring for the infant. It turned out that she was from Tabaco, a town thirty kilometres from Legaspi and had never previously even given a baby a bottle. Her older sister lived in Manila and she was taking the sister's baby, her niece, back to Tabaco to see the grandparents. This was to be the first time the grandparents would see their grandchild. Ina, observing the young woman's discomfort, played with the baby and helped her relax.

About a half hour into the flight, while looking out the window, to my great surprise I watched as half of the propeller fell away from the left wing. As a twin engine, the Fokker 50 aircraft has one engine on each wing. Fire immediately began shooting out of the badly damaged propeller. The plane sharply tilted to the left and started descending rapidly, very rapidly. Most of the passengers took immediate fright, none more so than the young woman with her niece. She was again panicking (who could blame her) and the baby screaming. Ina took the baby and tried to calm them both down.

The pilot turned on the loud speaker and with a composed voice announced that "there was no real emergency, we have a technical problem with one of the engines but I am correcting it and the plane can fly perfectly on one engine." This reassured no one as the plane continued to lose altitude. It was obvious we were in deep trouble when I looked at one of the Filipino stewardesses who was a pretty brown skinned woman when we boarded, but was now ashen white in colour.

The Fokker 50 normally cruises at about 20,000 feet and within two minutes, we had descended to 5,000. At that point, the pilot was able to level the plane. He called Manila for instructions and was told to return because Manila airport had better emergency facilities than Legaspi's small airport. A few minutes later he announced that since the plane had already travelled more than half way, we were proceeding to Legaspi. To his credit, the rest of the flight was smooth and the landing was perfect with Legaspi Airport's one fire engine sitting out on the runway waiting for us. Ina handed back the baby and helped the woman off. The stewardess did get her colour back.

Two days later, there was a knock on our door. Standing on our doorstep was the young woman from the flight, her parents (the baby's grandparents), the baby, and other assorted relatives. Each had a handful of different goodies, which were presented to Ina as appreciation for the help she provided for the baby. It was a wonderful gesture of Filipino generosity.

CHAPTER 9

DOGGIE, DOGGIE...
WHERE ARE YE?

Rats, snakes, geckos (small lizards), roaches, chickens, dogs, and about every insect conceivable played a big part in our lives. Our apartment was next to a huge rice field and rice fields normally have rats and snakes as inhabitants. Kids being kids, they were always playing in the field with their friends. It was impossible to keep them out. There was little we could do but let nature take its course. Gratefully we got through the three years without any confrontations with cobras.

Rats, however, were a different story. The first time one appeared before me in the Philippines, I mistook it for a cat. In New Jersey, all we saw was an occasional tiny mouse. But now we were to live with the largest rats imaginable. They were everywhere and one soon took them for granted, accepted them as part of the family. On our first venture to the cinema in Legaspi City, we noticed that all the patrons were sitting barefoot with their two feet up on the backs of the chairs in front. In the movie theatre, if you put your head back, you had a pair of bare feet cuddling each of your ears. We soon learned an important reason for the "foot on the back of the chair" practice.

"Chinillas," called rubber thongs or flip-flops in the U.S., were the footwear of preference for a majority of Filipinos. They were inexpensive and could be removed easily. Never was easy removable more important than in the movies. For we quickly learned that continuously scurrying under your seat in the theatre were the cat-sized rats, attracted by the trash dumped on the floor. It was an unequivocally wise move to watch the entire movie with your feet up on the back of the seat in front of you. You learned to live with the smell coming from other people's feet on either side of your ears. The boys, whose legs were too short to

41

reach the seats in from of them, learned to quickly sit crossed-legged with their feet tucked under them on their seats.

One of our favourite restaurants was in the centre of town. They served the best siapo, a stuffed rice-dough dumpling. The restaurant had two floors and we always ate upstairs. In the middle of the wooden floor, surrounded by tables, was a rather smallish hole. Periodically popping its head up through the hole was the restaurant's resident rat. It became a favourite of our kids' and they used to toss it food when he (or she) popped up.

Nothing in our apartment was safe from rodents or insects. One morning, upon rising, I noticed a trail of strange looking droppings. The trail went from a utility closet across to the living room. Upon further examination, it proved to be animal droppings but what was unique was that the droppings were in a variety of colours. Technicolor animal shit. Ina immediately recognized the residue as cockroach turds. The critters had been in the closet, eating the boys' wax crayons, and we found the results of their digestive systems.

Rats in the house were always a nuisance. It was hard to believe such large rats could find a way in but Ina, our resident rat expert, explained that they could easily get under the one-inch space between the door bottom and the floor. I remained unbelieving until, sitting up reading late one evening, one of our rat friends twisted its body into all sorts of contortions and quickly slipped underneath the door and into the house.

Ina, in her determination to combat these large critters, bought a couple of large rat traps from the local market. She loaded each of them with pieces of cheese and placed them in strategic locations throughout the house. In testing one of these large traps, the spring snapped prematurely and almost took off a couple of her fingers.

One evening, as we were sleeping in the upstairs bedroom, we were awoken by a large thunder-like crash. Hearing no rain outside, we hypothesized that perhaps it was one of the rat traps and that maybe we had actually nailed our first giant rat. So warily we went downstairs and turned on the light. Sure enough, the trap had sprung. But the rat was not in the trap. It was actually lying deathly still right next to it.

"Congratulations, we got it," I said.

"No we didn't," said Ina, our rat expert.

"What do you mean? Look, it is lying there dead."

"Its not dead, it is acting like it is dead."

"What do you mean? Rats can't act."

"Oh yes they can."

"Go pick it up by the tail and we can throw it in the rice field," I said.

"You go pick it up by the tail," responded Ina.

"Let's forget about the tail. I'm sure you have a better idea."

Ina did have a better idea. Cautiously she picked up a long handled broomstick and carefully reached out to poke the dead monster rat. But do you know what? It wasn't dead. As quick as a flash, it scooted to the front door, contorted its body and slid under the small crack between the door and the floor. That night I learned that rats can act.

Dogs were a constant worry, with most dogs left unattended in the streets. Peace Corps gave each volunteer three rabies shots upon arrival in the Philippines. These were the first shots in a series of twelve that would be necessary if bitten. The shots were given in the stomach and the thought of nine more of those jabs was just as frightening as rabies itself.

A dog actually figured prominently in one of my job related assignments. Besides the university, I also served as a consultant to the Bicol Regional Department of Education. In the early 1970s, the Philippine education system was undergoing significant reforms. One of the reforms involved changing the way social sciences were taught, from elementary school right through to university. A unified curriculum was being adopted throughout the country and it was based on scientific inquiry methodology made current by Jerome Bruner and others in the United States. The Department of Education asked me to help them introduce the new curriculum throughout the Bicol region. It provided an opportunity to visit just about every school, even the most remote, as we held orientation workshops for administrators and teachers.

One of the remotest school districts was on an island called Rapu Rapu, about four hours out into the Pacific Ocean from Legaspi City. I was invited to Rapu Rapu for a workshop. There was no problem getting there on a scheduled commercial boat but coming back two days later would present a problem. I had a morning graduate class at the university and the boat from Rapu Rapu would not return to the mainland on time. The elementary school principal was kind enough to offer her own small banca, basically a dugout canoe with an outboard motor and her boatman, to get me back. With that offer in hand, I left for Rapu Rapu.

Rapu Rapu was an extremely poor island. The inhabitants were primarily fishermen and they eked out a subsistence living. During a break in the workshop, everyone was outside having refreshments. I noticed a lone dog walking around licking people's feet, including mine. That evening, as an appreciation for the consultant team including myself, a lavish feast was laid out. This was done despite it being obvious that there was little to spare in this town. But that is how Filipinos are. They will give the shirt off their backs to a guest. It was expected that there would be fish, rice, and noodles but surprisingly, there was also meat on the table. At first one wondered where it came from. And then noticing the dog from the afternoon was no longer around, the wonderment ended. Surely, to honour a guest, meat had to be served and it was. By the way, it tasted quite good.

The trip home from Rapu Rapu was one of the most spectacular I have ever made. True to her word, the principal told me her boat and boatman would be waiting at the pier at 3:00 am in order to get me back for my class in the morning. We left under the most brilliant moonlit night with a magnificent sky filled with stars. The boatman started the put-put engine and off we went into the Pacific. It was truly breathtaking. Only later did I stop to think about what would have happened if the engine failed, and we were stranded in the ocean. But our arrival in Legaspi was in plenty of time for me to teach my class.

CHAPTER 10

RELIGION NUMBER ONE

As previously mentioned, Spain and the United States each bequeathed a similar legacy to the Philippines. That legacy was a form of "religion." In Spain's case, it was a conventional religion, namely Roman Catholicism. In America's case, the religion was non-traditional, basketball. For there is no country in the world more fanatical about basketball, none, without exception, and that includes the United States. My supposition is that more people in the Philippines are devoted to basketball than they are to the conventional religion left behind by the Spanish.

During the 1950s and 1960s, the Philippines had the best basketball players in Asia, often winning the Asian championships. That only started changing in the 1970s and not because Filipinos became worse basketball players but because South Korea and Japan were much more developed economically. The overall standard of living in those countries was a good deal higher than in the Philippines. With better diets, South Korean and Japanese players were becoming taller and stronger than their Filipino counterparts year by year. Before long, while the skills of Filipino players were just as good, these other countries were producing larger players. And of course, in recent years, the Chinese have become the best team in Asia. Nevertheless, basketball remains the number one passion for Filipinos.

It just so happened that I had a personal interest in the game, having started participating quite young, then going on to play for my high school and college varsity teams. In college, we played against teams that went on to both the National Collegiate Athletic Association (NCAA) and National Invitation (NIT) tournaments. A number of players on opposing teams went on to professional basketball careers in the National Basketball Association (NBA). As a 6'1" guard, my strength was a fairly decent jump shot from long range. After graduating, getting married and raising children, I stayed in shape, continued to play competitively and was doing so when we became volunteers. After all, thirty was not such an old age.

Although knowing nothing about Filipino fanaticism for basketball until after we arrived, did I learn quickly! While training in Iloilo, games were organized everyday after classes for the volunteers and Filipino instructors. Shortly after establishing residency in Legaspi City, I laced up my sneakers and went over to the nearest court at Divine Word College. That was my second immediate acceptance into Filipino society (eating Balut was the first). Basketball became an important part of my three years as a volunteer and in effect, became a second job after the university commitments. At times, basketball seemed to be the number one job.

My involvement with the game was not exactly the same as it had been in the United States. Basketball in the Philippines had it own distinct flavour. As a guard in college, I was usually one of the shorter players on the court. Now, in this new adopted country, my 6'1" height made me one of the tallest players. Word quickly spread around town that there was a new "Kano" (short for Americano) in town who could play basketball.

The game actually helped me graduate from "Hey Joe" to "Hey Mike." Along with the jeepney, another remnant left over from the Second World War was "Hey Joe." Filipino kids, from the time they could speak through their teenage years called any white male stranger walking down the road either "Hey Joe" or "Kano, Kano." American soldiers in the war were referred to as "G.I. Joes." In 1970, twenty-five years after it ended, all unknown white males were still "Hey Joe." It did not matter if one was Swedish, German, English, Italian, or Greek, it was "Hey Joe" or "Kano." With basketball, at least in the region where we lived, for me it was now "Hey Mike." Today, in 2007, the "Hey Joe" greeting no longer seems to be in vogue. It has not been passed on to the new generation of youngsters. A white stranger can walk around without causing any stir at all.

Every public school, high school, college, and university in the country had basketball teams. In the 1970s, there was no formal professional basketball league but big corporations sponsored teams so the players were paid as employees of the companies, not as basketball players. This was not dissimilar to the old Amateur Athletic Union (AAU) teams in the United States, such as the Phillips Oilers. This arrangement helped Filipino players keep their amateur status for the Olympics. Today, the Philippines has not one but two organized professional leagues with a number of imported players. The imports are mostly from the United States.

Basketball became an entrée into making friends and meeting new people. From pickup games, participation quickly moved into an organized league and we were soon playing in towns all over the Bicol area. A group of us, about the same age, played on a team that was sponsored by Philippines Airlines (PAL). Ben Rosalio, the station manager for PAL, had been a player on one of the semi-professional teams in Manila.

Some of my most interesting exposures to the Filipino way of life came from involvement with basketball. One of these was trying to come to grips with a much different sense of time. Each town in the Philippines has an annual fiesta honouring its patron saint. During fiesta time, it was common practice to sponsor a basketball tournament. The town invited teams to come and play in the tournament, which was normally held over three or four days. Games were always played at night because of the daytime heat. Such an arrangement also allowed more people to attend.

Our team became enormously popular and we were invited to participate in many tournaments. People wanted to see the "tall Kano" scoring a lot of points. One of the most popular annual tournaments was in Tabaco and we would travel there each evening to play our games. Our games were often scheduled as the second or third on the evening's schedule. The first game was declared as starting at 7:00 pm, the second for 9:00 pm, and if there was a third game, at 11:00 pm. My team mates would all meet at about 7:30 pm in a restaurant in Legaspi owned by one of the players. We would sit around a table with everyone except me drinking San Miguel beer. If we were to play the second game at 9:00 pm, by 8:15 I was anxious to leave for the half hour drive to Tobaco. 8:30 would come and go; then 8:45 but no one would move. Then, at some moment, unfathomable to me, without any visible signal, the group would rise in unison and it was off to Tabaco. No matter what time we left Legaspi, our arrival was never late. So much for schedules. I was never able to figure out the internal clocks of my team mates.

Playing games away from Legaspi always proved interesting and different. The locals all came out to yell and jeer. As one of the tallest and the only white guy on the court, it was easy for the crowd to find a target to jeer. Scoring a lot of points against their favourites did not help either. But when the game was over, the crowd was always friendly. We went away for one tournament and to my great surprise, the U.S. Army had entered a team. They were part of a civic action group sent to the Philippines to help repair school buildings that were damaged in a recent typhoon. Competing against the U.S. Army proved to be a role reversal for me. Playing with a group of Filipinos against five Americans, I had the whole crowd cheering and rooting for me. It was a nice change and we won the game.

After being together for about a year, we were winning a lot of tournaments. The biggest tournament in the area was about to take place during Legaspi City's fiesta. Teams were coming from as far away as Manila to play and big money was going to be bet. Gambling was always popular, with cockfighting and basketball being favourites for the gamblers. One of the teams coming from Manila had recruited five players from the semi-professional league for the Legaspi tournament. We won our first game quite handily against a weaker opponent and were scheduled the next evening against the "big bad guys" from Manila.

There was great excitement in Legaspi City and a large crowd was going to turn out for the game. Since the town plaza and basketball court were close to our apartment, I walked over to the court just as the preliminary game ended. We were now scheduled as the next contest. As we went out to warm up, wearing the same uniform as myself were four guys I had never before seen in my life. If they had the same uniform as I did, we must have been on the same team. Right? But who were these players? And where were my regular team mates, my friends?

It seemed that because this game was such a big thing for Legaspi, our PAL coach did not want to lose to a team from out of town. That morning, he quietly called his contacts in Manila and recruited four players from the semi-professional league to come and join me for the game (he probably flew them down for free on Philippine Airlines). My regular teammates, whom I thought would be upset for being replaced, were actually quite pleased with the situation. They were happy to sit on the bench and watch what turned out to be an exciting game, played at a high level. We won, the trophy was ours, and the four fellows who were my team mates, whose names were unknown to me, disappeared, never to be seen again.

Sometimes the betting stakes were so high that things got out of hand. At one tournament, there was big money being placed on the games. Tension was high among the people watching. We were playing a strong team and with about three minutes left in the first half, were ahead by four points. While running down court, there was a loud bang and within thirty seconds, hundreds of people had cleared out of the stands and disappeared, including all the players from both teams. There was no one else left on the court besides me. The other team and my team mates were no where to be found. Someone who had a bet on the game and was not satisfied with what was going on, had fired off a shot. I was later told he fired in the air but no one really knew. He might have been firing at one of the players. Perhaps at me. One of my co-players eventually grabbed me from the court, threw me into his car, and we were out of there. It was the end of that tournament for our team.

CHAPTER 11

RELIGION NUMBER TWO

There really were "other religions" besides basketball. The Catholic Church could count the largest number of faithful. Yet missionaries from various Protestant denominations were not discouraged and popped up in abundance. They viewed the Philippines as ripe for picking off converts. In day-to-day life, there was little contact with the Muslim population that was primarily located on Mindanao, Jolo, and some other islands in the south. When visiting these areas, which was possible in the early 1970s, one was immediately struck by the strong Muslim influence and cultural practices similar to such countries as Indonesia and Malaysia.

Historically, there has always been conflict between the "Muslim south" and the "Christian north." There have been insurrections and conflicts throughout the past few hundred years and certain Muslim groups have, off and on, threatened secession. Southern Mindanao has again been a war zone for the past twenty years. It has been easy to label these problems as religious conflicts. In truth, they have been more of a struggle over economic development and land rights, with Mindanao feeling it has been exploited by those from Manila and the north. All Philippine Presidents since independence have had to deal with this thorny issue, and true integration has never really happened.

In both our daily living and our work situations, we were in close contact with many Catholic priests, both Filipinos and expatriates. I came to have great respect for the priests working in the towns and barrios away from the church hierarchy in Manila (and Rome). They easily fit in and were almost always an integral part of the community. Most of the Catholic priests we met were hard working, hard drinking, down to earth and not at all full of themselves. The same could be said later for my experiences with priests in Africa.

In the Philippines, priests in the countryside were adaptable. Catholicism was often Filipino Catholicism, blending in local culture. The priests did not fight the local traditions but adapted a number of them into the church. On a few occasions, one encountered priests who did not hide their human failings; they maintained "unofficial wives." The Philippines had one of the highest birth rates of any country in the world and the Church's official policy was strongly anti-family planning. This policy was pronounced loud and clear by the Cardinal in Manila, Cardinal Jaime Sin (Yes, there was a Cardinal named Sin). He passed away in 2005). At the local level, the priests turned their heads the other way and never really proved a stumbling block to family planning activities.

After about a year in Legaspi City, two priests whom I knew quite well on the faculty of Divine Word College asked me to help them out by teaching a course in their newly developed education programme. Fr. Joe Bates was an American priest and the second was an English priest whom I will call Fr. Rick Frye. As friends, it was not easy to say no to them. The College's President, Fr. Camacho, also backed their request. We worked out a time, which would not conflict, with my Bicol University commitments (or basketball games).

The class at Divine Word only had about ten students but they were exceptionally bright and highly motivated. All were eager to graduate and start teaching. One young woman, I will call her June, especially stood out because of her keen mind and intellect.

About two months into the semester at Divine Word, Fr. Rick asked if he could have a quite conversation with Ina and myself. We had become quite friendly with Fr. Rick and saw each other on numerous social occasions. Our private conversation with him turned out to be quite a shock and began a serious of episodes that belong in a spy movie.

Rick admitted that he was in love with a young woman, a student at Divine Word College. Ina asked Fr. Rick if he knew she loved him and his answer was "definitely, yes." . Being nosy, my next question was "Do we know her?" And he said "of course, she is in your class." The young woman in question was June.

Silence reigned for sometime as we tried to think of something to say. When we finally asked what he planned to do, Fr. Rick who was a caring and compassionate individual and somewhat of an idealist answered, "I am petitioning Rome for a dispensation to allow us to get married." Being a non-Catholic but knowing something of the Church's track record on married priests, I told Fr. Rick he was dreaming about something that will never happen. He, however, was full of confidence and declared he planned to go to Rome to plead his case.

While waiting for word on his dispensation, Fr. Rick swore Ina and I to secrecy. He basically could trust us because as non-Catholics, there could not be a threat of excommunication. Neither Fr. Rick nor June had shared their involvement with anyone and we were the only ones besides the two of them to know. Her parents were very traditional and conservative. The consequences for June as well as Fr. Rick would have been grave had anyone found out. The two of them honestly believed that if Rome approved, they could then go public and everyone would continue doing what they had done before, including Fr. Rick remaining a priest.

We were really curious as to why Fr. Rick would reveal his secret to us at this time. He explained that the first reason was before leaving for Rome, there was really no place where he and June could meet and speak privately. "Could we come over here from time to time?" We had no objection and when they did come, they were always well chaperoned. The second reason was that he expected to be in Rome for an indefinite period and had no way to communicate with June. "Could I send letters for her to your house?" Again, we had no objection and told him to address any mail from him to Master Matthew Gerber. Matthew was only seven years old and didn't receive letters from anyone. If a letter came for Matthew, we would not open it. I would then quietly let June know after one of our classes and she would later come over to the apartment, go upstairs, and read it. Our place was being used as a "dead letter drop," just like in the movies.

This story had both a sad and a happy ending. The sad part for Fr. Rick and June was, as expected, the Church denied any dispensation and refused to allow this priest to be married. After much deliberation and soul searching, Rick decided to leave the priesthood. He and June were married. They moved to England and the last we heard, he was continuing his following by working with troubled youth and she became a midwife.

Besides priests, there was frequent contact with strong advocates of other religions. The Church of Latter Day Saints was quite active in the Philippines. We met many young men who were spending a year away from college doing missionary work. It was always easy to spot these Mormon missionaries. They were dressed in identical fashion, short white sleeve shirts, thin black ties, long black pants, and carried black attaché cases. The Mormon missionaries were the only people I ever saw wearing ties in Legaspi City. When some of the young men came around knocking on our door, we frequently invited them in for discussions about their religion's policy towards race, namely who could or could not be full members of their church. While we never saw eye to eye and they never made any converts at our home, the young men were always polite, well spoken, and intelligent. We enjoyed their company.

The same could not always be said about some missionaries from other

Protestant sects. Unlike the low-key demeanour of most Catholic priests, these missionaries seemed to take great pleasure in calling attention to themselves. They often rode around in large, four wheel drive air-conditioned vehicles, hidden behind tinted windows drawn up tight. Painted in the biggest possible letters on the sides of their vehicles was the name of their church or their sect. A number of them lived in particularly large houses with servants. Their life styles were markedly different from those they were trying to convert. The Catholic priests we knew were always able to separate their religious duties from their social lives. Not so these missionaries. Whether in church or at a dinner party, they were sure to make their conversion pitch. As with the Mormons, none had any success with us.

There were a number of interesting indigenous religious sects. One of these was the Rizalista Church. Jose Rizal was a great 19th century Filipino writer and nationalist leader. The followers of this Church, which had all the trappings of Catholicism, worshipped Rizal. When attending a mass, the rites appeared to follow those of the Catholic Church with the exception that Rizal replaced Jesus.

One Peace Corps volunteer, Randy Schwartz, a nice Jewish boy from New York City, married a Filipina who was a Rizalista. Like many of those belonging to this Church, she came from a poor farming family. Our youngest, Daniel, was asked to serve as ring bearer and we had a first hand look at the Church's marriage rites. Randy's mother had come from New York for this wedding. During the ceremony, we wondered what she thought about all that was going on. It wasn't exactly your typical Jewish wedding. But Randy's mom seemed to take it all in good stride and the newly married couple appeared to be more than happy. Daniel, who was two years old and blond, proved to be a popular choice as a ring bearer. He went on to perform the same service admirably at a number of other weddings. We actually thought of renting him out.

Regarding mixed marriages, a number of male volunteers married Filipinas. The women were beautiful and without sounding like a male chauvinist, had traditional Asian values towards men. This meant worship your husband and do everything to please him. Most of these marriages worked out well. The males liked being worshipped and taken care of. But the women also came out ahead. They now had a guaranteed entrée , a green card, into the United States. There were fewer mixed marriages between female volunteers and Filipinos. These often did not work as well. The Filipino male had his traditional attitudes towards women. The American females usually did not believe in blind obedience and servitude.

CHAPTER 12

OUR OLD FRIENDS – THE PEACE CORPS ORGANIZATION

Once we became volunteers, fortunately there was minimal contact with Peace Corps as an organization. The Peace Corps Philippines had its office in Manila. The head was a Country Director who was responsible both to the U.S Ambassador in the Philippines and the Peace Corps Asia Director in Washington. The Manila office had a sizable number of other paid staff made up of both Americans and Filipinos. In addition, there were a number of regional offices throughout the country. There was such an office in Legaspi City. Heading the Regional Office was a Regional Director who reported to the Country Director in Manila. During our time as volunteers, the Regional Directors were all Americans.

Paid staff must have totalled about fifty. Throughout the country, there were almost 300 volunteers. There always seemed to be tension between the two groups and many volunteers felt the staff's primary concern was to justify their own existence.

We thought we had learned enough about the Peace Corps organization during our application period and training. My attitude now as a serving volunteer was that my responsibility was my university, whose Deans were my bosses. As long as Peace Corps made sure we received our monthly maintenance allowances and took care of any health problems that arose, our paths needed to cross as little as possible. They did not cross often but when they did, it was not always a smooth crossing.

An example of these sad crossings arose over an incident related to the health of our eldest boy. Matthew became sick one day with a high fever. When the fever did not subside, we took him over to the local hospital. After an examination, the doctor presented us with his diagnosis, namely appendicitis, a common diagnosis for many ailments. We were concerned that the local hospital was not geared up to cope with any post-operative emergencies, should one occur.

Peace Corps had a policy, which stated that if a volunteer or dependent was seriously ill and they could not be treated locally, an immediate medical evacuation to Manila would be arranged. If the problem could not be dealt with in Manila, then the volunteer would be evacuated outside of the country, to the U.S. if necessary. Such a policy was always reassuring given that our kids would be living in places where health and medical facilities could not always cope with emergencies or complicated cases.

Hearing of the need to immediately remove his appendix, we asked the hospital and the local Peace Corps office in Legaspi to contact Manila and have Matthew evacuated to the capital. It was now about 5:00 pm. Around 7:00 pm, a message came back from Peace Corps Manila, which said "Gruber child? There is no Gruber family in Legaspi City." The idiots either misheard or misread the name and could not figure out the name was Gerber, as if there were so many Peace Corps Volunteers in Legaspi (we were the only ones). By now, given it was already dark, it would have been too late to evacuate by air. Matthew stayed in the hospital overnight and miraculously by morning, his fever was gone. No appendix and no evacuation. It left us rather skeptical about both the local diagnosing capabilities and Peace Corps' evacuation policy.

In theory, there was nothing wrong with the medical policy, it was actually quite good. The problem rested with those who were implementing the policies, such as in the case of Matthew's "non evacuation." Another aspect of the policy stated that if a volunteer contracted an illness or medical problem while in service, Peace Corps would pay for dealing with that problem even after the volunteer left service. I was to develop some pilonidal cysts on the base of my spine soon after leaving the Philippines. The doctor asked if I rode horses every day because the constant pounding of bumping up and down could be the cause. I told him no, but explained that I had just spent three years riding in jeepneys over some of the roughest, isolated rural roads imaginable. "That could do it," he said, adding, "Riding in jeeps was the leading cause of pilonidal cyst occurrence among servicemen in World War Two." Peace Corps did pay for the surgery to remove those cysts one year after we had finished our service.

Toward the end of our second year, the Director of Peace Corps, Joe Blatchford, visited the Philippines. Blatchford was a former Congressman from California and a Nixon appointee as Peace Corps Director. One of his primary objectives for coming to the Philippines at that time was a photo opportunity with some of the Peace Corps families. Peace Corps was trying to justify to Congress that while the families were more expensive to support than other volunteers, the new programme was a success. Since we were only one of two families to have requested a third year of service, the bigshots in Manila figured we were happy volunteers and Blatchford should be brought to Legaspi to visit with us. Did they make a mistake! We were in the main, happy volunteers but as you have read, it was not because of the Peace Corps organization but rather the contrary.

Well, the big day finally came. A three-car motorcade pulled up at our door and an entourage poured out of those cars, which included Blatchford, a number of his aides, the Philippines Peace Corps Country Director, the Bicol Regional Director, and a photographer. It was like a scene out of the circus where about ten clowns emerge from a tiny car. This was that scene with a twist. It was like a lot of clowns stuffing themselves into our small apartment.

If Blatchford thought he was going to hear from us about how wonderful his organization was, he was in for a big surprise. Ina did most of the talking and gave him a litany of most of the experiences you have read about in these pages, beginning with the initial application process and finishing with the botched medical evacuation of Matthew, with many things in between. Blatchford's ears were ringing by the time she finished. No one waited for photos to be taken. They beat a hasty retreat, looking for greener pastures elsewhere.

The Peace Corps experimental family programme turned out to have mixed results. Of the six families, two terminated before their two years were up, two finished the two years, and two extended for an additional year. The family with the most problems had the oldest children. Their three kids were teenagers and it proved problematical for kids of that age to adjust, given the Peace Corps volunteer status of the family. The kids were placed in the International School in Manila. Their classmates had plenty of money, being the sons and daughters of diplomats and wealthy business people. The teenage years are awkward enough and to place those youngsters in a situation where they did not have the means to do what their classmates did was a big mistake. They were one of the families that terminated before their tour ended.

With young children, there was a great advantage. At six, three, and two, the boys were extraordinarily flexible and adapted to most new situations quickly. Living in a small rural city, we did not have to compete with the wealthy and our kids quickly became part of the local society. They were easy to travel with, would sleep anywhere, and eat almost anything. Our boys, with the exception of their skin colour, really became Filipino kids.

Upon returning to the U.S. and putting them into school, Ina received a call from Adam's teacher after only the second day of the term. We couldn't believe he was in trouble after just two days in his American school. Ina went in expecting the worst and was totally unprepared for what she heard. The teacher could not figure Adam out. He always called her "maam," was exceptionally polite, never raised his voice above a loud whisper, and always did everything he was told. She wanted to know what was the matter with the boy. Unfortunately, that lasted about three weeks. He quickly adapted to his new culture and became a typical, loudmouthed American kid in a short time.

Peace Corps phased out the family programme after only a few years. It proved difficult to justify the additional expenses for maintaining a volunteer family overseas. In reality, the organization was not terribly well equipped to support such a programme, which was obvious to those on the inside.

CHAPTER 13

RESEARCH AND POLITICS

At the start of our third year as volunteers, in August 1972, discussions took place in our family as to what should be done when our service ended. It was agreed that the Gerber family should return to the United States rather than seek paid employment overseas. This decision was reached primarily for educational reasons. It was felt the boys would now benefit from returning to an American school system. Ina wanted to pursue a Masters Degree in biology. And I wanted to finish my PhD degree, having completed almost all of the course work at New York University before we left in 1970. Regarding the latter, left in limbo was the identification of a research proposal for a dissertation. My interests were closely related to Asian culture and education. Somehow, I wanted to link the three, but had no idea of a specific topic when we left for the Philippines.

* * *

While in Legaspi City, two factors influenced the identification of a topic and the advancement of my doctoral dissertation. The first was an invitation to assist the Regional Department of Education with their new social science curriculum. The second was a declaration of martial law in the Philippines during September 1972.

It was quickly obvious to a number of people that the new comprehensive social science programme being adopted for Philippine schools and colleges had some problems. The curriculum was based on scientific inquiry methodologies and rational questioning, encouraging students to think for themselves and not accept things on face value. This was the latest trend in the United States, and was promoted in the late 1950s and throughout the 1960s. It was advocated because the United States was in a "space race" with the Soviet Union. The Russian Sputnik of 1958 had a profound impact on American education. There was panic that American education was falling behind the Russians. American kids would need to become more scientifically oriented so we could catch up. The scientific thinking was applied to social science methodology.

Given close historical ties between the Philippines and the United States, many Filipino leaders in government, universities, and business, received their graduate education in America. This was especially true for the leading thinkers in Philippine education who were influenced by scientific inquiry models being propagated in the U.S. A number of the key educators who helped develop the new social science curriculum, both from the national Department of Education and from leading Philippine academic institutions, were PhD holders from places like Stanford, Indiana, and other American universities.

As the new curriculum was introduced nationwide, it was fairly obvious to observe that there were a number of discontinuities or conflicts between the educational methodology of the new social science curriculum and prevalent Filipino values. Teaching youngsters in America to question, to not accept things on face value, was acceptable. It was not alien to American values, even if it meant questioning a teacher in the classroom. Children are always questioning their own parents. Why not question teachers? But it was a different story in the Philippines.

Filipino society was traditional, formal, with particular attention given to respect for age and authority. Children were acculturated to be seen but not heard, and when they were heard, it was barely above a whisper. Unquestioned allegiance was given to grandparents, parents, teachers, and anyone else older or in authority. No child would question his parent or a teacher, either in the classroom or outside. Every teacher in every classroom throughout the country was addressed as "Sir" or "Maam." Even if a student went on to become President of the Philippines, and if he or she met a former elementary school teacher, it was still "Sir" or "Maam."

Observing such conflicts between the culture and the social science methodology being proposed led to serious consideration regarding a PhD dissertation topic. While in the Philippines, I stayed in close touch with my doctoral adviser at New York University. Then on home leave in 1972, after completing our first two years of service, we met to discuss a proposed topic. He encouraged me. It was now going to be necessary to collect enough data to write my dissertation after completing our last year of service as volunteers. It was a sad and unfortunate occurrence in the Philippines that provided enough time to start collecting data.

In September 1972, President Ferdinand Marcos declared martial law throughout the entire country. What did this have to do with the furtherance of my doctoral dissertation? Well, the declaration of martial law forced the closure for a few weeks of all universities in the country. With no classes, I was able to start on the data collection.

Ferdinand Marcos had become President of the Philippines in 1965. He had been a brilliant student at the University of the Philippines and became an equally brilliant lawyer, being the only person in the Philippines ever to defend himself successfully in a murder trial. From the Province of Illocos Norte in northern Luzon, he was first elected as a Congressman before becoming President. The Philippine Constitution was modelled after that of the U.S., with a separate Executive Branch, two houses of Congress, and an independent judiciary. There were fixed limits set for a President's term.

Marcos had married a beautiful model from Leyte, Imelda Roumaldez. She was from the poorer branch of a prominent Leyte family. Marcos, after being elected President, was easily re-elected for a second term. Philippine politics were a tricky but predictable business. It was said that 100 families owned 95 per cent of the wealth of the Philippines. These families aligned themselves into two political parties but party loyalty was not often firm. Filipino politicians changed parties as quickly as a rabbit scoots across a road.

From 1946 onward, while the Presidents might be elected and then replaced, there was little effect on policy or action. It was just one of the parties replacing the other with little difference between the two. The one exception was Ramon Magsaysay. Magsaysay led a Filipino guerrilla movement against the Japanese invaders during World War II. After the war, he was named Secretary of National Defence in 1950 and completed a successful campaign to defeat the communist inspired Hukbalahap (Huk) rebels. Elected President of the Philippines in 1953, Magsaysay was a strong advocate of land reform, which made him suspect among the wealthy elite but popular with farmers and the common people. Sadly, he died in a plane crash in March of 1957 before seeing his reform policies come to fruition.

During Marcos' second term, strong rumours abounded that he was going to try and have the Constitution changed in order to remain in power. There was strong political opposition to the Marcos regime as well as a communist insurgency (the New People's Army) active in different parts of the country, including Sorsogon Province, which was also part of the Bicol Region, and the Province next door to where we lived in Albay.

* * *

Vociferous anti-Marcos sentiment continued to grow. Much of the press was critical of both him and Imelda. The Philippines had one of the freest and most irresponsible press of any country. There were a number of English language dailies and one of them ran an article that was truly unforgettable.

Imelda Marcos had an uncle whom the President had appointed as the Philippine Ambassador to the United States. Like every other Filipino, the Ambassador had a nickname. Ambassador Roumaldez's nickname was Kokoy. A small, but vociferous segment of society expressed strong anti-American sentiments and was critical of what they perceived to be a one-sided relationship between the two countries. One day, an anti-Marcos Manila newspaper ran on its front page a lead article headlined in big bold letters. The article was entitled "The Thoughts of Kokoy".

Below the bold headlines of this article was a wide column that ran the length of page one. It was completely blank, not one written word, just white space except for the very bottom of the column. Appearing were four small words, "continued on page 6." Upon turning to page 6, all that was found was another wide column, as blank and as stark white as on page one. Enough said about the thoughts of Kokoy.

Just prior to the declaration of martial law, a bomb exploded during a political rally held at the Plaza Miranda in Manila. Some people were killed and many injured. Marcos blamed the bombing on the communists and shortly afterwards, declared martial law and among other actions, closed the universities for a number of weeks. Marcos (and Imelda) remained in power until overthrown by a popular and basically peaceful revolution in 1986. It was the August 1983 assassination of Benigno (Ninoy) Aquino, a popular opposition leader, who was gunned down at Manila's international airport upon returning home from three years in exile that sparked the "people power" revolution. It culminated in 1986 when Marcos and Imelda had to flee to Hawaii, without her infamous shoe collection, where he eventually died. Corazon (Cory) Aquino, wife of the slain opposition leader, then became the first woman President of the Philippines. .

It was possible to use those few weeks of marital law to begin data collection. In the provinces, there was little indication of what martial law actually was. True there was a curfew at night but there were few soldiers evident (a few appeared in the market) and no presence of extra police. Worried relatives in the States, upon hearing what happened in the Philippines, anxiously contacted us but we alleviated their fears. For those not involved in politics, life went on as normal.

During the weeks that no classes were held, I travelled to Manila to use the library at the University of the Philippines (UP). It was the best library in the country. The Philippines had a number of prominent universities of which UP, a public university, was the most well known. The best of the private universities were Santo Tomas, the oldest in the country, founded in 1619 by the Dominicans and Ateneo de Manila, opened in 1859 by the Jesuits, and one of the most demanding academically.

Because the university was officially closed to students, the library was also off limits to all. But some friends on the faculty helped. They were able to get me in and it was an eerie feeling being a lonesome soul using this vast collection. I used the next few weeks to advantage and, along with other opportunities during the year, my data was collected by the time we eventually left the country in July 1973.

With a commitment to continue teaching, I sent out resumes to numerous colleges and universities at the end of 1972, seeking a position for the academic year beginning September 1973. During the time we were in the Philippines, I had kept in touch with a number of former faculty colleagues at Brooklyn College, and to my great surprise, was invited back to rejoin the faculty. The former Dean had left and the School of Education was looking to introduce a more international flavour into its comparative education courses. They already had a Latin American expert on staff and I would add an Asian dimension. I agreed to the offer and it was nice to know that when we left the Philippines, there was a job to go back to which would put food on our table.

As an aside, I only again started working for real wages in September of 1973. During that entire year, our total family income was about £2,100 and taxes were withheld on this amount. Would you believe that six months later, after filing our income tax forms, we were called down to the Internal Revenue Service (IRS) for an audit? We read the audit notice with disbelief. How do you audit a family of two adults and three children earning a total of £2,100? The sad explanation given to us by the IRS investigator was that since we earned so little, the computer picked us out. We told him what we thought about the IRS and its computer.

CHAPTER 14

THE END GAME –
A DEATH IN THE FAMILY
AND GETTING OUT

Having been granted an extension as volunteers for one year, we now planned to leave the Philippines towards the latter part of April 1973, when classes for the academic year ended at the university. In March of that year, the Dean asked if it would be possible to stay for an additional eight weeks in order to teach some courses in the summer session. I told the Dean it would be no problem as long as Peace Corps approved. We applied to the head office in Manila through the regional office and within a week, the approval was granted. Our departure date was now scheduled for mid-July, after summer session ended.

Just as summer classes began in early May, one evening there was a knock on our door. It was the Regional Director who had rarely shown up on our doorstep before. He told us he had some bad news for Ina. A call was received in Manila with information that her father had died. Peace Corps Manila was organizing compassionate leave for Ina to immediately travel to New York City, where her mother and brothers lived and where the funeral would take place. I said to him, "It was also my father-in-law that passed away. And according to the Peace Corps by-laws, surely we were both entitled to attend the funeral." The Regional Director replied that Manila had only approved Ina's flight. Upon hearing this, he was told that we wanted to speak to Manila and since we had no phone, it was off to his house. On the phone, the administrative office in Manila was told what we thought of them denying me the right to attend my father-in-law's funeral. They said they would have to clear my going with Washington. An hour later, a call came back saying not only could the both of us go but we could take the children as well. It seemed as if Peace Corps was trying to play games. The Manila office was informed that the kids were in school and they were too young to be travelling close to 10,000 miles for a funeral.

That evening, we asked our neighbours, Drs. Johnnie and Ludi Estevez, who had children friendly with ours, if they would allow Matthew, Adam, and Daniel to stay with them for a week while we were away for the funeral. They were accommodating and their kids were ecstatic that ours would stay in their house. We flew to Manila the next morning, left for San Francisco in the afternoon, and arrived in New York a day later, in time for the funeral. We stayed a few extra days so Ina could be with her mom and brothers.

Before leaving Manila, a Peace Corps staff member gave us the telephone number of Peace Corps Washington's emergency office. He asked that we call the number after reaching the U.S. to check in with the office, explaining such a call was standard procedure. However, with a deep distrust of what Peace Corps was up to, we waited until the morning of our return to the Philippines before calling the Washington number, actually dialling from John F Kennedy Airport prior to boarding a flight to San Francisco.

A woman in the emergency office answered the phone. Our conversation went like this:

"This is Mike Gerber. We are volunteers in the Philippines, now here in the U.S. on emergency leave attending my father-in-law's funeral. We were told to call in to inform your office. Whom am I speaking with?"

"Hi! I'm Peggy Sue (Peggy Sue seemed to be a common name among staff in Washington). What did you say your name was?"

"My name is Mike Gerber. My wife and I are volunteers based in Legaspi City, Philippines."

Peggy Sue: "Could you please wait a minute Mr. Gerber." (pause)

One minute turned into five and Peggy Sue finally came back on the phone.

"We had expected you to call the day you arrived in the States. We want to inform you that since you only have seven more weeks to go, it doesn't make sense for you to go back to the Philippines so we will terminate your services as of now. We normally do this for volunteers who take emergency leave close to their termination dates."

My response to the young woman was as follows:

"Well, Peggy Sue I am going to give you three reasons why you will not terminate our services right now. First of all, a professional commitment has been made to teach summer semester at the university. They are depending on me and students have already enrolled for the courses. We realize that people in Peace Corps Washington are not overly concerned about what a professional commitment means but perhaps this can serve as a good example."

"Secondly, we have three kids, aged nine, six, and five as well as all of our other worldly possessions back in Legaspi City. Peggy Sue, are you telling us to abandon our children in the Philippines?"

"And thirdly, Peggy Sue, and most importantly, right now I am holding in my hand two confirmed return tickets back to the Philippines. Your 'suggestion' to terminate us early was anticipated so we were not going to leave Manila without return tickets. And do you know where we are calling you from? That's right, JFK Airport. We did not call you when we arrived in the States. We are calling you as they are making the boarding announcement for our return flight that is now leaving. Sorry to upset your routine and your questionable termination policy but don't despair, we will send you a nice picture postcard from Legaspi as soon as we get back home."

We arrived back in Legaspi City, safe and sound, to three happy kids, our apartment, and the last seven weeks of summer session. I didn't think much of Peace Corps' compassionate leave.

During our last few weeks in Legaspi, friends and colleagues gave us a number of going-away parties called "despedidas". These despedidas were part of the culture and gifts were always given. We had to find a third duffle bag to carry the gifts. On the day of our departure for Manila, my basketball buddies showed up at the airport carrying a case of San Miguel beer, twenty-four bottles, and gave it to us as a going away present. Now how could we carry a case of beer on the airplane? After offering profuse thanks and convincing them it would be impossible to get the bottles back to the U.S. unbroken, it was suggested the beer be opened right there and that we have one last party. They were still drinking along-side the runway as our plane taxied for takeoff.

Normal procedure for volunteers leaving service was to spend the last week in Manila undergoing debriefing and medical exams. Sometimes what was supposed to be normal turned out abnormal.

The final medicals were enormously important. Peace Corps wanted to make sure every terminating volunteer was healthy. Since they had a commitment to continue caring for any medical problems contracted while in service, the staff wanted to ensure we were cured of all ailments and rid of bugs and other parasites before flying out of Manila. The final examinations were thorough, with volunteers undergoing all kinds of tests. One had to produce both a urine and stool sample for analysis. Everyone was given a little brown canister, which we carried all over in order to be ready for collection of the latter.

Producing the stool sample was a dreaded affair for more than a few volunteers. There were rumours about some who were ready to leave but had to remain in Manila for an extra month just to produce that stool sample. Why would a little piece of turd cause so much anxiety?

You have to understand the environment in which some single volunteers lived during their two years of service. Many were assigned to the remotest of rural areas. A number were sent to such out-of-the-way islands like Mindoro or Palawan. They often lived with extremely poor families whose diet was simple and unvaried. For their two years, a number of these volunteers ate nothing but the staple Filipino foods, namely rice or camote (a form of sweet potato) and some fish. Both rice and camote are starches. A steady diet of either can bind one's stomach harder than a rock. Producing a stool sample on demand was not an easy trick for the rice and camote-eating volunteers. When ready for their exit, there was a great deal of uneasiness about the final physical examination and other tests.

A story had been circulating about the departure of a female volunteer. She had actually served for two years in a remote part of the Bicol Region, about forty kilometres from where we had been stationed. Those who told the story swore it was true but since the volunteer in question had left before we did, there was no way for me to corroborate it. Without doubt, it does capture the flavour of the final examination week and is worth telling.

Susan Laury, the volunteer in question, was one of those who had been eating rice and little else. Being ready to leave, she went to Manila with more than a little anxiety for the final week. One advantage of the last week was it gave volunteers an opportunity to meet old friends who were also leaving. Susan made an appointment to have lunch with two female volunteers. After lunch, she was to proceed to the Peace Corps office for a medical examination in the afternoon.

To Susan's good fortune and relief, that same morning she produced her stool sample. It was loaded into the canister and then placed into a plain brown paper bag. She would bring it along to her appointment and then turn it over to the Peace Corps doctor at her examination. Susan carried that brown paper bag with an iron grip as if it was filled with gold, which for us volunteers in the last week, was more precious than gold.

Susan and her friends were to meet in a restaurant not far from the American Embassy on Roxas Boulevard. In 1972, Roxas Boulevard was an attractive avenue, which followed along the contours of Manila Bay. It was a famous place for watching the most beautiful sunsets. On one side was the city of Manila and on the other a seawall. At one point, the seawall separated Roxas Boulevard from a small sandy beach and the ocean. Getting to the appointed meeting place early, Susan sat up on the seawall with her back to the sea, waiting for her friends to arrive. She placed the precious brown bag right next to her. Without concern for anything behind her, an unknown person wearing a wet suit, goggles, and flippers came out of the water, walked up to the seawall without Susan seeing, snatched the brown paper bag, ran back into the ocean with Susan in pursuit, and disappeared below the waves.

I am not sure who was the bigger loser, poor Susan, who was traumatized and would now have to produce another stool sample, or the thief? One can imagine the reaction of the poor fellow when he opened the bag to count his loot and found what was inside. Poetic justice?

Over the past twenty five years there have been many projects to reclaim land from the sea and now, much of the seaside of Roxas Boulevard has benefited or suffered from such projects. In many places, Manila Bay no longer laps its waves against the seawall. If Susan's thief is still alive and up to his old tricks, upon leaving the water he would have to run about a kilometre across reclaimed land in his wet suit and flippers to steal more shit.

As to our family, we produced everything that was necessary, passed all the tests, and were cleared to leave. Our plans were to travel for about forty-five days, ending up in the New York City area at mid-September for me to start work and the boys to enrol in school. Our journey to the U.S. took us through Thailand, India, Afghanistan, Iran, Turkey, Israel, Greece, Germany, France, and England. Some interesting things happened on this long journey home.

CHAPTER 15

THE LONG WAY HOME

Bicol University attracted a handful of foreign graduate students each year. There were, at any one time, at least three or four from Thailand. The Thais viewed speaking English as a distinct advantage. For those who wanted to pursue further education in the English language, the United States, Australia, Canada, or Great Britain were countries of choice. If those options were not available, the Philippines was another possibility since all university instruction was in English. The Philippines also had other advantages. It was much closer to Thailand, getting home was easier and less costly, and tuition and maintenance expenses were about a third of those in North America or Europe.

Besides advising Filipino graduate students, I also served as thesis adviser to three Thais during my years as a Peace Corps volunteer. They each came to Bicol University to obtain a Masters Degree. There was a subtle reluctance on the part of some Filipino faculty colleagues to mentor the Thai students. This might have been due to a lack of command of the English language on the part of the latter. As far as I was concerned, there was no reluctance. It was not all giving on my part. While I served as an academic adviser, the students would, from time to time, share their Thai food with us, which Ina and I loved to eat. We eventually became good friends with two of the students.

One was a remarkable woman. She was in her mid-thirties, married with four children, and a teacher by profession. With education given great importance, the whole family sacrificed so she could spend two years in the Philippines getting her graduate degree. Her husband, who worked for the Thai Government, and her mother took care of the children. She was able to get home only once in two years to see the family. Struggling with English at the beginning, she worked extremely hard and eventually graduated with honours. It was rewarding to see the excellent job she did on her thesis.

Given the friendship she developed with our family, we had an open invitation to visit her home in Thailand. She lived in Udon Thani, in northeastern Thailand, not far from the Mekong River. Since we would be travelling to Thailand for a second time on our way home, Udon was placed on our itinerary.

With typical Thai hospitality, the family treated us like honoured guests. Our boys had a great time with their children even though neither set of kids could speak a word of the other's language. While only in Thailand for a few days, our hosts arranged two "unique" excursions for us.

Outside a small village, about forty kilometres from Udon, archaeologists had uncovered a site that revealed findings of a civilization dating back just about 4,000 years. The site was declared an historical monument by Royal decree, which meant it was forbidden to remove any of the findings. In general, Thailand had exceedingly strict laws prohibiting the removal of antiquities, with harsh punishment for any one trying to take something out of the country. Signs at the airport so informed anyone entering or leaving.

*   *   *

We were taken to visit the site. It was located just at the edge of a typical small Thai rural village. There was one dirt path, which was sort of Main Street. On either side of the path were rows of wooden houses with thatched roofs. The houses were off the ground on stilts, to protect from flooding and to allow animals underneath. There were probably a maximum of about twenty houses in all. Walking down "Main Street," there were whistles and calls from each of the houses. Looking up, it was usually an old woman in the doorway motioning for us to come in. Entering two of the houses, we saw exactly the same thing. Pieces of pottery and other artefacts were being offered for sale. The villagers either looted a good part of the site before the government sealed it off or they were making good imitations. They had developed a cosy little cottage industry. Obviously, we good-naturedly refused all offers to buy.

The next morning our hosts had another trip scheduled. We were informed to leave everything behind – passports, wallets, money, children, anything that could identify us. Hearing this, we diplomatically asked,

"Where are we going?"

"To Laos" was the answer.

"Don't we need visas to enter Laos?"

"Not today" came back the response.

"Shouldn't we have our passports with us?"

"No, do not worry."

"Then, let's go."

This was 1973, the year the last American troops left Vietnam and two years before the fall of Saigon to the North Vietnamese. A clandestine war had been taking place in Laos. The U.S., with the C.I.A. playing a major role, had secretly trained about 30,000 Laotians, mostly Hmong tribesmen, to fight the North Vietnamese regular army, the Vietcong, and their Pathet Lao allies. The Ho Chi Minh Trail actually ran through a part of Laos. Americans definitely needed visas to get into the country. In fact, the only legal point of entry was through the capital, Vientiane, and one was only permitted to arrive by air. It appeared that morning our journey into Laos was not going to take place through official channels.

The boys were left with our hosts' children and their grandmother. We drove to Nong Khai, a small town on the Mekong River. The Mekong separated Thailand and Laos. Our host got out and spoke to a few officials whom he seemed to know quite well. After a lengthy discussion, it was back into the car and a further twenty-minute drive to a second village on the river. The discussion here was shorter but much more animated. It did not seem to go well. At a third stop, we were told to leave the car and come down to the river. The four of us got into a small dugout canoe with an outboard motor and headed across the river. In less than fifteen minutes we were in Vientiane, Laos. No passports, no immigration, no customs, no questions asked on either side.

For sure, the discussions on the Thai side of the river involved friendships with officials, cajoling, and most likely, money passing hands. Whatever was involved, we were across. After about twelve hours in Laos, the process was reversed, back into the boat, to the other side of the river, and into Thailand. Upon returning to our friend's home, we found our children almost sorry to see us. They had a great time with their friends and grandma. She would give them a few baht and off they would run to the market. Our boys each had red mouths from the beetle nut the old lady had given them to chew. A wonderful time was had by all.

Afghanistan was the most difficult country we ever visited. In 1973 the war with Russia had not yet started. It was possible to travel everywhere but getting around did not prove easy. Ina found herself the victim of cultural bias. Even in the capital, Kabul, adult women were basically invisible. If they did appear in public, they were covered from head to toe with a chador. The city had a popular park where people went for an outing each Sunday. We visited the park and everyone was sprawled out on the grass, eating and drinking. But we only saw men. The woman were hidden away, either behind bushes or behind blankets that were strung up between two trees.

If a western woman was married and had children, that was usually enough to act as a legitimising agent. But not in Afghanistan. Even with three kids in tow, on occasion Ina was given a hard time. There was a lot of subtle but inappropriate touching by Afghan males, though it did not stop us from visiting various parts of the country, which is ruggedly beautiful.

An eventful, or rather uneventful trip, was the one we were to make to Bamian in the north. Bamian was the famous site having the world's largest stone Buddhist statues. Sadly, these were destroyed in 2001 by the religiously fanatical Taliban regime in Afghanistan. Because our time was limited, we booked to fly to Bamian on the local airline, stay overnight, and return the next day.

The one flight a day to Bamian was scheduled to depart Kabul at 8:00 am. Being told to get to the airport no less than thirty minutes before the scheduled departure, we arrived by 7:00 am just to be safe. Upon arriving, we seemed to be the only ones in the airport terminal. By 7:30, we were still the only ones. Finally, finding an airline representative, we inquired about the flight to Bamian.

"Oh, the flight has already gone," we were told.

"Gone? It is scheduled to leave at 8:00 o'clock."

"Oh, the plane filled up early and left."

"And what time did it leave?"

"At about 6:00 am."

Keen to see the statues, we rebooked for the next day. The following morning, now older and wiser, we arrived at the airport by 5:00 am. By 5:30, four more people had arrived. We were now nine. By 8:00, there were still only nine of us. At 8:30, the same airline representative appeared and announced there would be no flight that day because there were not enough people to fill up the plane. That was it for scheduled air service in Afghanistan. I believe we were just not destined to ever see those statues.

*   *   *

Arriving in Israel was the beginning of a weeklong culture shock. After three years in Southeast Asia, we were used to people speaking softly, being overly polite to one another, and avoiding confrontation at all cost. Hello Israel, goodbye Asia. This was our introduction into another world.

At Lod Airport, there was more shouting, yelling, and confrontation than we had ever seen before. The Israelis were the polar opposites of Filipinos. Staying in Jerusalem, we decided to take a bus and visit Tel Aviv. Upon boarding the bus, in the second row of seats was a woman sitting near the window. In the seat right next to her was a dog. Yes, a dog sitting on the seat. Our kids were flabbergasted.

While travelling in Asia and then Africa, I have been on crowded public transport with live chickens, goats, even a pig at one time. But it was accepted practice that humans had preference over animals. People on the seats and animals on the floor, under people's legs. But I guess preferences were different in Israel.

As the bus was not yet full, we took seats about five rows back. Within a few stops, more and more people got on and all the seats were taken. Eventually there were more people than seats so some had to stand, hanging on to straps. The standees were giving the lady and her dog all sorts of dirty looks. But that lady never moved her dog. We told the boys to stand up so the adults could take their seats. That action drew all kinds of surprised looks, as if it was the first time such a gesture had occurred. The kids could not understand how a dog could sit while people stood.

Another bus trip gave us a further glimpse into Israeli life and interpersonal relationships. Having never seen a kibbutz, we chose one from a guidebook to visit. A bus leaving from Jerusalem would take us to our destination. While waiting at the bus station, an elderly couple who appeared to be in their eighties started speaking to the boys. Adam came over to us and said they could not understand what was being said to them. It seemed the couple first started speaking in Hebrew and when our boys didn't understand, switched to another language. The second language was Russian.

Ina, born in the Ukraine, speaks both Ukrainian and some Russian. When she started speaking to the old lady in Russian, the woman greeted Ina like a long-lost daughter. They told an amazing story with Ina acting as translator.

To escape Czarist Russia, this couple with a number of other people, went first to Turkey and then trekked on foot across that country as well as Syria to reach Palestine in 1905. The journey on foot took them over two years. Upon arrival in Palestine, the group founded a kibbutz which turned out to be the second oldest kibbutz in what is today Israel. They told us of the first two winters, when settlers had only tents to sleep in. All of the first-born children died, not being able to survive the cold. The old woman lost her first child, a girl. Perhaps that was why she took such a liking to Ina. It was both a marvellous and heartbreaking story.

When they heard we wanted to visit a kibbutz, our travel plans were changed instantaneously. It had to be their kibbutz we would visit and since they were going home on the bus, our new friends took us along. We were not prepared for what we saw. Over the years, the kibbutz had grown into a large business enterprise. There was actually a hotel with a swimming pool and sports facilities for tourists to use. There was a professionally run dairy which bred champion milking cows. Various other businesses were going on. This was nothing like we had envisioned.

Yet on the kibbutz, interpersonal relationships were not much different than those observed on our previous bus trip or at the airport. As the old couple took us around, we would walk past other old people. They would point out that this person was in the group that walked to Palestine and that person walked to Palestine, that one lost her first two babies and the other lost her husband soon after arrival. Yet as these old people walked past each other, not only did they not speak but would not even acknowledge each other's presence with a glance. After all the hardships that they had in their earlier lives, we expected they would have bonded closely together. But the opposite was the case. They would have nothing to do with one another. How sad! Our time in Israel proved to be an eye opener for us in terms of how human beings reacted to each other.

Thus, a most interesting chapter in our lives came to a close. It was not really the end but a beginning, a beginning that kept me involved with development work in Asia and Africa for another thirty-plus years.

BOOK TWO

MAKING OF A SKEPTIC: THE AFRICAN YEARS

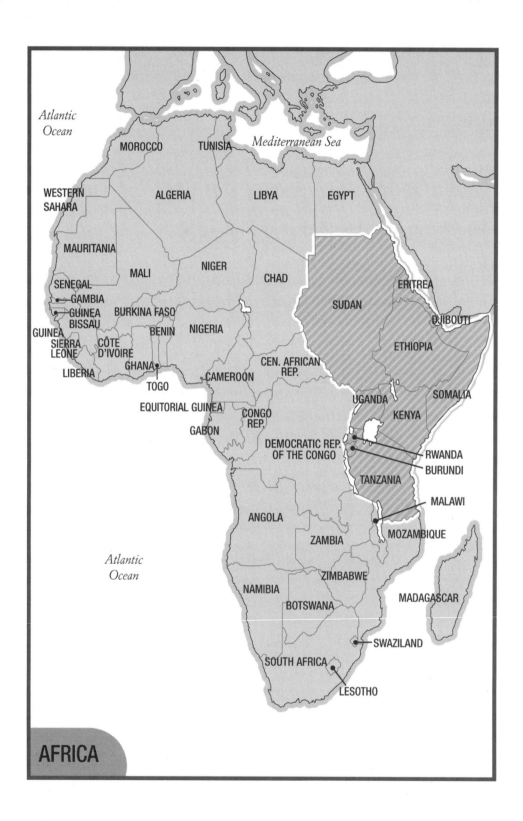

Atlantic
Ocean

MOROCCO   TUNISIA   *Mediterranean Sea*

WESTERN
SAHARA   ALGERIA   LIBYA   EGYPT

MAURITANIA

MALI   NIGER   CHAD   ERITREA

SENEGAL   SUDAN   DJIBOUTI
GAMBIA
GUINEA   BURKINA FASO   ETHIOPIA
BISSAU
GUINEA   BENIN   NIGERIA
SIERRA   CÔTE   CEN. AFRICAN   SOMALIA
LEONE   D'IVOIRE   REP.
LIBERIA   GHANA   CAMEROON   UGANDA   KENYA
TOGO

EQUITORIAL GUINEA   CONGO
REP.
GABON   DEMOCRATIC REP.   RWANDA
OF THE CONGO   BURUNDI

TANZANIA   MALAWI

ANGOLA   MOZAMBIQUE

ZAMBIA

Atlantic
Ocean   ZIMBABWE

NAMIBIA   MADAGASCAR

BOTSWANA

SWAZILAND

SOUTH AFRICA
LESOTHO

AFRICA

CHAPTER 16

THE NEXT LIFE: FIRST STOP INDIA

Returning to familiar ground at Brooklyn College made for an easier readjustment to the faster pace of life in the U.S. My university career was definitely moving forward. With the finishing of my PhD degree not long after returning, I received a promotion and tenure could be expected within a few years. The university demanded publications and outside professional involvement by faculty. With luck my teaching schedule allowed time for both.

Part of each academic year was spent in Asia, either in India or the Philippines, doing research or organizing short-term Fulbright programmes. From 1974 through 1977, the South Asia Department at Columbia University's School of International Affairs received Fulbright funding from the U.S. Government. Summer study programmes were developed to provide university and high school teachers with first hand knowledge of India. Columbia University asked if I would act as the Programme Director for their summer Fulbright grants. I did so for three consecutive years with each programme lasting about ten weeks. In addition to the summers in India, it was necessary to spend parts of January and February in that country as well, organizing for the following summer. Participants were selected in a competitive process and each group limited to twenty. Those selected received awards covering all expenses.

India, unlike any other country I have ever visited, has a unique effect upon people. Those that visit for short periods have very predictable reactions. Their reactions are either black or white with no shades of grey in between. From 1969 to 1978, my time in India was quite considerable and provided ample opportunities to witness the behaviour of western visitors. They either fall in love with the culture, the people, the history, the arts, or hate everything about India. I have never heard anyone, after being asked how he or she liked his or her visit, answer "Oh, it was alright." There is no middle ground in peoples' reactions – it's love it or leave it.

One might expect that twenty selected individuals chosen in a highly competitive process, individuals who had been teaching American students about India, individuals who were given an all expense paid trip for over two months, would all fall into the first category above, "Love it." False expectation.

Leading my first Fulbright group in the summer of 1974, we landed in New Delhi during late June at about 3:00 am. When the plane door opened, it was like stepping out of an air-conditioned room into a blast furnace or like walking into a brick wall of heat and humidity. Along-side the aircraft's parking apron, there were probably more than 100 people asleep on the grass.

Driving into town from the airport, the bus passed by some large "bustees," or slum areas. Slum areas in Asian and African cities cannot be compared to what are referred to as slum areas in the United States. One has to picture thousands of people, packed into the most densely populated space, with cardboard shacks for homes, if they are lucky, or just sleeping on the ground, if not so lucky. With little running water, no sanitary facilities, the streets and houses flooded during the monsoon season, such sights are not an easy thing to accept even for the most seasoned traveller. For the uninitiated, it can be unsettling to put it mildly.

During our orientation sessions at Columbia University, we tried to prepare the participants for many of the things they would experience. I guess for one fellow, the preparations were not enough. Passing the slums on the drive in from the airport proved too much for him to take. We reached the hotel in downtown New Delhi about 4:30 in the morning. Everyone was given the key to their rooms. Having travelled for about twenty-four hours straight, most just went upstairs and right to bed. Making sure all participants were settled, I stayed behind in the lobby. Out of the corner of my eye was this man pacing around near the door. His key was still on the counter.

"Robert," I said, "aren't you going up to your room to get some rest? We have a busy day tomorrow."

"I'm not going upstairs," replied Robert, "I'm leaving."

"Leaving for where?" I asked.

"Leaving for home," answered Robert.

"Do you mean your home in the U.S?" I responded.

"Yes."

"When?"

"Right now."

"But there is no flight right now."

"Then I will just go to the airport and wait."

Nothing was going to keep Robert in India. After travelling for more than one day, through nine time zones, this guy was turning around, reversing the nine time zones and travelling back for another twenty-four hours. Appealing to his better judgment got me nowhere. My first approach was the "guilt trip" angle. "Do you realize how much of the taxpayers' money was invested to get you to India? It is too late to find a replacement." That didn't work. Secondly, I just pleaded with him to stay. "Robert, give it a chance. Things will definitely appear brighter tomorrow." No good.

The best I could do was have him sit in the lobby until the airline offices opened a few hours later. He was re-booked and flew out for the U.S. the same evening. I always wondered if he suffered double jetlag. Or perhaps no jetlag at all because it was too quick for his body to even realize he had gone someplace. It did leave questions about our sound screening process.

Since the group was comprised of twenty academics (reduced now to nineteen) that knew about India, at least from books, time should have been taken up with the programme's educational aspects. Was I mistaken! More time was spent acting as tour guide, doctor, psychologist, and father confessor, than anything else.

Medical problems, or rather perceived medical problems, were the most common concerns to deal with. However, there was always access to well-trained doctors. One woman, Marion by name, was notorious for contracting a different ailment each day. She was given the nickname of "Miss One-a-Day." Immediately upon our arrival in Delhi, she came down with something. I initially ministered to her needs but a doctor was then called in. Second day, second ailment. Third day, sick again. This went on and on, continuing as we left Delhi for Jaipur and Agra. About two weeks later, in Benares, "Miss One-a-Day" was working on her 16th disease. It was not only becoming farcical but was taking too much of my time away from the other participants.

That evening in Benares, I visited Marion in her hotel room sick bed "Marion, I am really sorry you are so sick. The doctor who was here earlier recommended two options. Option number one: we immediately hospitalise you here in Benares. Tonight, into the hospital with you. The group leaves for Calcutta in the morning but you will stay behind in the Benares government hospital until you are better. Once cured, you can then catch up with us."

Upon hearing option one, Marion, who actually looked fine before this conversation took place, now turned a deathly white in colour. I surmised that the thought of going into a hospital in Benares was just too much for her. "What is option two?" she quickly asked. "Option two" I replied "is you making an immediate recovery, getting out of bed, joining us on the plane to Calcutta tomorrow, and never again complaining about being sick while in India. So it's the hospital or immediate recovery. Your choice?"

Marion was the first to board our Indian Airlines flight the next morning. She miraculously enjoyed excellent health for the next eight weeks.

There was never a day in India without some type of surprise. Often it seemed I was involved in playing children's games. As youngsters, one of our most popular party games was Musical Chairs. Two rows of chairs were laid out back-to-back. Children marched around the rows while music was played. When the music stopped, everyone had to quickly find an empty chair. Most of the time one was always finding a different chair to sit in. The game always had one more player than there were chairs. Whenever the music stopped, whoever was left standing is eliminated from the game. Another chair was removed and the music started again. It was over when only one child, the winner, was sitting in a single chair.

Travelling in India, there were times when it seemed as if a similar game was always going on but of an Indian variety. Instead of Musical Chairs, it was Musical Rooms and Musical Cups.

Checking into hotels with twenty participants was always time consuming, yet interesting. Ten double rooms were always booked and the reception desk had keys waiting with room assignments. As leader, that revered status entitled me to my own room. This at least allowed me some peace and quiet in the evenings.

It was inevitable that someone was going to be unhappy with his or her room at each hotel we stayed in. I would always remain in the lobby with my key for at least fifteen minutes after the last person was supposedly settled. A lot of time was spent standing around lobbies. For it was inevitable that within fifteen minutes after distributing keys, one pair of participants was sure to come marching downstairs, complaining about their room. My response was "don't fret, here take my room, it is much nicer." I would just hand over my key and take theirs in exchange. Of course, as yet I had not even seen my room.

Remaining in the lobby, a few minutes later the next pair would march down. "Our room is terrible." "Don't worry, here take my room, it is much nicer." And I again handed over the key in my hand. Off they went satisfied thinking they had the leader's room. After about two or three more switching of keys, I could finally go to bed knowing the game of "Musical Rooms" was over for the evening. It would just continue at the next stop.

In January 1974, while between semesters at Brooklyn College, I was in India organizing the programme for participants who would come in the summer.

We would do our academic study at the University of Rajasthan in Jaipur. Besides work in the classroom, field visits in various parts of the country needed to be arranged. The type of field visits depended on the major themes being studied.

For the 1974 summer programme, one of the themes to be studied involved comparative farming methods. Large, mechanized farms would be contrasted with small-scale subsistence farms. That January, a friend from another American university was also in Delhi arranging a summer Fulbright programme. He joined me on a trip about 150 kilometres north of Delhi to an area near Karnal. We were in a region of noticeably small farm holdings and these basically provided families with bare subsistence but little more. Most of the villages were extremely poor.

While passing through a small village, we entered into a discussion with one farmer. With traditional hospitality, he invited us to his home. It was a typical poor north Indian home. There were just two rooms, one where the animals were kept and one for the family. The rooms fronted onto an open courtyard. Cooking was done in that outdoor yard.

Upon entering, the farmer said something to his wife. She went outside to prepare refreshments. It was obvious that this was a poor household and we both felt guilty about our hosts depleting their meagre food stock for strangers. But it would have been an insult for us to refuse.

The wife seemed quite frail and sick. She was constantly coughing and spitting on the ground. It appeared to me that she might have been suffering from tuberculosis, which was quite prevalent in that rural part of India.

The woman was wearing an old sari, a traditional dress for Hindu women in India. The sari is a long piece of cloth, most often six yards in length (there is also a nine yard variety). It is wrapped around the lower half of the body and then draped over a small blouse, called a choli, which covers the chest. The top end of the sari is then passed over one shoulder. It can be used to cover the head. That top end also serves a clearly utilitarian function in daily life. A mother can use it to wipe a child's runny nose, or to clean a cup or glass.

Our hostess was sitting on the floor in the courtyard, preparing tea for her husband's two guests. There were only two cups on the ground. While preparing the tea, she was constantly coughing and spitting, coughing and spitting. Then after each cough and spit, she used the end of her sari to wipe her mouth. Cough, spit, wipe the mouth, attend to the tea.

My friend and I both knew what was about to take place. While talking to the farmer, we never for one moment took our eyes off that woman. Just as the tea was about ready, between a cough, spit, and wiping of the mouth, she took the same end of that sari, put it into one of the teacups, and wiped it. For some reason unknown to the both of us, the other cup was left untouched.

Keeping up polite conversation, there were two sets of eyes glued to that one teacup – the unwiped one. Who was going to get it? She poured the tea and brought both of the cups inside. Each of us thought we knew which cup was which. She placed the two cups on a small table in front of us. To my horror, what I thought was the "wiped" cup was placed in front of me. Nonchalantly, I pushed the cup across to my friend. Seeing what I did, he just as nonchalantly reversed the cups. This went on for about five minutes, while our discussion with the farmer did not miss a beat. Perplexed at these two strange Americans, he must have thought we were crazy while watching our version of a new game called Musical Teacups.

After a few minutes, neither of us could really tell which cup had been "sari wiped." We just drank our tea. In the end it didn't matter. The tea was so hot, it would have killed anything living in either cup. And we both survived.

In 1946, with the encouragement of Senator William Fulbright, the Fulbright Fellowship Programme had been established. This allowed for a U.S. Government sponsored exchange programme for scholars from the U.S. to study and do research abroad and for foreign scholars to come to the United States. Then in 1954, PL 480, also known as the Food for Peace Programme, was signed into law by President Dwight D. Eisenhower. During the 1950s and 1960s, sales of surplus wheat were common. Because third world Asian and African countries could not pay in dollars, PL 480 allowed for payment in local exchange. These local currencies were not convertible and therefore were kept in U.S. Government accounts held in the foreign countries. Its implications for India allowed the importation of American wheat by the Indian Government, which paid for it in rupees. With PL 480 in effect, educational activities in India sponsored and paid for by the U.S. Government such as Fulbright grants, were now done so using PL 480 local rupee funds.

Because India was one of the major purchasers of American wheat under the PL 480 programme, wheat that was sold at concessional prices and paid for by the Indian Government in local currency, there was a large pool of funds from which to fund the Fulbright programmes in India. The U.S. Government, at one time, held millions and millions of dollars worth of rupees in India. The account was finally eliminated a number of years ago. The remaining millions in the account were given to the Indian Government.

American universities administering summer Fulbright programmes received grants from the U.S. Office of Education, which was given a budget from the rupee account held in India. All participant expenses including in-country transportation, room and board, fees to Indian universities, and payments for lecturers and cultural performances were provided for in local currency. When an American University was awarded a summer programme, it negotiated an overall rupee budget with the U.S. Office of Education.

A number of these summer programmes ended with pleasant surprises for the participants. Because PL 480 rupees were plentiful, and it was beneficial to get them back into the Indian economy, allocated budgets were never skimpy. At the end of each summer's programme, if no emergencies or contingencies occurred, it was almost inevitable to have rupees left over. Because of contractual arrangements with the U.S. Office of Education, the funds needed to be spent. About two days before a summer programme was to end, the surplus rupees were distributed in equal amounts to each participant, usually about the equivalent of £60. Not having known about the possible windfall, all at once, there were twenty people scattering in all directions, trying to figure out what to do with their rupees before getting on a plane for home in forty-eight hours.

CHAPTER 17

WHO TURNED OUT THE LIGHTS?

Everything seemed to be going well. I enjoyed Brooklyn College and my students. Opportunities were plentiful to be in Asia with the Fulbright programmes, and on other consultancies in the Philippines. There was even time to produce publications and teaching materials on India. But all good things have to come to an end.

The end of my university career was inexplicably linked to a financial crisis in the City of New York. By the mid-1970s, the city was undergoing hard times. It was running out of money. This impacted all public services. Under the administration of Mayor Ed Koch, budgets were slashed for subway and bus systems, for police and fire departments, and for the entire City University of New York. Brooklyn College was the largest campus within the City University system. Therefore, it was to become victim of the largest budget cuts. By 1976, plans were being drawn up to reduce faculty and other staff. Within the School of Education, rumours were rife that there would be a faculty reduction of 25 per cent. Morale was not exactly high.

One day, upon entering my office, I tried to make a phone call. A recorded announcement on the other end said "Sorry, no outside calls can be made from this phone. Please contact the operator." No longer was it possible to make a direct call. The only way to contact someone on the outside was to go through the college operator. This was an institution of about 25,000 students and hundreds of professors and staff. It was not a strain to imagine the hundreds all trying to get the college operator at one time.

Nor was it an arduous task to imagine that in the next few days, the university would order us not to turn on lights before 6:00 pm. Not the best environment in which to enjoy one's job. It was time to get out. My senior colleagues were reassuring me that I was not on the 25 per cent hit list for staff reductions. Perhaps I wasn't; perhaps I was. Either way, my mind was already turned elsewhere.

With great reluctance, it was goodbye to academic life and hello to the world of charity, the world of NGOs or non-governmental organizations. With my Asian experience, I was invited to join a well-established organization in 1978, the International Institute of Rural Reconstruction or IIRR.

Dating back to World War One, IIRR was founded by a remarkable Chinese individual, Dr. Y.C. James Yen. Dr. Yen began his life's work in France. Sent there by the YMCA, he helped illiterate Chinese labourers communicate with their families back in China. They had been recruited by the Allies to repair railroads. At the end of the war, he returned to China and founded the Mass Education Movement. This later evolved into one of the first integrated rural development programmes aimed at uplifting the rural poor. In the 1950s, Dr. Yen moved to the Philippines and helped establish the Philippine Rural Reconstruction Movement. By 1960, he founded a new international NGO headquartered in the Philippines, the International Institute of Rural Reconstruction.

Located in Cavite Province, IIRR registered itself in the United States and maintained an office in New York City. This office helped raise money for the Institute's programmes in Asia, Africa, and Latin America and assisted in the recruitment of international staff. Having been familiar with the organization while living in the Philippines, I was hired to work out of the New York office.

On rare occasions, one can find oneself in the right place at the right time. Unfortunately, with IIRR, I was in the right place at the wrong time. Full of enthusiasm and ready to move forward quickly, I had joined a quite conservative organization that was only prepared to move slowly. The leadership was elderly and the Board of Trustees was divided into two camps – those who wanted to push forward more quickly and those who were tied to the old traditions. I found myself trying to walk up a down escalator, one step forward and four steps backward. It was not a good fit and I left within a year, probably one step ahead of being fired.

Life is full of ironic twists. Sixteen years later, I was asked to become the President of IIRR. While serving in Kenya as the Chief Executive of AMREF, the African Medical and Research Foundation, IIRR invited me to head the organization. I really could not accept because of my commitment to AMREF. But how many individuals get the opportunity to become President of an organization that had been ready to fire him? While not able to accept the offer, I became a Trustee of IIRR upon retirement in 1998. Then in 2002, I was elected Chairman of the Board of Trustees. I had now come full circle. While being in the right place at the wrong time ended my employment with the Institute, it never ended my belief and commitment to what it did for the lives of the rural poor. And that commitment always kept me interested in what IIRR was trying to achieve and it remains as strong as ever today.

CHAPTER 18

HELLO AFRICA

Out of a job and out on the street. Not a good position for someone with a wife and three sons to support. But life is full of unexpected twists and turns. My temporary unemployed status actually turned me away from a ten-year engagement with Asia and pointed me towards a twenty-year connection with Africa. How did that happen?

All of my energies at this point were devoted to finding employment. In the end, there was a good possibility that new employment would have me leaving the non-profit world of teaching, universities, and NGOs and moving into the private sector. One of the major U.S. banks, Chase Manhattan, had recently started a new subsidiary called Chase World Information Service. It was founded to conduct political risk analysis and to sell its findings to current and potential investors in developing countries. The information would supposedly be helpful to those doing business in Asia, Africa, and/or Latin America. Investors would use the information to determine how risky their investments might be. Individual country profiles would be made available.

Chase World Information Service hired a brilliant mathematician from Shell Oil as technical adviser. His job was to develop a scientific methodology to be used by social scientists for analysing risk potential in a given country. Data would be collected through interviews of key nationals from a specific country, then analysed, and a report prepared.

Where did I fit into all of this? Chase was in the process of recruiting geographical area specialists with social science backgrounds. Their jobs would be to target a country, interview the appropriate nationals of that country, and put together a country risk study. The bank's interest was not only in the expertise of the new potential hires but most importantly, in the contacts he or she had at high levels. Such contacts were important in order that the most appropriate nationals would provide data for the analysis.

Chase had recently hired a Latin American expert. After a number of interviews, I was in the final process of being considered for the Asian specialist position. They were particularly interested in my Philippine contacts. There was a large American business presence in that country.

* * *

My introduction to a corporate environment proved an eye opener. Money had never figured prominently in my previous career choices, namely teaching, serving as a Peace Corps Volunteer, and working for a charitable NGO. In this new environment, money did not seem to present a problem. Budgets for travel to Asia, lodging, and entertainment were no obstacle. I had to remind myself of the contrast to when our family of five tried to make do on £3 a day when travelling during our Peace Corps years.

While involved in discussions with Chase, I expressed serious concerns that given political problems in a country such as the Philippines, certain important people might not be comfortable providing information on sensitive issues. And interviewing people in their own country might make them more reticent to speak. Without inputs from such people, the political risk studies would be lessened in value.

"Don't worry about that," I was told. "If someone in the Philippines is reluctant to meet with you there, just fly them to Hawaii, or the U.S., or anyplace else where it would be more comfortable to speak." "And what if it was four or five individuals?" I asked. "Just fly them as well," was the answer.

When it came to specifics about the remuneration package for what might be my new job, it was easier said than done to take it in with a calm demeanour. My first reaction was to ask "How much did you say?" but I did not want to look too unsophisticated. The figures were more than double that of my last position with IIRR and about triple my salary at Brooklyn College.

During the final days of negotiations, an old friend called. He informed me there was an NGO looking for a chief executive and felt that the job suited me perfectly. I told him of my discussions vis-à-vis Chase but was urged to at least speak with this NGO. "What organization is it?" I asked. "AMREF USA" he answered. "What is that? I never heard of it." "Never mind, just call" and he gave me a phone number.

On a Thursday afternoon I called Dr. Mickey Alderman at Cornell University Medical School. Mickey was the Vice-Chairman of the Board of AMREF USA. He asked a few questions and then invited me for an interview the next morning. On Friday, I met with Mickey Alderman, Dr. Jim Sheffield, who was Chairman of the Board, Dr. Tom Rees, one of the founders of the organization, and another Board member.

My first question was "What is AMREF and what does it do?" "AMREF is the African Medical and Research Foundation" it was explained, and information about what it did was provided. During the course of our conversation, I openly described my on-going discussions with Chase. The meeting lasted about three hours and I went home. On Monday, I was scheduled for a final meeting at the Bank.

Friday evening the phone rang. It was Mickey Alderman. "We want you to become the President of AMREF USA" Mickey said. "Can I have some time to think about it?" "No problem, just let us know as soon as possible."

Less than twenty-four hours later, on a Saturday afternoon, I called Mickey Alderman and accepted the position. As an NGO, AMREF's financial package was less than half of what we were discussing at Chase. Was I crazy? Why not just wait until after Monday's meeting at the bank before reaching a decision? I didn't think I was crazy and this decision turned out to be one of the best I have ever made.

"Corporate culture" was the most influencing factor in my choice. There was on one hand, the for-profit corporate culture of Chase, my first real taste of the private sector environment. On the other hand was the corporate culture of non-profit service organizations. The first choice held the possibilities of earning a large salary within a highly aggressive atmosphere, working with intelligent people who were under pressure to be concerned first and foremost with the bottom line. While the salary was attractive and the aggressive atmosphere a challenge, the primary objective of a bottom line was personally uncomfortable. In the end, it was really no contest.

There was one more task to be undertaken before joining AMREF USA. A call to Chase was in order. I had to inform them of my decision and cancel a final meeting. During previous discussions, the lead person in recruiting area specialists for Chase's World Information Services was a woman Vice-President. It was to her that my call was made early Monday morning. I have never forgotten that discussion.

"Hi, this is Mike Gerber. I have to inform you that I cannot come for our meeting today. After careful thought and much consideration, I am removing myself from consideration for the Asian specialist position. My main reason for doing so is that I have accepted another position."

"What?" a somewhat agitated voice replied. "Why would you do something like that before we had our final meeting? It is most likely that after you came in today, an offer was to be made. We were prepared to do that."

Hearing her tone of voice, diplomacy was now called for.

"That is much appreciated. I was impressed with what you are trying to do at Chase and with the people I met. However, all of my professional life to-date has in some way, involved service to people who do not or cannot afford to pay for such services. This is something I feel comfortable with and want to keep doing."

A voice, now tinged with some anger asked, "Would you mind telling me who offered you a job?"

"No, I don't mind. It was the African Medical and Research Foundation."

"The African Medical what? What kind of organization is that?"

"It is a non-profit, charitable organization that works in Africa trying to improve the health of Africa's neediest people."

"You are going to do that instead of coming to work for Chase?" my angry phone partner asked. "And what are the African Medicals going to pay you?"

I mentioned the figure and waited for her to erupt into a fit of laughter. Instead, with all composure gone, she exploded, "Are you for real?" she screeched. "You are going to work for peanuts in an organization no one has ever heard of. You are actually giving up the possibility of joining Chase to do that? There has to be something wrong with you." And on and on she went for another two minutes. I was now even more assured that my choice had been the right one.

In the end, Chase Manhattan Bank held no grudges. They became AMREF's bank in the United States and, for a number of years, made donations to support our activities in Africa.

*   *   *

It was now hello to Africa.

CHAPTER 19

WELCOME TO THE NGO WORLD

The African Medical and Research Foundation or AMREF is more popularly known as The Flying Doctors. My association with this NGO, which lasted for approximately twenty years, provided a wonderful introduction to the continent of Africa. That introduction led to a continuous, on-going education. From Sudan in the north, to Ethiopia, Eritrea, and Somalia in the horn of Africa, to Kenya, Tanzania, and Uganda in eastern Africa, to Rwanda and Burundi in central Africa, to Zimbabwe, Malawi, Mozambique, Lesotho, Swaziland, Namibia, and South Africa in the southern part of the continent, AMREF took me on a journey never to be forgotten.

Never to be forgotten does not imply that each thing experienced and observed was pleasant. Too much of it was not. I sadly had a front row seat for such man-made disasters as a continuous war in Sudan, genocide in Rwanda, the disintegration of Somalia, massive refugee populations, the bombing of American Embassies in Nairobi and Dar es Salaam, and the devastation left behind by AIDS. Still, that front-row seat was greatly appreciated when one witnessed Uganda emerge from the devastation brought about by Idi Amin to a country held up as a model for economic development and as a leader in the battle to combat the AIDS pandemic. It was also appreciated when one was able to contribute to the development of health care in the newly independent country of Namibia. And it was a privilege to be involved in South Africa from the time of Nelson Mandela's release from prison, to witness the end of apartheid, and the transformation to today's Rainbow Nation.

With AMREF as the focal point of my involvement and observations, some background on this organization is warranted. It was founded by three plastic surgeons: Michael Wood, Archibald McIndoe, and Thomas Rees. Besides surgery, all had a common love for East Africa. Archie McIndoe was a specialist in burn reconstructive surgery. He organized the famous burn center at East Grinstead Hospital during the Second World War. The center did pioneering work on badly injured RAF pilots. At a later time, both Michael Wood and Tom Rees studied with McIndoe.

Mike Wood moved to East Africa after the Second World War, bought a farm in Tanzania at the foot of Mt. Kilimanjaro, learned to fly, and "commuted" to Nairobi to perform surgery. In 1957, Drs. Wood, Rees, and McIndoe formed a non-governmental organization, the African Research Foundation, which later became the African Medical and Research Foundation, or AMREF. Their first objective was to establish a reconstructive burn unit in Nairobi. Burns were, and still are, an unfortunately common occurrence in Africa. Many tribal groups have fires burning continuously, some even having open fires burning inside huts to keep mosquitoes away. Children often incur burns when falling into these fires.

Michael Wood became AMREF's first Director General and set up the organization's headquarters in Nairobi, Kenya. Tom Rees returned to his practice in New York and established AMREF USA, with the intention of raising funds to support AMREF's work in Africa. Archie McIndoe did the same with the establishment of AMREF UK, headquartered in London.

It was soon realized that while burn reconstructive surgery was important, it was only a drop in the ocean in relation to the major health problems of East Africa. There were only a few doctors and the few who practiced were mostly found in towns and cities. But 90 per cent of the people did not live in towns or cities; they were out in the rural areas. With poor roads and unreliable communications, it meant that the great majority of people in truth had no access to medical care.

Michael Wood quickly came to appreciate that medical services had to be brought to where people lived. With road transport being gruelling or sometimes impossible, small or light aircraft were the most reliable methods of reaching isolated areas. Why not use light aircraft to bring badly needed doctors and nurses to the people, rather than have people come to the medical providers? Hence, the birth of AMREF's Flying Doctors.

From 1957 to the early 1970s, AMREF was synonymous with the Flying Doctors. Its aircraft brought surgeons and other specialists to remote hospitals, both government and missionary, throughout Kenya, Tanzania, and at times, Uganda and Ethiopia. AMREF surgeons specialised in burn, leprosy, and polio reconstructive surgery. Ground mobile teams, using Land Rovers converted into small ambulances, brought health care to hard-to-reach nomadic tribes in Kenya, such as the Maasai and Turkana.

In the early 1970s, AMREF began to transform itself. While the work of the Flying Doctors became well know and was highly regarded, the organization began to realize that with limited resources, the numbers it could treat would be small compared to those that needed care. Direct delivery of medical services began to give way to training and education. By working with African governments in training health workers, a multiplier effect would take place. Train one person who could then care for a hundred. Train a hundred who could then care for 10,000.

A second transformation saw a shift from treatment to prevention, from the delivery of medical care to health education and primary health care. Working closely with African Ministries of Health, by the beginning of the 1980s AMREF was one of the major health training institutions in Africa. Its Flying Doctor programmes were maintained but with growth and a shifting of priorities, they were now only a small part of the larger AMREF.

Upon my retirement as Director General towards the end of 1998, AMREF employed about 600 full time staff of which over 95 per cent were African. It had an annual budget of close to £7.5 million (since grown to over £12 million) and received funding from major western government donors, from foundations, corporations, and from individuals. Its activities stretched from Sudan to South Africa and across to some West African countries. The Foundation had programmes relevant to all of Africa's major health problems, of which malaria and AIDS were at the top of the list.

With its headquarters in Nairobi and a predominantly African staff, AMREF is, in reality, an African international NGO. To assist in finding necessary resources for its programmes in Africa, a family of AMREF organizations were established in North America and Europe. The first two were AMREF USA and AMREF UK. These were later joined by AMREFs founded in Germany, Canada, Holland, Sweden, Denmark, Italy, France, Austria, and Spain, and more recently, Monaco.

After becoming President of AMREF USA in 1979, we initially focused on the development of large projects in Sudan, Somalia, Kenya, and Tanzania. These were funded by the United States Agency for International Development (USAID). Although the AMREF USA office was located in mid-town Manhattan, I spent most of my time commuting between New York City, Washington, D.C., and Africa.

After ten years as President of AMREF USA, I became Director General of the organization in 1989, based at the headquarters in Nairobi. But even while at AMREF USA, life was still full of surprises.

CHAPTER 20

TRANSPORTATION AND TRAVEL – ACT II

Two months after starting at AMREF, I was scheduled to visit Africa for the first time. USAID had provided us with a large grant to do primary health care in the southern Sudan. Khartoum would be my first port of call. There I would review the project with the USAID Sudan staff, then fly to Juba in the south to see the project activities, and lastly to Nairobi for my first visit to AMREF's headquarters.

Getting to London for a connection to Khartoum was uneventful, flying overnight and landing at Heathrow in the morning. The following evening I was scheduled to depart London on Sudan Airways. In twenty years of travelling to and within Africa, that was my first and next to last trip ever booked on Sudan Airways. On the evening of our scheduled departure for Khartoum, the passengers showed up at Heathrow only to be sent away with a brief explanation, "the flight is delayed for twenty-four hours." Back again the next night only to be sent away with the same explanation, "flight delayed for twenty-four hours." Finally, on the third try, seventy-two hours later, we boarded the plane for Khartoum.

It was only after arriving in Khartoum that I learned the cause of "flight delayed for twenty-four hours." With the loss of three days, my visit to Juba in southern Sudan was put off. Plans were now made to fly directly from Khartoum to Nairobi on my least favourite carrier, Sudan Airways. On the day of departure for Nairobi, passengers were actually checked in for the flight. However, taking off did not naturally follow checking in. We sat in Khartoum airport and sat and sat – for two more days. But at least the reason for all the delays became clear.

Sudan Airways' international fleet consisted of two old Boeing 707s. One of the planes had been grounded for six months so only one was in service. And the one in service was diverted away from regular scheduled flights for what was considered a higher priority.

Sitting in Khartoum Airport for two days, I watched that plane come and go on three separate occasions. It would land empty, taxi to the far end of the runway, and stop. The front and back doors were opened. Through a big cloud of dust, a bus would pull up to the aircraft. Village people would get off the bus and get onto the plane, men up through the front door and women through the back. The doors would close, the plane would take off, and five hours later return empty. Another bus would pull up and the same scenario unfolded again.

This went on with frustrating repetitiveness. It was the Hadj period, the time when Muslims make the pilgrimage to Mecca. And Sudan Airways was using its one serviceable aircraft to carry the Mecca bound pilgrims. All scheduled passengers just had to wait. When we finally departed, I quickly fell asleep on what was supposed to be a three-hour non-stop flight to Nairobi. Upon waking, the plane was already in its descent. After landing, the doors were opened and I moved out onto the staircase. Upon looking around, I saw nothing but desert. From my little prior knowledge of Nairobi, I knew that city was not in the desert. Asking the stewardess where we were, she replied "S'ana."

"S'ana? Isn't that in Yemen?"

"Yes," I was told.

"Aren't we supposed to be in Nairobi?"

"We had to make a stop first."

It was back into the plane and off to sleep again. About two hours later, another descent and landing. With more hesitancy this time, I walked to the door and looked outside. In the distance was a sparkling blue ocean. I understood enough to know that Nairobi was not within 500 kilometres of any ocean.

"Where are we now?" I asked.

"Djibouti."

"Djibouti? Aren't we supposed to be in Nairobi?"

"Yes, but we had to make another stop."

So, back into the seat, one more take off and landing, and finally Nairobi. Because of the Hadj flights, what Sudan Airways did was to combine a number of regularly scheduled flights into one and cram in as many passengers as possible. Of course, the passengers for Nairobi were never informed of this new sightseeing excursion. It was like taking a local bus, making one stop after another.

Experienced travellers, upon hearing of my tale, just laughed and referred to Sudan Airways as the IBM airline. This IBM was not the same as the highly successful computer company. The "I" stood for Inshallah, which in Arabic means "God willing." The "B" was for Bokrah, meaning "tomorrow." And the "M" for Maalesh was often interpreted as "who knows," said with a shrug of the shoulders. God willing, tomorrow, and who knows are fitting descriptions for flying Sudan Airways.

While still based at AMREF USA in New York, it was actually possible to work one week in the United States, the following week in East Africa, and the third week back in the USA, all without missing one day in the office at either end. I would leave Kennedy Airport in New York on a Saturday evening, arrive in London on Sunday morning, depart London on Sunday evening, and arrive in Nairobi early Monday morning, in time to reach the AMREF office by 9:00 am. After a week in East Africa, the process was reversed. Leave Nairobi late on Friday evening, arrive in London on Saturday morning, immediately connect for New York, and land on Saturday afternoon. Then back to work in the New York office on Monday morning. It was not a routine I would highly recommend to others.

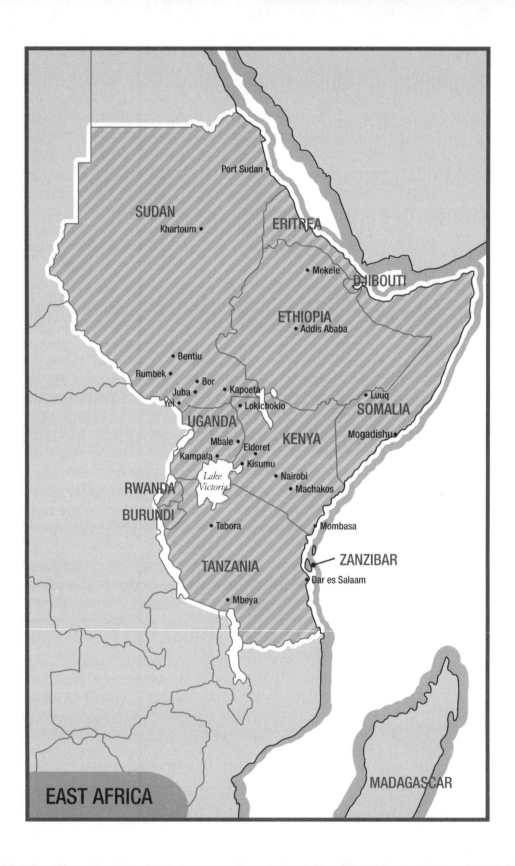

EAST AFRICA

CHAPTER 21

THE SUDAN –
NEVER A DULL MOMENT

As Africa's largest country, the Sudan is a vast land of contrast. Since its independence from Britain in 1956, it has also been a nation of conflict. The north is predominantly Muslim, Arabic speaking, and Arab in temperament and culture. The south is largely African, with many tribal languages. The Dinka and Nuer are the largest tribal groups. Southerners are mostly Christian or animist. English is often used as the lingua franca in the south.

Shortly after independence, civil war erupted. A number of southerners, not wanting to be dominated either religiously or economically by the north, were interested in some form of autonomy within a federated Sudan. Others saw a separate country as the only solution. Fighting went on for sixteen years, when in 1972 the Addis Ababa Accord was signed, signalling an end to the war in Sudan. The result was a semi-autonomous region for the south within the larger Sudan nation. Juba, the largest town in the south and situated on the Nile River, became the seat of a new southern regional government. Southern Sudan now had its own government ministries. These assumed responsibility for such services as health, education, and economic development. National portfolios like foreign affairs, defence, and internal security remained with the federal government in Khartoum.

Khartoum, the national capital, sits at the confluence of the White Nile, originating from Lake Victoria in Uganda, and the Blue Nile, emanating from Lake Tana in Ethiopia. The two rivers join and then flow over 2000 kilometres into the Mediterranean Sea near Alexandria in Egypt. Khartoum, a dusty city capital with wide boulevards, is surrounded by desert. The desert actually moves into the city during the Haboub season, when a fierce wind covers everything in sand. Khartoum has always been one of the safest cities in the world. It is possible to walk anywhere, day or night, without feeling threatened. Northern Sudanese are warm, friendly people, remaining so throughout changes in Governments, which have brought about political and economic turmoil since the time of independence.

With temporary peace between north and south agreed after a truce was signed in the Ethiopian capital of Addis Ababa in 1972, the United States Government began pouring millions of dollars annually into Sudan in the form of foreign assistance. The United States Agency for International Development had its biggest African programme in Sudan. Official U.S. aid started flowing in mid-1970s and at that time, continued until the mid-1980s. Assistance was split between north and south. Politically, Sudan was seen by the United States as a moderate Arab state, counterbalancing some of the more radical nations of the Middle East region.

This began to change in 1983 when President Ja'far Nimeiri adopted the most important features of Islamic law or Sharia for the northern part of Sudan. Nimieri, who had come to power in a coup in 1969, was himself deposed by a similar plot in 1985. With the introduction of Sharia, the tensions between the south of Sudan and the North again came to the forefront and a resumption of the civil war was inevitable. The war worsened following the taking of power in Khartoum in 1989 by Omer al-Bashir, who as Chairman of the Revolutionary Command Council for National Salvation, used the Islamic fundamentalist movement in Sudan to consolidate his position.

*   *   *

Al-Bashir became President and virtual dictator of the country in 1993. The threat of imposition of Sharia Law throughout all of Sudan was a stimulus for the war to escalate further. This next chapter in the fighting went on until May of 2005 when a peace agreement between the two sides was signed in Nairobi. Interestingly, the agreement gives a good deal of autonomy to the south while maintaining the Sudan as one country. If one looks at this accommodation, it is not unlike the similar autonomy given to the south in 1972 after the signing of the Addis Ababa accord. Independent Sudan has now suffered two devastating wars – the first from independence in 1956 to 1972 and then again from the mid-1980s until 2005. Will the latter be the last? Hopefully.

The south, which always felt it received an unequal distribution of Sudan's resources, is one of the poorest and least developed regions in Africa. The civil war following independence destroyed what little infrastructure the British had left behind. The United States and other western donor nations pumped in aid faster than it could be absorbed with the hope of rebuilding health facilities, roads, and schools and to train new cadres of health workers to replace many killed in the war.

Working for a large health NGO headquartered in Africa, I was involved with Sudan from 1979 until retirement in 1998. Our projects were centred in the south and my travels brought me to all parts of that region. In addition, it was necessary to visit Khartoum frequently for consultations with various Government Ministries as well as with such donors as USAID and the European Union.

From my very first visit via Sudan Airways, travelling in Sudan always left memorable impressions. If one anticipated fifty things that could go wrong, there was always a fifty-first waiting in surprise. Because AMREF ran a Flying Doctor Service, we had our own aircraft. During the period of relative calm in Sudan, from the late 1970s to the late 1980s, it was possible to travel throughout the southern region using our own light planes. I often flew from Nairobi to Juba and then on to other locations in Southern Sudan.

Arriving in Juba was always an adventure, leaving even more so. As the major town in southern Sudan, it was both a commercial and military centre. About three times a week Sudan Airways had scheduled flights from Khartoum to Juba. Scheduled as in Sudan Airways' "IBM" system of operation. One flight a week was usually the norm, if it was a lucky week. While the airport facilities consisted of one old dilapidated control tower and a small one story building for arriving and departing passengers, the runway was tarmacked and quite long. It could handle commercial jet aircraft and military flights as well as light aircraft.

My first arrival at Juba airport in 1979 was a rather lonely one. We flew from Nairobi in a Cessna 404, a small, twin-engine plane. On approaching Juba Airport, it appeared that not a soul could be found. There was no one in the control tower to direct our approach. Sitting next to the pilot, I could hear him screaming or rather cursing at the empty control tower for instructions. No response. Flying low, he circled the town three times to wake everyone up even though it was around eleven o'clock in the morning. Finally, he just landed. There was not another aircraft parked on the apron. No one was to be found on the ground.

Coming from Kenya, our arrival was technically an international one. Government health officials should have been checking for yellow fever and at that time, cholera vaccinations. Immigration officials should have been checking passports and visas. And of course, customs officials should have been looking for contraband, or arms, or whatever. The only person waiting was a driver from our project who was there to take us to town. The pilot and I took the jeep, drove into town, and basically did a house-to-house search for the airport officials. The only one to be located was the immigration chap. We drove him back out to the airport and after a delay of about thirty minutes, while he tried to locate his entry seal, our passports were duly stamped and we were now entered into Sudan legally. We could have been infected with bubonic plague while smuggling AK47s at the same time, but that did not seem to concern anyone.

Leaving for Nairobi a few days later, the same process was reversed but with a new twist. The immigration official was having lunch at the time we wanted to go. He was located at his favourite eating-place. Knowing nothing would come between him and his lunch, we bowed to the inevitable and just joined him. When all were fully satiated, he was driven with us out to the airstrip. This time his stamp was close at hand so passports could be quickly processed.

The pilot flying me on that trip was Captain Joe Moran. Joe was an old Africa hand who knew much of the continent well. He had been in a religious order at one time and was totally committed to the health work AMREF was doing. Nothing fazed Joe. He had seen it all, been through it all, landing and taking off from the most isolated places one could imagine, on every type of conceivable airstrip including grass, beaches, even roads. Joe was never one to hold back when bureaucracy got in his way. He could smoothly cajole officials to get his way or fiercely berate them when necessary, all done in his wonderful Irish accent.

Ready for departure, Joe and I boarded the aircraft. Joe was in the left hand seat and I was sitting next to him. He taxied the plane out to the end of the runway to position for takeoff.

"Juba tower, this is 5Y DOC [the plane's registration] requesting permission to take off."

No answer.

"Juba control, this is 5Y DOC requesting permission to takeoff."

No answer.

A third time, "This is 5Y DOC requesting permission to takeoff."

Still no answer.

"The hell with them," muttered Joe and after checking visually, moved the Cessna to the takeoff position.

As the Juba airstrip was quite long, the control tower was now at the far end of the runway from where we were ready for takeoff. It was just barely visible to us.

"Juba tower, for the last time, this is 5Y DOC requesting permission for takeoff."

Again, no response.

"For the last time, Juba tower this is 5Y DOC requesting permission for takeoff," screamed Joe into the mouthpiece.

More of the same – nothing.

Turning to me, Joe said, "The hell with those bastards, let's go."

Just as he was about to rev the engines up to full power, something appeared to be sticking out of the control tower window in the far distance. Lo and behold! It was a hand. And the hand was waving a big green flag.

"I imagine that means we can go," said Joe.

Joe released the brakes and our Cessna started moving down the runway for takeoff, slowly at first and then more quickly. About ten seconds into the takeoff, again a hand comes sticking out of the control tower window. This time it was waving a big red flag.

"Joe, I think the guy is now waving a red flag."

"Holy shit," shouted Joe, looking up.

Joe quickly hit the brakes and just as he did, a terrifically loud noise was heard from above our heads. The Cessna started shaking violently. Zooming in over our heads and landing just in front of where Joe stopped our plane was a Sudan Airways 737 passenger jet. While not scheduled for that day, to our surprise, Sudan Airways had decided to fly to Juba. But fortunately for us, we saw the red flag in time. Had Joe not been able to stop, we would have been one crushed Cessna.

I never thought that even an Irishman was capable of heaping the kind of curses Joe directed upon the control tower through his radio mouthpiece. After a five-minute tirade, we reversed back to the end of the runway. This time, Joe just took off without asking for clearance. And no flags were waved out of the control tower.

That Cessna 404 and its pilot, Joe Moran, were destined to provide other interesting adventures. On one trip, we needed to fly from Juba to Rumbek, about 300 kilometres by air and in the middle of nowhere. Trying to find Rumbek, all of three or four buildings, a small hospital, and a few thatched huts, was like looking for a needle in a haystack. After about fifteen minutes of circling and searching, Joe proclaimed, "There it is." Looking out, all I could see was the few mud walled, thatched roofed huts and a large heard of cattle grazing.

"There what is?" I replied.

"Rumbek, down there."

"And where are you going to land the plane?"

"Down there."

"Where's the airstrip?"

"The cattle are grazing on it."

Joe did a low flyover, chasing the cattle off what I thought was a bumpy road. "Welcome to the Rumbek airstrip," and down we came in a perfect landing. About 50 Dinka tribesmen, who had formed as our greeting party, immediately surrounded the Cessna. Also on hand was the Rumbek hospital administrator who put us into his Land Rover and off we went to the hospital for meetings and discussions.

The next morning, we were to fly back to Juba. Joe turned the key to start the engines. Nothing happened. Turned the key a second time and again nothing. After about ten minutes, Joe announced that the battery was dead and would need recharging. I knew about car batteries needing recharging but never witnessed a dead airplane battery.

"How do you charge an airplane battery, Joe?"

"We use cables to connect Land Rover batteries to the plane's battery."

"No problem, let's just bring the Land Rover over to the plane."

"Well, it is not as easy as that."

"Why not?"

"Because the Cessna's battery is 12 volts and the Land Rover's is only 6 volts."

"Oh! We need two Land Rovers."

"Brilliant deduction."

Sadly, the only other Land Rover in the vicinity was over 100 kilometres away. After consulting with the hospital administrator, we realized it would only return the next day at the earliest. So it was back to the hospital for another night. About noon on the following day, the second car showed up. Both vehicles were driven up to the aircraft and two sets of jumper cables were attached, one from each Land Rover. Here in the middle of the bush in Southern Sudan, there was this airplane being charged from the batteries of two Land Rovers, all the while surrounded by hundreds of local Dinka who miraculously appeared from out of the bush to witness this spectacle.

It did work. That night we were back in Juba, safe and sound.

CHAPTER 22

HOW THE OTHER HALF
OF 1/10TH OF 1% LIVES

Generally, health care in Africa suffers from many constraints. These include a shortage of trained personnel, poor facilities and equipment, and inadequate drug supplies. There are few doctors, especially in the rural and peri-urban areas where most of the people live. Health care, when provided, is most often done so by non-physicians.

The lack of access to safe water and proper sanitation are also major contributing factors to poor health. While in recent years there have been campaigns to inoculate children against preventable diseases, many remain unvaccinated. Deaths from measles or diphtheria, almost unheard of in North America and most of Europe, occur all too often in Africa. And, as is well known, Africa has the highest incidences of both HIV/AIDS and malaria in the world.

Recognizing that treating people after they were sick wasn't feasible to improving overall health standards, the World Health Organization launched a "Health for All by the Year 2000" strategy at a conference in Alma Ata (in present day Kazakhstan) in 1976. The emphasis for health services in the poorer countries of the world was now shifted away from curative medicine toward prevention. "Prevention rather than cure" became the catch phrase.

Primary health care, starting at the village level, was to be adopted by Governments and their Ministries of Health. Many NGOs had for years already been involved with community-based health care. They were to become important players in implementing the "Health for All" strategy.

With too few trained health personnel, African countries realized that new cadres of workers would be needed to impact conditions in the villages. In addition, those health workers already in service would need to be re-orientated away from curative medicine to a mind set which emphasized health promotion.

AMREF had been promoting community care through its projects in Kenya starting in the early 1960s. It quickly realized that with limited resources, trying to treat the sick would minimize the organization's impact. Therefore, by the start of the 1970s, its focus moved away from direct delivery of medical services to one of training and health education. When in the late 1970s and early 1980s, governments moved to a primary health care approach, AMREF was well situated to provide assistance.

*   *   *

In 1978, AMREF received a three-year grant from USAID for a primary health care project in Southern Sudan. The award was for £1.7 million (eventually increased to £2 million), at that time the largest ever made by USAID to a non-governmental organization. The major components of the programme included the training of hundreds of primary health care workers, strengthening the capacity within the Regional Ministry of Health to support primary health care, and the development of a drug distribution system for the southern region.

By 1981, the project was evaluated and proved to be successful. USAID then expressed interest in funding a second and much larger phase. It wanted to initiate a £8.5 million five year health project which would have two components, one for northern Sudan with funding of £3.2 million, and one for the south amounting to almost £5.3 million. Since we were successful in the first project, AMREF was approached and asked if it wanted to continue with the second phase.

Now the U.S. Government's strict rules and regulations began to kick in. In its relationship with NGOs, USAID almost always made grants. The NGO would, in consultation with its partners (local governments, communities), submit a proposal for funding. USAID would consider the proposal and decide whether or not to fund it. This was the preferred arrangement for a non-governmental organization because the initiative was taken by the NGO. It was the NGO's project.

With such a large project for phase two, USAID would not consider a grant arrangement. It wanted to have more control over the project, which would be possible only if it was designed as a contract. Contracts, with few exceptions, are offered after an open and competitive bidding process. USAID itself designs the project, publicizes the terms of reference without indication to cost, and requests proposals with budgets from prospective contractors. A contract is basically USAID's project.

We were not interested in either implementing someone else's programme or bidding to become a USAID contractor. But this now presented a dilemma. Because of our success in Southern Sudan, and the fact that few, if any, health organizations knew as much about the region as AMREF did, USAID was very keen that we implement phase two. An interesting compromise plan was devised.

USAID's Mission in Khartoum came up with a creative strategy. To overcome our reluctance to enter the bidding wars, we were informed that AMREF would be requested by USAID to implement the project on a "non-competitive waiver" basis. This meant that a special request would be made to the U.S. Congress asking for a waiver in order for AMREF to implement the southern component of phase two. We would not have to compete against other bidders. While such a waiver was not often requested by USAID or granted by Congress, it was possible.

To overcome our concern about implementing someone else's project, AMREF was assured by USAID that it would consult closely with us during the design stage, thereby guaranteeing our input and ideas. Because of the amount for the southern component (£5.3 million), USAID was insistent it had to be a contract rather than a grant. Contract regulations were much more stringent than those for a grant. Given that we would be awarded the project without competing, it was agreed to accept the contractual arrangement. The other part of the project, the northern component, was to be offered to prospective contractors through the normal bidding process.

In June of 1982, I joined some AMREF colleagues in Khartoum for consultations with USAID on the preparation of the new venture. Given that AMREF had extensive experience in Southern Sudan and knew the cost of operating there, USAID asked us many questions regarding budgetary items. We gladly provided information on salaries, vehicles, petrol, etc. They were grateful for the realistic appraisal provided because none of our figures were inflated beyond actual costs.

Because AMREF had not worked in the Arabic speaking part of Sudan, USAID hired an American consultant, Dr. Greg Pontos, to assist them in preparing the northern component. Dr. Pontos was supposedly an expert on Sudan, especially on the north.

It was agreed that before commencing separate consultations on the northern and southern components, all parties would meet for two or three joint sessions to discuss overall conditions in Sudan. Assuming the meetings would take place at the USAID offices in Khartoum, our three-person AMREF team showed up on time and ready for work. We were then informed that the group would not meet at the USAID offices but rather in room 307 at the Khartoum Hilton Hotel.

"Why meet at the Hilton?" we asked ourselves. "Perhaps it will be more comfortable than the USAID offices," we rationalized. Room 307 at the Hilton turned out not to be a conference setting but rather the bedroom of Dr. Pontos.

Opening the door, we found the good doctor sitting in a chair. Slung over the ceiling chandelier was an intravenous (IV) bottle. A long thin tube connected from the IV bottle to a needle stuck in the arm of the good Dr. Pontos. There was a constant drip of IV fluid entering his arm.

"This guy must be really sick," we thought to ourselves. "And what a brave man, still willing to work while being fed intravenously."

It turned out the special consultant USAID hired for Sudan, Dr. Pontos, was not sick at all. He just never left his hotel room at the Hilton. Dr. Pontos was phobic about getting sick and feared eating or drinking anything prepared locally, even at a hotel of international standards such as the Hilton. His only concession to food was French fried potatoes. Three times a day Pontos ordered French fries from room service.

To supplement his steady diet of fries, he stayed hooked up to the intravenous drip, having brought the fluids and needles with him from the United States. We had to meet in his room so he could "drink from his drip." A most interesting introduction to the world of so called development specialists. Dr. Pontos was only one of numerous dysfunctional "development" specialists I came to know.

This new project in Sudan not only introduced us to some special characters, it also allowed a first hand look into the bureaucracy and regulations of the U.S. Government.

"Mike, its USAID on the line."

"Please put them on."

"Good morning. Is this the head of AMREF?"

"Yes, Mike Gerber speaking."

"This is the office of USAID's Inspector General. He wants to meet with you as soon as possible."

The Inspector General's office serves as a sort of internal auditor and watchdog of the government agency. About two months prior to our eventually signing a contract with USAID to implement the £5.3 million second phase project in Southern Sudan, the above conversations took place. I presumed the Inspector General was anxious to see me because two days later he was sitting in my office.

The first question from the Inspector General was, "How did you know that the amount in USAID's contract budget for operating a four wheel drive vehicle in Southern Sudan was exactly £3,900 for one year?"

"Easy answer," I said. "We gave USAID the figure. About 25 gallons of fuel a week times 52 weeks times £3 a gallon totals £3,900."

"You calculated and gave the figure to USAID?" he responded with a look of incredulity on his face.

"Yes."

The second question was, "How did you know that the exact cost for constructing a two bedroom house in Juba in the USAID budget was £12,900?"

"Easy answer. After building four houses in 1979, we know what building expenses are in Southern Sudan and we told USAID how to calculate that cost."

"You told USAID?" said this now shell-shocked Inspector General.

"Yes."

And for the next thirty minutes, he fired similar questions on various other cost items and received similar responses.

It did not take long to figure out what was going on. This gentleman had come to my office to investigate what he thought was a huge fraud. In USAID contracts, the prospective contractor cannot have any prior knowledge of the cost calculations determined by USAID itself. The prospective contractor is required to do his or her own costing. Part of the evaluation process by the U.S. Government is to evaluate the prospective contractor's cost estimates in comparison to what USAID determines it will actually cost. The prospective contractor's figures are an important component of USAID's determination in deciding who eventually wins the bid.

Now here was a situation where the new contractor to be, AMREF, submitted figures which matched exactly with the figures in the USAID calculations. USAID's figures were supposed to be top secret. Fraud? Collusion between some USAID employees and AMREF? Tricky business had to be going on.

From our perspective, we could not understand why this guy was getting himself into a tizzy. The explanation was simple. AMREF was approached by USAID Khartoum with a request to act as implementors of the second phase project for Southern Sudan. Responding we were not interested in a USAID contract, they offered the carrot of taking it on through a non-bidding, non-competitive waiver passed by Congress. When both parties agreed, it was natural for USAID Khartoum to ask our help in putting together the actual project, given our experiences working in the region. We had much better knowledge than USAID about calculating costs so they asked our advice and used what we told them in their own budget for the project. Naturally, when AMREF was then asked to submit a budget, we again gave them the actual costs, the same ones presented to USAID when our advice was sought.

When I told this story to the Inspector General, he was stunned. Never before had he seen a prospective contractor's budget match exactly with USAID's own figures on key cost items. All he could say was, "highly unusual, highly unusual." Jokingly, I told him that if we had been wiser, we would have inflated the AMREF figures by 20 per cent and then negotiated down to the USAID figures (which we helped them prepare). He wasn't too appreciative of this joke and was gone in a huff.

Not long after, the Congressional waiver was approved, we signed the contract, and began implementation. I am sure that within USAID itself, some people must have had their knuckles slapped for taking initiatives and working out a special kind of contractual relationship with an NGO. It was effective, but as the Inspector General said, "highly unusual."

Sadly, the big USAID project was never completed. By the mid-1980s the conflict between the north and south in Sudan started resurfacing. All of the old issues re-emerged and a new one added – oil discovered near Bentiu, in the northern part of the southern region. The leading southern faction, the Southern People's Liberation Army or SPLA actively took on the national Sudanese army and round two of the bloody conflict caused untold suffering for millions. By 1989, the SPLA and some other dissident groups had forced the army to concentrate its strength in Juba and a few small towns, with the rebel forces controlling the countryside.

Our activities, originally planned throughout the southern region, were by now pretty much confined to the Juba area. The reason for this was not so much the war but rather the bilateral agreement for the project signed between USAID and the Sudan Government. At the time of the agreement's signing, it was an official government programme. Now the Khartoum Government was basically confined to Juba and we were pretty much at a standstill. USAID and other major western donors, disaffected with the Government of Sudan, were closing down their official aid programmes. Many started and/or continued helping the SPLA and other groups in the south.

In February 1991, I received a telegram from the Office of the Ministry of the Interior in Khartoum. It was basically a summons, requesting me to come to Khartoum to discuss the de-registration of AMREF as an NGO working in Sudan. Reading between the lines, it appeared as if the government wanted to throw us out of the country.

Off I went to Khartoum for a meeting with the Minister.

"Why is AMREF aiding and abetting the enemy?" was the first question he asked.

"Aiding and abetting the enemy? What do you mean?"

"Why are you training staff at Kapoeta Hospital on the eastern side of the Nile while Kapoeta Hospital is controlled by the SPLA?" was his second question.

"There is a good reason for that. Anything else?"

"Why are AMREF vehicles being used by the SPLA to attack Sudan's Army?" was the third question.

"There is also a good reason the SPLA had our vehicles. Anything else?"

The Minister's questions, which to me seemed ridiculous, and the tone of this initial exchange made it obvious that AMREF's days, or rather hours of officially working in Sudan, were numbered.

When the civil war started for the second time, the SPLA captured many of the health facilities outside of Juba and some other larger towns in the south. Kapoeta Hospital was one of those facilities captured. A number of western donors, wanting to provide assistance to the south while trying to retain influence in the north, worked with UNICEF (the United Nations Children's Fund) to establish a humanitarian project called "Operation Lifeline Sudan." The Sudanese Government accepted UNICEF as the lead agency to coordinate relief efforts to war-torn areas in the South. It was under the Operation Lifeline Sudan umbrella that a project to assist Kapoeta Hospital was approved by all parties, the government, donors, and UNICEF.

UNICEF approached AMREF and asked if we could participate in the Kapoeta venture by providing two training officers for the hospital. Given that we were still working in Juba under a Khartoum Government sanctioned project, an arrangement was reached with UNICEF. Rather than have AMREF staff work in Kapoeta, two of our training officers were given an indefinite leave of absence. They then joined UNICEF as temporary employees and went to Kapoeta as UN workers.

One day, these two staff members were seen in Kapoeta wearing AMREF T-shirts (more on T-shirts later). This was somehow reported to government representatives in Juba and word was sent back to Khartoum that it was AMREF working in Kapoeta.

When the Minister confronted me with "aiding and abetting the enemy" at Kapoeta Hospital, I duly explained that they were not AMREF staff members but rather UNICEF employees working under the Operation Lifeline Sudan agreement. It was an agreement, he was reminded, that was signed by his own government. He was not too thrilled that this point was brought up and immediately turned his attention to AMREF vehicles being used by the SPLA to attack the army.

One of the areas where we had been working was a town called Yei. AMREF had ten employees based in Yei. They were provided with staff housing and project vehicles. Yei eventually came under heavy attack by the SPLA and it became obvious that the Sudanese Army would not be able to hold the town. Through radio contact with our staff, they were advised to evacuate and get to Juba by any means possible. The staff members quickly hitched rides on a lorry convoy, having to leave behind all possessions, including vehicles.

Sure enough, within hours the attack on Yei began and it was soon overrun by the SPLA. To the conquerors go the spoils. The SPLA took everything they found abandoned in Yei, including four-wheel drive vehicles with AMREF's logo painted on the doors.

When confronted by the Minister with the fact that the SPLA was riding around in AMREF vehicles, my reply was:

"Mr. Minister, it is true the SPLA now has AMREF vehicles. Our staff was evacuated from Yei just prior to the outbreak of hostilities. We were primarily concerned with their safety at that time and not possessions. They had to flee quickly without taking anything along. Naturally, the SPLA forces took all that they found after moving into Yei. Don't all conquering armies do that? Why I have even seen the SPLA driving around in Sudanese army tanks. They captured those tanks from your own troops and are now using them against your army. Would I be fair in saying that your own tanks are aiding and abetting the enemy?"

These proved to be my final words. The Minister abruptly terminated the interview. If there had been a one in a million chance that we were not going to be thrown out before the interview, that miniscule possibility had now evaporated. De-registration of AMREF in Sudan was assured. It also officially marked the end of our relationship with the USAID project. We still continued to help in the south through cooperation with Operation Lifeline Sudan.

There was a postscript to this story. Four years later, in 1995, another telegram was received from the Ministry of the Interior in Khartoum. It again requested my presence at a meeting in the capital. This time though, the Ministry wanted to discuss the re-registration of AMREF. A new Minister was in office and he had known about AMREF's health efforts in Sudan dating back to 1976. His words were "I do not know why you were de-registered but the Sudan Government wants your organization to work here." We were quickly re-registered but continued to limit our activities to UN sponsored projects along with the training of southern Sudanese health workers who were brought into Kenya.

Nothing with regard to Sudan took place without one form of hassle or another. An old friend helped smooth the way for our re-born acceptance and re-registration. He was Professor Assad Ahmed Zeidi Anwar Mohammed, a prominent Sudanese medical doctor from the north. By 1995, Professor Mohammed had been appointed as Vice-Chancellor of the newly created

University of the Upper Nile in Malakal. He had been the Dean of the Medical School at Juba University for many years where AMREF worked closely with him in the south. Professor Mohammed was also an important member of our Health Advisory Committee.

In 1996, I personally invited him to spend a week in Nairobi for consultations and a review of some of AMREF's health projects. Knowing that tensions existed between the Governments of Kenya and Sudan, a formal letter of invitation was sent to Professor Mohammed with copies to the Kenyan Embassy in Khartoum, the Kenyan Ministry of Foreign Affairs in Nairobi, the Kenyan Ministry of Health, and to the Office of Kenya's Principal Immigration Chief. At certain times, the two governments made it arduous for each other's nationals to secure visas. On this occasion, to our surprise, a visa was issued fairly quickly and Professor Mohammed forwarded his date and time of arrival.

It all seemed too easy. About 10:30 one evening, I received a call at home in Nairobi. The AMREF staff person at the airport who was sent to meet our distinguished guest informed me that immigration officers at Jomo Kenyatta Airport refused Professor Mohammed entry into Kenya. The reason given was his visa, issued by the Kenyan Embassy in Sudan, was not recognized by Kenyan airport officials as being valid.

This was just an excuse. The real reason was that the two governments were in a period where they were just hassling the other country's nationals, no matter who the individual was. Mohammed was basically being held captive for the night, to be placed on the next flight back to Khartoum. Needless to say, this was a most embarrassing state of affairs for us, having this eminent senior Sudanese doctor and University Vice-Chancellor locked up in an airport. The only saving grace was the Kenyan officials at least locked him up in the First Class Lounge.

Some frantic calls to the airport were made but the immigration people claimed they were powerless to act. The only person who could free Professor Mohammed from airport captivity was Kenya's Principal Immigration Officer. Professor Mohammed had to be pried loose from the airport, not only to save face, but because he was an important member of our Health Advisory Committee.

It was now around midnight. I called AMREF's Personnel Director, who was a relative of Kenya's Principal Immigration Officer. "We need to find your uncle and have him release Professor Mohammed from the airport." This poor AMREF chap on the other end of the line was now in a state of panic, hearing his boss on the phone in the middle of the night, relating what had happened to our Sudanese guest.

"How can we contact your uncle?"

"What time is it?"

"Around midnight?"

"He is never home at this time."

"Then where is he?"

"In a bar in downtown Nairobi."

"Which bar?"

"I'm not sure. He frequents three or four different ones."

"Don't move. I will pick you up at your home in about twenty minutes."

Off we went to the bars of Nairobi at one o'clock in the morning, searching for Kenya's Principal Immigration Officer. He was located at the third place we visited. The Principal Immigration Officer took it all in stride, greeted us warmly, and after hearing my story, called the airport and had Professor Mohammed released. All's well that ends well. Mohammed took it all in good spirit and continued to assist us over the next few years.

Before moving on from these stories related to Sudan, there is one additional account that clearly illustrates the stark contrast between extreme poverty and extreme wealth in Africa. Here are a few statistics to set the scene. Sudan's infant mortality rate (number of children who die before age one) is 76 per 1000 live births. To compare, similar rates for Great Britain and the United States are 5.2 and 6.6 respectively. Life expectancy in Sudan is 54 years of age in contrast with the latter two countries' rates of 77 and 76 respectively. Annual per capita income in Sudan is £242, slightly above the average poverty level for the continent of £192, or a little over 50 pence per day. These types of statistics are all too familiar for NGOs working in Africa. Their employees spend a great deal, if not all of their time working with the poorest segments of populations given that the vast majority of Africans live at or below the poverty line. With few exceptions, the contrast between a majority of Africans living in abject poverty and the wealthy few can be shocking to the uninitiated westerner. The Sudan was not exempt when it came to glaring inequalities.

In the early 1990s, on a trip to Khartoum for discussion with Ministry of Interior officials, I was accompanied by my wife. We had one free evening and the both of us were invited out by a Sudanese friend, a well-respected academic leader in the country. He had originally intended to invite us to his home, but that same night he himself had been asked to attend a pre-wedding party and was obligated to go. He therefore requested that we join him. Reluctant to go as uninvited guests, there was some hesitation on our part but my friend insisted we would be more than welcome.

On the way to the party, it was revealed that the host was exceptionally wealthy, owning large sugar estates to the south of Khartoum. Upon arrival at the site of the party, held at an especially large house, it was in marked contrast to what we had seen on the drive over. Instead of entering the residence, Ina and I were first introduced to the host who was the father of the groom-to-be along with his about-to-be-married son, and then ushered into a sizeable courtyard. There we found tables and chairs set up for hundreds. At minimum, there were at least 500 people, all kneeling on the floor praying, appearing like a sea of white. Everyone in the courtyard was male, dressed in brilliant white Jalabiyas and matching turbans, the Sudanese national dress for men. There was not a woman in sight, except for Ina, who besides standing out as the only non-Sudanese and non-male present, was wearing a red top in contrast to the white sea of Jalabiyas.

To say she was uncomfortable was a gross understatement. Seeing her discomfort, both my friend and the host tried to reassure her it was not a problem to be in the courtyard because she was a western guest. But Ina politely asked to be able to join the women guests. They directed her to the house.

Inside there were countless women who were having their own party – singing, dancing, and telling seemingly naughty jokes in English. Ina was made to feel right at home, although she did politely decline an offer to have the soles of her feet and the palms of her hands painted with henna, a traditional practice among Sudanese women. From the size of the house, the number of people at the party, and the abundant amount of food being served, it was obvious that our hosts were more than a little comfortable. But it was the women who really gave away the "secret" of just how comfortable.

The beautiful traditional garments of the women present were of the highest quality. Ina, interested in possibly visiting the shops in Khartoum where the attire was purchased, asked one woman for the name of the places. "Shops in Khartoum? No, we go to London to buy our clothing," was the response. These people definitely belonged to the "half of the 1/10th of 1 per cent" of extremely wealthy Sudanese. And while our host was well to do, it turned out that the future bride's family was even wealthier.

This party was only the first in a number of pre-wedding receptions to be held for the betrothed couple. Before the night was over, Ina was invited to attend a celebration at the bride's parents' home the next evening. There were also parties planned by other family members and friends, and given gracious Sudanese hospitality, Ina was invited to attend them all. She did have a legitimate excuse for declining: we were off to Addis Ababa the next day. But one could not help thinking about how many poor could be clothed and fed with just the money that was to be spent on all of these pre-wedding parties. Between the opulence of the pre-wedding parties, the expensive clothing, and the trips to London, there would have been enough to fund any future health projects in Sudan for the next ten years. It was impossible not to keep asking ourselves "What was the actual wedding going to be like?"

The gap between the few very rich and the overwhelming majority of the impoverished, the marked inequality in the distribution of wealth, and the ostentation in the midst of poverty, are all an unfortunate fact of life in the world's poorest nations. Of course every country has both wealthy and poor but these terms are relative. The poverty in the industrialized nations cannot be compared to that in Africa. The absence of a middle class and the number of people living at or below a poverty line defined as 50 pence a day makes the disparity unacceptable for outsiders concerned about 99.9 per cent of the unfortunate in a country such as Sudan.

CHAPTER 23

WHAT ARE THOSE BIG BIRDS DOING?
AFRICA THROUGH A YOUNGSTER'S EYES

Once I started working in Africa, our son Daniel was keen to go along on one of my many trips to the Sudan. When he was about twelve years old, I agreed that he could come with me if his teachers would give him schoolwork to do while he was away for about two weeks. That was worked out successfully and we first went to Nairobi for a few days of meetings before proceeding to Juba and other places in southern Sudan.

With a free weekend in Kenya, I decided to take him on a safari to the Maasai Mara game reserve. We rented a jeep and set off about 6:00 am on a journey that should have taken us about four hours. The road as far as Narok was good but then there were about three more hours over a rough track until we reached our destination – Keekorok Lodge.

About an hour past Narok, the jeep started bouncing badly because one of the front tyres was flat. I changed the tyre in the heat of the morning sun while Dan sat comfortably reading a book. Setting off again for the Mara, we covered about thirty more kilometres when again the jeep began shaking. Now one of the rear tyres was flat. There was no other tyre to replace the second flat.

Dan and I then held a mini crises meeting and devised a plan. We would flag down the next tourist bus headed for Keekorok and ask if they would take Dan along. There was a petrol and repair station at the lodge. Dan would inform them of our problem and have them send a repair vehicle to help. It should have been about another hour to the lodge so we calculated that from the time Dan was picked up, a repair truck should have gotten back to me in about two hours. Good plans often do go astray.

We had no problem flagging down a vehicle within fifteen minutes and a group of German tourists were happy to take Dan along to Keekorok. It was now about 9:00 am and by our calculations, someone should be back to get me and the jeep by around 12:00 noon.

Twelve came and went and I was still stranded in the heat with the car. Twelve o'clock and no sign of a repair vehicle or Dan. Finally at about 12:30 pm, I was becoming frantic – what could have happened to a twelve year old boy on his own in Africa for the first time? So I decided to abandon the jeep, flag down the next tourist minibus, and ask for a lift to Keekorok. A nice Dutch group picked me up.

The petrol station and garage were just inside the front gate of the lodge. I got out of the minibus and went inside. Politely, the garage staff asked me what I wanted.

"Did a twelve-year-old boy come in here about two hours ago and tell you that I was stranded with a vehicle that had a flat tyre and no spare?"

"No sir, no boy has come in here today."

Now I was really worried – what could have happened to him? Off I went to the reception desk and asked if they had seen an unaccompanied twelve-year-old boy.

"No sir, we haven't seen an unaccompanied twelve-year-old boy but we have seen a boy of about that age in the company of a German tourist group."

"Do you know where they went?"

"Sure, they are in the dining room having lunch."

Into the dining room I marched and there at a big round table with about ten adults was Daniel, stuffing his face with a delicious lunch and carrying on a conversation with his new companions. Trying to control myself, I went over and asked him in the calmest voice I could muster:

"Hey Dan, did you tell the people in the garage that your father was stranded on the road with a flat tyre and no spare and that they should come and help fix the tyre?"

"Gee Dad, I forgot. I was hungry and my new friends invited me to lunch. And when we finish, they want me to go on a game drive with them to see the animals."

It doesn't take a great deal of imagination to figure out how this conversation ended.

After recovering from our outing to the Maasai Mara, Daniel and I flew to Juba in the southern Sudan. From there, we were scheduled to drive north along the Nile for a few hours to Bor in Jongli Province where some meetings were scheduled with the provincial hospital staff.

The trip to Bor proved uneventful until we actually reached the hospital. Even when supplies were available, hospitals in the southern Sudan lacked many basic necessities such as drugs, beds, sheets, blankets, water, and food. It was not a rarity to see two patients in one bed or more commonly, patients lying on the floor. Bor Hospital was no exception. I had briefed Dan so he would understand what to expect on our visit and that conditions would not be like those in an American hospital. He said he understood and to his credit, never made any comments while we were in the Bor hospital until the end of our visit. Because the hospital was never completed, one ward did not have a roof and the patients were lying outside, most of them on the floor. While speaking with the hospital administrator in this open-air ward I felt something tugging on the back of my shirt. It was Dan and he then asked me the question.

"Dad, what are those big birds doing?"

"What big birds?"

"Those big birds sitting over there on the low wall behind the patients."

And he was right. There were three big birds perched on a low wall at the back of this open-air ward. The big birds were vultures.

"Oh, those big birds. I'll tell you about them when we are driving back to Juba."

I did tell Dan what the vultures were waiting for. He reacted quite stoically.

CHAPTER 24

WAS *CATCH 22* A NOVEL ABOUT SOMALIA?

"Fasten your seat belts, we are about to land at Mogadishu Airport."

Looking out the window of a Somali Airlines Boeing 737, what appeared below was a scene from a picture postcard. The waters of the Indian Ocean were a brilliant blue and the city with its white buildings looked quite picturesque from the air. At that height it was not possible to see the sharks swimming just offshore from Mogadishu's beaches, waiting for unwary swimmers, or "human sharks" waiting to pounce on the unsuspecting on shore.

This was 1981 and my first visit to Somalia. A consortium of church related organizations had approached us for assistance. Church World Service, Catholic Relief Services, and Lutheran World Relief had become involved with the rehabilitation of a hospital in Lugh, the major town of Gedo Region in southwestern Somalia. The Church trio had contracted Vellore Christian Medical College in India to work in Lugh. The Indians had agreed to rehabilitate a hospital and then run it for the Somalia Ministry of Health.

A bitter war had been fought between Ethiopia and Somalia in the late 1970s. Hundreds of thousands of refugees had crossed from Ethiopia and were living in camps on the outskirts of Lugh town. The hospital had been severely run down because of the lack of support from the Health Ministry in Mogadishu.

The Vellore medical team came from India, travelled to Lugh, took one look at the hospital and town, turned around, and immediately returned to India. They didn't want to have anything to do with working or living in Lugh.

Having been friends with staff at Lutheran World Relief, they asked me if we could help them out of their predicament. Not interested in only running a hospital, AMREF proposed a broader project whereby the hospital would become the focal point for a region-wide community health care project, including training, maternal and child health care, and water and sanitation components. The Church consortium agreed to the broader proposal and we began our involvement in Somalia.

In 1981, Mogadishu Airport consisted of one runway and one small terminal building with a flat roof. Leaving the plane, we saw there were a few hundred Somalis crammed on the rooftop of the building who were awaiting our flight from Nairobi.

Big signs greeted us with warnings not to change money illegally. Currency controls were in strict effect. Every entrant into Somalia had to declare all foreign currency in his or her possession down to the last penny or pence. A form had to be filled in, listing all foreign currencies. Each time one wanted to change dollars or pounds sterling or deutchmarks for Somalia shillings in a bank, the form needed to be produced. The amount of foreign currency changed was recorded and shillings given. Upon departure, one had to change any Somali shillings left over back into foreign currency. It was illegal to take these shillings outside of Somalia. Before being allowed to board a flight out of the country, the form had to be produced and the amount of foreign currency one had remaining needed to coincide with the amount changed as duly listed on the form. If it didn't balance, one could be punished as a "black marketeer."

Each new arrival was, by Somali law, obligated to change the equivalent of about £30 of foreign currency upon entering the arrivals building. Locating the long line for changing money, I waited almost an hour before reaching the window. I asked the teller for a currency declaration form and requested to change my £30 for Somali shillings.

"You must buy a currency declaration form," said the Somali teller.

"OK. How much?"

"Forty Somali shillings."

"But I don't have Somali shillings. That's why I need the form, so I can change my pounds for shillings. I will give you the pound equivalent of 40 shillings for the form."

"Sorry, you can only buy the form with Somali shillings."

"Hey, the sign says its illegal to take shillings out of Somalia. If you cannot take shillings out, how does someone coming in have Somali shillings to buy the form?"

"Sorry, only Somali shillings can buy this form."

Now I understood why it took an hour to get up to the counter. You cannot take shillings out of Somalia so anyone coming in cannot have shillings in their possession. Yet one coming in needs shillings to buy the currency declaration form. Figure that one out. In this situation it wasn't a case of which came first, "the chicken or the egg?" It was a case of which came first, "the shillings or the currency declaration form?" Did Joseph Heller conceive of writing "Catch 22" after a visit he made to Somalia?

The solution to this dilemma was actually quite simple once one understood the Somali system. Remember all those people standing on the roof of the terminal building when we arrived? They were there for a purpose. It was necessary to have a Somali friend or a "fixer" waiting on the rooftop to greet you upon arrival. Being already in Somalia, he had shillings. His most important task was to buy a currency declaration form and send it down from above into your waiting arms. Retreating back outside, I observed a profusion of paper airplanes being flown down off the roof into the hands of arriving passengers. Those paper planes were the needed declaration forms. Welcome to Somalia.

Somalia was a world unto its own. We eventually employed a project manager named Al-Hadji Sani and stationed him in Mogadishu. Al-Hadji, from the Gambia in West Africa, was a health sanitation officer by training. He worked for some time in Lugh and then transferred to the capital where he helped AMREF liase with various government and UN agencies. Al-Hadji was a friendly, outgoing fellow, well liked by all; Somalis and expatriates alike.

As a fellow Muslim and one who had made the pilgrimage to Mecca, he had special standing in the eyes of many Somalis. He eventually left AMREF's employment to work for the United Nations High Commission for Refugees (UNHCR) after President Siad Barre fled Somalia in 1989. The country had degenerated into devastation and chaos as different warlords and factions wrecked havoc throughout. Sadly, while with UNHCR in the mid 1990s, Al-Hadji was killed in Kismayo in southern Somalia. He was on a UN chartered plane that landed for a brief stopover. Sitting in the aircraft while it was on the ground, a shot was fired into one of the plane's windows, hitting Al-Hadji and killing him instantly.

During his stint as AMREF's representative in Mogadishu, he was the "fixer" supreme. There was nothing that Al-Hadji could not get done nor anyone of importance he did not know. One day I accompanied him to the Ministry of Interior on AMREF business. As we were walking down the hallway, very loud shouting was coming from a room at the end of the corridor. Curious, we had a look.

Inside was a friend of Al-Hadji's who was also from the Gambia. The friend, who worked for one of the United Nations agencies based in Mogadishu, was standing in someone's office carrying on a heated shouting match with a Somali official seated behind a desk.

Somalia was one of only two African nations that I frequently visited where one had to get an exit visa to leave the country. Sudan was the other. Just about every African country required visas to enter. But a visa to leave was unusual. Al-Hadji's Gambian friend had a Belgian girlfriend. He wanted to travel to Brussels to pick her up and bring her back to Somalia. They were planning on a wedding in Mogadishu. He went to the Ministry of Interior to apply for his exit visa to leave and re-entry visa to return, an entry visa for his fiancée, and permission to hold a wedding, which was required of foreigners.

Immediately after seeing Al-Hadji's friend's passport, the Somali official told him he was under arrest and would either spend the rest of his life in a Somali jail, or if lucky, be deported back to his country in chains. This poor fellow had only gone to the Ministry for a visa and permission to marry. Now he found himself under arrest and threatened with life imprisonment.

Seeing the friend in a state of panic, we went into the room where Al-Hadji, in his diplomatic mode, greeted the official with a warm smile. Asking what was the problem, he was shown a piece of paper with a picture on it. The paper was a "wanted poster." The picture was completely fuzzy. It was only possible to distinguish the vague outline of an African male. The poor reproduction could have been any African man.

What happened was that about twenty years before, a national of the African nation of Zambia was accused of armed robbery. Zambia, not Gambia. The thief ran away from Mogadishu and had not been found. Wanted posters were circulated but to no avail. The Interior Ministry official had one of these twenty-year-old wanted posters in his desk.

When Al-Hadji's friend presented his passport to apply for the exit visa, the official looked at it and put him under arrest. When Al-Hadji asked why, the official replied that he was the man in the poster from Zambia. Pointing to his friend's passport and showing the official that the man was from Gambia, not Zambia, Al-Hadji politely stated that perhaps there was a mistake.

"Gambia, Zambia, it is all the same" said the official. "We have to arrest somebody."

After about three cups of tea for each of the four people in the room, and an hour of quiet diplomacy from Al-Hadji, the friend was released. Oh yes, he also had his exit visa and permission to marry his fiancée.

What would have happened if we had not wandered by at the precise moment the argument was going on in the official's office? What would have happened if Al-Hadji had not accompanied me to the Ministry of Interior? His poor friend would have been bundled off to a Somali jail and who knows when anyone would have discovered his disappearance. Here was a case of pure chance getting the better of instant Somali justice.

Getting out of Somalia often proved to be more difficult than getting in. Trying to leave on a departing flight from Mogadishu Airport was often a five to six hour ordeal. On my first trip, before AMREF had staff in the capital, flying off was an all day affair. With little regard for ticket confirmations, no computerized passenger lists, few flights to anywhere, and the hassles of money exchanges, passport checks, customs, and hundreds of people milling around in a chaotic state, departing proved challenging and exhausting.

To help cope with the bureaucracy and unique Somali systems, Al-Hadji hired an assistant named Ali. Ali could arrange anything. It seemed he had a key to get through all "back doors" and the wit to outflank all obstacles. To compliment Al-Hadji's stature, cool nature, big smile, and charming personality, Ali contributed smarts, daring, cunning, and knowledge as to where every shortcut was. They proved a formidable one-two punch, as good as Wayne Rooney and Christiano Renaldo for Manchester United or Mickey Mantle and Roger Maris during their heyday with the New York Yankees.

On one visit to Somalia in the mid-1980s, I arrived from Nairobi and after a few days, was scheduled to go on to New York. Few airlines serviced Mogadishu and there were only limited flights each day. From Mogadishu there were three scheduled flights a week on Somali Airlines (or I should say there were supposed to be three flights a week) to Nairobi, twice weekly service to Jeddah on Saudi Arabian Airlines, and an Alitalia Airlines weekly flight to Rome.

Getting from Mogadishu to New York was a challenge because of the limited flight schedules. It would have been easiest to go back to Nairobi, then on to Europe with a connection to the USA. However, such a routing was not possible because it would have meant waiting an additional two days in Mogadishu and hoping the flight would come from Kenya. A decision was made to fly on Saudi to Jeddah, connect to London, and on to New York.

Scheduled to depart on a Thursday afternoon at 5:30 pm, we left Lugh at 4:00 am that same morning for the eight-hour trip by road. Hoping to reach Mogadishu between 12:00 noon and 1:00 pm, and remembering some of my earlier departing adventures, I expected to be taken directly to the airport to begin the going-away ordeal. Instead, to my surprise, we went to Al-Hadji's house where a lovely lunch was laid out.

At 2:00 pm I asked, "Shouldn't we be going to the airport?"

"Don't worry," said Al-Hadji.

At 3:00 pm, "Shouldn't we be at the airport?"

"Relax and have another lemonade."

This went on until about 4:30 pm, an hour before my scheduled departure. All I kept thinking about was the free-for-all that must have been going on at the airport, and about me not being there. Just then, in walks Ali and says, "Let me have your passport, your ticket, all Somali shillings, your currency declaration form, and your suitcase."

Turning everything over to him, he disappeared from Al-Hadji's place. At 4:45 pm, I asked, "Shouldn't we be going to the airport?"

"Don't worry, relax and have another drink."

"OK," and I sat back and took more lemonade.

Five o'clock came and nothing happened. Five fifteen and now I was starting to sweat more than a little. Then at 5:20, Al-Hadji stood up and said, "Let's go."

With no passport and no ticket, I asked him, "Where are we going?"

"To the airport of course," he responded with some puzzlement on his face.

We drove about ten minutes and the airport terminal came into sight. But we did not drive up to the terminal door. Instead, we zipped right past and travelled for another half mile. Then quite suddenly the car made a left turn, through a gate in the airport perimeter fence, and came to a stop in front of a large Saudi DC10. I got out and Ali was waiting by the steps with my passport, plane ticket, and £30 he exchanged for Somali shillings, all in hand.

"You are in seat 10C," he smiled and handed me the documents and money. Onto the plane I went and into seat 10C, the only available place in an aircraft with about 280 other souls already buckled into their chairs, all looking at me as if I were either being forcibly deported from the country or the President of Somalia. The door closed, the plane taxied, rose into the air, and we were on the way to Jeddah. Looking into my passport, I found a Somalia exit stamp. My money receipt for changing shillings back to pounds was also duly stamped as having departed Mogadishu. I was totally stamped out of the country while sitting in Al-Hadji's house drinking lemonade. Good old Ali, master fixer. Never again was leaving Somalia a hassle.

CHAPTER 25

A COUNTRY THAT IS
NOT A COUNTRY

There is an old Somali proverb, which goes something like this:

"Me and Somalia against the rest of the world.
Me and my clan against Somalia.
Me and my family against my clan.
Me and my brother against my family.
Me against my brother."

Such is a generalized statement of a Somali's priorities. The country has a number of factors that should contribute towards a unified nation: one language, Somali; one religion, Islam; and one ethnic group, the Somalis. Society is organized around kinship ties, with family being the strongest of these. Groups of families form clans. Clan identity is strong and historically there have been tensions and warfare among the Somali clans. Primarily nomadic, disputes often arose over territorial issues, with watering rights for camels and goats often at the centre of clashes. When the weapons of battle were spears and old rifles, the damage resulting from clan warfare was limited. In recent years, when the weapons of choice have included AK 47s, mortars, hand held rocket launchers, and four wheel drive vehicles converted into mini battle wagons, the results have been the disintegration of a nation.

Proudly independent, Somalis have a reputation of being fierce warriors and the smallest perceived slight to self, family, or clan can lead to violent blood feuds. On the other hand, the kindest generosity is often shown to total strangers and the poorest nomads will share their meagre rations with someone they have just met. The contradictions are great.

In the eyes of many Somalis, the "Greater Somali nation" has always extended beyond the borders of Somalia as drawn on most maps. For Somalis, Greater Somalia includes everywhere there happen to be ethnic Somalis. This meant Somalia itself, much of the Ogaden region of southwestern Ethiopia, the Haud Desert area in eastern Ethiopia, Djibouti in the northwest, and a great portion of northeastern Kenya. The Somali flag is a white, five-pointed star on a light blue background. Each point of the star represents one of the regions of Greater Somalia. Ethiopia, Kenya, and Djibouti have differing opinions as to what the point of each star means.

Both Kenya and Ethiopia have had their historical problems with Somalia, resulting in outright war or frequent raids and counterattacks across borders. The Kenya Government is always coping with the "shifta" or bandit problem along the Somalia border. Since the late 1970s, frequent conflicts have created serious refugee problems both in Somalia itself and in northern and northeastern Kenya.

Siad Barre came to power as President of Somalia in 1969 after a military coup. He used the dream of a Greater Somalia to rally his cause and tried to unify the various clans. Attempts to weaken the clan structure were never really successful, proving impossible to undo after centuries of built up loyalties. By 1974, Siad Barre had signed a treaty with the Soviet Union, which then provided him with a modern weapons arsenal. This was at the height of the Cold War, with the Russians and Americans continuously jockeying for position in the region known as the Horn of Africa. While Somalia had little in the way of resources, it did sit in a place of geopolitical importance. At the entrance to the Red Sea, and bordered by the Gulf of Aden and the Indian Ocean, it was strategically located for access to the Middle East.

After World War Two and in the first few years of the Cold War, the United States had been one of Ethiopia's key supporters. Once Emperor Haile Salassie was overthrown by a group of army officers, Cold War rivalries began to shift in the Horn of Africa. When Mengitsu Haile Sellassie Mariam emerged as the head of the revolutionary Derge regime in Ethiopia, the Soviets began courting him, and tried to bring about some type of Marxist alliance between Siad Barre and the new regime in Addis Ababa. Somalia wanted nothing to do with such an alliance. It attacked and captured the Ogaden region of Ethiopia in 1977 and the hope of a Greater Somalia was partially realized.

Not being able to control Siad Barre, the Soviets shifted allegiances and threw their total support behind Mengitsu and his regime in Ethiopia. Beginning in 1978, the United States stepped into the void left by the Soviet Union in Somalia and over the next ten years, granted hundreds of millions of dollars to the country in both military and development aid. It was now the U.S. that represented Siad Barre's principal backer while the Soviets propped up a rapidly growing repressive Derge Government in Ethiopia.

With military backing from both the Russians and Cubans, Ethiopia was able to recapture the Ogaden and force hundreds of thousands of Ethiopian ethnic Somalis to flee across the border into Somalia. By 1982, when AMREF began its work at Lugh Hospital and in the Gedo Region, there were four major camps surrounding the town with, according to U.N. statistics, a total population of just over 400,000 refugees.

Modern African history is marked by people fleeing from one country to another. Much of Africa south of the Sahara had gained independence from former colonial masters beginning in the late 1950s and early 1960s. Ghana was the first to be granted freedom by the British in 1957. Since that time, the continent has experienced a series of wars and crises, resulting in mass migrations of populations and the creation of either refugees, those who cross borders, or the internally displaced, those forced to relocate within their own country. The Biafra war in Nigeria caught the world's attention in 1967. Mass murders of Tutsi and Hutu moderates in Rwanda during the early 1990s by the Interahamwe, the Hutu extremists, resulted in over a million people leaving that country and moving into both Zaire (now the Democratic Republic of Congo) and Tanzania. That was one of the most widely publicized chapters in Africa's refugee history.

Angola, Mozambique, Sierra Leone, Burundi, and Sudan, among others, have all written their own refugee chapters. And Somalia deserves a book all unto itself. Through the actions of its leaders and the resulting clan warfare, it has been both the recipient of and the cause for mass migrations of people, into the country, out of the country, and within the country.

The politics and "business" of refugees are dealt with later in this book. At this point, a few words about the situation in Gedo Region in the beginning of the 1980s are in order. When AMREF took up residence in Lugh, combining a programme to rehabilitate a hospital in particularly poor shape and providing primary health care services to settled villagers and nomadic groups, we found two health systems in place. Hospitals such as Lugh were the responsibility of Somalia's Ministry of Health. Health care for refugees in the camps surrounding Lugh were the responsibility of a special quasi-government ministry that had been created and called the Refugee Health Unit (RHU). It was theoretically under the Ministry of Health but was basically autonomous, with its own leadership and its own resources for refugees. The RHU's resources were much greater than those available for the non-refugee population of Somalia, namely the great majority. Much of the funding for the RHU was provided by the office of the United Nations High Commissioner for Refugees (UNHCR), western government donors, and NGOs.

At times, refugees have captured the world's attention and almost always the interest of major donor countries. Under the coordination of UNHCR, both western governments and NGOs usually mobilize resources quickly. Conditions in camps are always incredibly testing following the initial influx of people, with high rates of both morbidity and mortality. But these problems can be dealt with fairly quickly and conditions stabilized as services become organized.

When AMREF was asked to become involved in Gedo Region by the consortium of Church organizations, we were concerned with rehabilitating the hospital, providing services for a scattered local population, and health care in the four refugee camps surrounding Lugh town. These refugees were ethnic Somalis who had crossed over from the Ogaden in Ethiopia during the war. Working with both the Somali Ministry of Health and the special Refugee Health Unit, we tried to coordinate health services both in and out of the camps. It was a thankless job because, without doubt, much greater resources were available for refugee care than for the indigenous Somalis.

At one point during the mid-1980s, the Somali Government, with the backing of UNHCR, decided on a resettlement plan for the Ogadeni refugees. A great portion of northern Somalia was unpopulated. The influx of 400,000 people was causing severe degradation of the land area around Lugh town. This is a phenomenon that occurs almost every time large refugee camps are established. There was also the danger that the camps could become permanent settlements, something that happens all too frequently in refugee situations. Why not move as many of the migrants as possible to the north?

The initial strategy of UNHCR and the Somalia Government was to voluntarily relocate the Ogadeni refugees. Incentives such as cash and the possibility of land were offered. Everyone wanted the cash. No one was interested in the land. These were nomadic people. A fixed piece of land meant little. The refugees did not want to move far from their original home territory, harbouring the hope that some day they would be able to move back across the Ethiopian border. There were few, if any, takers for the voluntary resettlement scheme.

The next strategy saw the Somalia Government select "volunteers" to be moved. This, of course, did not go over too well. But one day, trucks showed up in the camps, guarded by soldiers. Refugees were selected for resettlement and forcibly loaded up onto the trucks. And the trucks rolled out of the camps on the main road toward Mogadishu and then north.

Somalia's roads were not exactly super highways. Often there were more potholes than actual road. Trucks had to move at a snail's pace. At each slow down, off the back of the truck jumped a number of people. They would then quickly disappear into the bush (rough vegetation of the surrounding countryside). Another half kilometre, another slow down, and more people off the back of the trucks and into the bush. Within five kilometres the trucks were practically empty.

Were those disappearing into the countryside refugees who couldn't bear to leave the camps close to the Ethiopian border? In reality, no. They were in fact not refugees from the Ogaden but local Somalis who had moved into the camps. And why would anyone want to move into a refugee camp? Why not? There were daily rations of free food in the camps. Outside, there was no guarantee of where one's next meal was coming from. Free health care was provided and of a quality that could not be matched outside the camps. For those with an entrepreneurial bent, a lot of money could be made in refugee camps by illegally selling donated goods. Who wanted to live a life of "poverty" in the countryside when such "luxuries" as listed above were available in the four refugee camps? Is it any wonder that the local population just moved in?

Somalis, whether living in Somalia, Ethiopia, Kenya, or Djibouti all speak the same language and follow the same customs and traditions. So it was impossible for the camp officials to determine who was a refugee and who was not. When the resettlement scheme was introduced, among those picked for relocation were some local people who had moved into the camps. They were loaded onto trucks with legitimate refugees and told they were to be moved to northern Somalia. Fat chance. The locals just jumped off the trucks and headed back to their homes. For these Somalis, the "riches" of the refugee camps came to an end.

The regime of President Siad Barre was one that became more and more repressive. By 1988, there were hostilities between Barre's Marehan clansman and other competing clans. In that year, the Somali air force, as ordered by Barre, levelled the city of Hargeisa in the north in an effort to destroy opposition coming from an Issaq clan rebel group. With the destruction of Hargeisa, U.S. military support for the Barre Government came to an end. Still, during the previous ten years, a limitless supply of weapons had found their way into Somalia and into the hands of the various clan factions. Somalia was an armed camp.

Besides armed rebellion in the north, resistance forces took up arms in the south. By 1991, armed groups were invading Mogadishu and President Barre was forced to flee the capital, first to Kenya where he lived in luxury at the Safari Park Hotel on the outskirts of Nairobi, and then to Rome. Before independence Somalia had been an Italian colony.

What followed was the destruction of at least a nominal nation, which now disintegrated into open clan warfare, with on-going battles for control of both Mogadishu and the countryside. The arrival of international "Peace Keeping" troops in 1993, including the American army, was at first welcomed as the saviour of Somalia. Yet, what followed was even more bloody warfare. The killing of Pakistanis, U.S. troops hunting for the warlord Mohammed Farah Aided, the massacre of American soldiers and the dragging of their bodies through the streets of the capital, brutal killings of foreign newspaper reporters and photographers, the American pullout, and the slaughter of thousands and thousands of innocent Somalis, all form a recent and all too vivid history. Hundreds of thousands of Somalis fled their country, moving across the border into northern and eastern Kenya. In 2005, the various clan factions, after years of on and off discussions, had with great difficulty finally reached an accord to form a "National Government." It will not be easy to put into practice and only time will tell if Somalia will ever again be a functioning nation state.

As in the rest of the country in the early 1990s, neither Gedo Region nor Lugh were spared from the nightmares of Somalia's clan warfare. Forces allied to Mohammed Farah Aided came through Lugh and devastated the town, which included shooting up the hospital. Lugh was eventually retaken by a group of Somali Islamic fundamentalists who established tight control over the town and surrounding countryside.

Through all the problems of this period in Somalia, AMREF stayed and tried to continue its activities in Gedo Region. For a short time, while Lugh was a battleground, we evacuated our staff, which consisted of both Somalis and East Africans. When the town was retaken by the fundamentalists, their leaders specifically requested that AMREF return. After funding by the Church consortium ended in the mid-1980s, USAID became the major donor. Regular U.S development assistance for Somalia came to an end with the chaos of 1991. The European Union then provided us with aid from a special humanitarian fund it established for rehabilitation of the country.

Working under a Somali Islamic fundamentalist regime proved to have both advantages and disadvantages. Lugh and the surrounding countryside were now safe places to operate. Strict law and order were established. Staff could carry out their activities without fear of coming under attack.

Sadly, during the fighting, much of the rehabilitation carried out on Lugh Hospital from 1984-1986 was destroyed. Work on the hospital had to be done again. Another example of the "one step forward, two steps backward" scenario.

There was also a downside to working with Lugh's new rulers. Our staff had a complicated time living normal lives, or as close to a normal life as was possible. Besides the general harsh conditions for anyone staying in Gedo Region, the fundamentalists imposed their own strict codes of behaviour. No radios, no music, no mixing of sexes, no unmarried males and females together even in private, and the worst of all, in a very hot and very dusty climate, no beer or any alcohol.

AMREF's senior staff consisted of two medical doctors, Willis Ouma Agutu from Uganda and Francis Kazito from Kenya. There were also two female Kenyan nurses and a number of local Somali staff. Neither the Kenyans nor Dr. Agutu were Muslim. The Kenyan nurses had the toughest time of all, forced to cover themselves from head to toe at all times. They were not allowed to treat any male patients. That had to be done by Drs. Agutu and Kazito. Since an important part of the project was the delivery of maternal and child health services to the rural areas, previously the nurses would spend many nights away from Lugh town. Now with the fundamentalist in control, that was no longer possible. It became too unmanageable for the nurses to do their jobs.

Our solution was to replace the Kenyan female nurses with a female Somali nurse who would have a better understanding of the cultural context one had to work in. That was much more complicated to do then it sounds. Firstly, with all the problems in Somalia, it was almost impossible to find a Somali female nurse with a specialization in maternal and child health. Secondly, the fundamentalists were not keen on any females working in public, Somali or non-Somali. We were fortunate to locate and hire a Somali nurse who had lived in Kenya for a long time. She was highly trained and committed to helping. She also had enough experience and composure to handle the male fundamentalists "watchers."

Calm did not last for too long. One day in 1997, while working at my desk in AMREF's Nairobi headquarters, I received an internal call from our radio room. We had an extensive two-way radio network, with over 100 out-stations in Kenya, Tanzania, Uganda, Sudan, and Somalia hooked up to the control room in Nairobi. It was originally set up to backstop the Flying Doctors Service, linking aircraft, hospitals, and headquarters. The network grew over the years and we were usually connected to every AMREF project site with a two-way radio.

An anxious voice said, "Mike, this is the radio room. You better get down here quickly. There are real problems in Lugh."

"What is the situation?"

"We just had a call from Dr. Agutu in Lugh. The town is under fire from Ethiopian helicopter gun ships. The airstrip is being bombed along with the hospital and town. Our staff are frightened and want to confer as to what they should do."

Fortunately, we were able to get back to them on the radio. After consultation, it was decided that flying into Lugh with an AMREF aircraft was just too dangerous. The EU Emergency Office in Nairobi was the coordination point for United Nations flights in Somalia. They too had the same reports we did and could not fly. Our Somali staff was advised to try and reach Mandera, which was just over the Kenyan border, a trip of about four to five hours by road. We organized an AMREF plane to pick them up in Mandera and bring them back to Nairobi. They were able to leave Lugh during a lull in the bombing and just before Ethiopian ground troops invaded the town. The staff made it to Mandera and were flown back to Nairobi, unharmed but badly shaken.

A week or so prior to the Ethiopian attack on Lugh, a pipe bomb had gone off in Addis Ababa. The Ethiopian Government blamed the explosion on Ethiopian Islamic fundamentalists, whom they said were trying to foment unrest among Ethiopian Muslims. Southern Ethiopia has a large Muslim population. The government also claimed that the Ethiopian fundamentalists were being supported by their counterparts from Somalia. Therefore, the invasion across the Somalia border resulted in air and ground attacks on Lugh.

It all happened so quickly, with hardly a mention in the western press. It barely received any coverage in Kenya and the Ethiopian Government denied the "incident" had ever happened. We learned from our evacuated staff and others who fled Lugh during the invasion, that the Ethiopian troops were assisted by Somalis from a faction opposed to the fundamentalists. These Somalis had given the Ethiopians the names of the fundamentalist leaders as well as the names of "foreigners" who were helping the fundamentalists. The Ethiopians had the names of the two AMREF doctors and were searching them out. Dr. Aguta and Dr. Kazito's lives had seriously been at risk.

Further investigation proved conclusively that the Ethiopians troops were really going after the AMREF staff. As a non-political, non-governmental organization, our position had always been that we were a humanitarian agency. Our purpose was to assist in the delivery of health services. Neither race nor religion was a factor with regard to those we helped.

A meeting was immediately arranged in Nairobi with the Ethiopian Ambassador to Kenya. AMREF's Chairman of the Board was Bethuel Kiplagat, an experienced diplomat. Bethuel had been Kenya's Ambassador to France, High Commissioner in London, and Principal Secretary in the Ministry of Foreign Affairs, the highest civil service position in the Ministry. He advised that we make a formal protest to the Government of Ethiopia.

The encounter with the Ethiopian Ambassador, whom I had known for some time, was unsatisfactory. While not denying outright that there had been an Ethiopian incursion across the Somali border, he was emphatic in his denials that

Ethiopia would ever physically harm any staff of an NGO. The Ambassador went on to state that his government had only the highest respect for AMREF's work. After all, AMREF had been working in his country for a long time and the government appreciated what we did. We went round and round, finally ending with the Ambassador saying "he would look into it further."

Although there was never any official recognition of what happened, AMREF was shortly back in Somalia. The Ethiopians withdrew after having made their point to the Somali Islamic fundamentalists. The fundamentalists moved back into Lugh, two out of our three non-Somalia AMREF staff returned (one never wanted to go back again), and our work continued. AMREF is still working in Somalia today, and the situation is more chaotic than ever.

CHAPTER 26

TRAVEL – ACT III

With projects ranging from Sudan to Namibia, Nairobi is better located than most cities in Africa for travelling north and south. Taking into account the normal hardships of moving around, and the special cases of Sudan and Somalia, reaching cities such as Addis Ababa, Entebbe, Asmara, Dar es Salaam, Kigali, Harare, Maputo, Johannesburg, or Windhoek from Kenya was relatively easy. Trying to get from east to west or visa versa on the continent was another story altogether.

On the occasions when it was necessary to travel west, creativity and ingenuity were helpful attributes. While AMREF's activities were limited in West Africa, there were occasional training programmes in countries such as Sierre Leone and Ghana or meetings to attend on the other side of the continent. At that time, the United Nations' World Health Organization (WHO) had its Africa regional headquarters in Brazzaville, Congo. For a health NGO like ours, constant dialogue and collaboration with WHO was expected.

The problems of travelling east to west across Africa stemmed from a lack of frequently scheduled flights. Ethiopian Airlines, one of the best of all the African carriers, normally flew twice a week across the continent from Addis Ababa and Nairobi to Lagos in Nigeria and Accra in Ghana, with intermediary stops (depending on the day) in places such as Kigali, Rwanda; Bujumbura, Burundi; Kinshasa, Zaire; Brazzaville, The Congo; and Yaounde, Cameroon.

For a meeting at WHO headquarters, one had to be lucky to catch the once a week Ethiopian Airlines flight to Brazzaville. If timings were not right, it might be necessary to spend an entire week there, in a city that was probably the most expensive in Africa. In addition, the West African flights were so crowded that it was often necessary to book three months in advance, not always easy to do when one had to travel on short notice.

The actual flying distance from Nairobi to Brazzaville is about 2,600 kilometres. Some people who in their desperation to get to WHO, would fly overnight from Nairobi to Brussels or Paris (about 6,700 kilometres). They would then catch a connecting flight the next day from one of those European capitals to Brazzaville (approximately 6,200 kilometres). To meet a schedule, they would have to travel approximately 13,000 kilometres to cover a distance of less than 3,000.

In the mid-1990s, I was asked to deliver a speech in Brazzaville at a WHO meeting. Thinking it would be a nice "holiday" for my wife, she purchased her ticket to come along. The only problem was that the flight schedules did not coincide with the time we needed to be at the conference. Not wanting to incur the expense or the wear and tear on one's body by travelling to Brazzaville by way of Europe, we looked for other options, including the possibility of making the journey in one of AMREF's small planes.

Our travel officer came up with something that appeared the best and cheapest solution. Cameroon Airlines flew twice a week from Nairobi to Yaounde. It also flew twice a week from Yaounde to Brazzaville. To reach Yaounde was an all day affair because of stopovers in Bujumbura, Burundi and Libreville, Gabon on the way. It was necessary to overnight in Yaounde and then backtrack the following day to Brazzaville, with another stopover in Libreville. It took thirty-six hours to cover the direct Nairobi-Brazzaville distance of 2,600 kilometres. But at least the schedule on Cameroon Airlines would mean spending only three days at WHO.

Leaving Nairobi, after ninety minutes of flying the Cameroon Airlines 737 made its scheduled stop in Bujumbura. We took off again and expected the next scheduled stop to occur in about three hours in Libreville. Settling back for a nice nap, I was surprised to be awoken by the aircraft's descent after less than two hours. Coming to a stop, the doors opened but no one moved on or off the plane. It was now 2:30 in the afternoon. Curious, we asked the stewardess:

"Where are we?"

"Kinshasa," she replied.

"Kinshasa?" I gasped with disbelief. "Isn't this the capital of Zaire?"

"Yes."

"What are we doing in Kinshasa? There was never any mention of Cameroon Airlines landing in Kinshasa."

"That's correct. We are really not here. Our airline does not have rights to drop or pick up passengers in Zaire. This stop in Kinshasa is only to refuel the plane."

Kinshasa, the capital of Zaire, or since the overthrow of former President

Mobutu Sese Seko, the Democratic Republic of the Congo, sits on the banks of the Congo River. And if you stand on the riverbank and look across the water, almost within spitting distance on the opposite side is Brazzaville, capital of the Congo and our destination. You can cross by boat from Kinshasa to Brazzaville in about thirty minutes.

We pleaded with the stewardess:

"Can we please get off? We are destined for Brazzaville and it is just across the river."

"Sorry, it is not allowed."

"But we now have to go all the way to Yaounde, stay over night, and then fly all the way back tomorrow to disembark within less than a few miles from this same spot."

"Sorry, no. Regulations you see. And besides, your baggage cannot be removed from the hold."

"Please let me speak to the Captain."

The Captain came out and the same unsatisfactory discussion took place.

"Let me speak to whoever is in charge of the airport here in Kinshasa."

We could have spent the next hour speaking to a 100 people but nothing was going to change if normal procedures were followed.

"Rules and Regulations, you see. No one can embark or disembark on Cameroon Airlines in Kinshasa. This is only a refuelling stop."

As the plane lifted off the runway, we waved goodbye to Brazzaville across the riverbank. It was on to Yaounde after a stop in Libreville. The next day, at about noon, or almost twenty-four hours after we had been on the ground in Kinshasa, the plane landed across the Congo River in Brazzaville.

Returning to Nairobi was more of the same but without an overnight stop in Yaounde. The Cameroon Airlines schedule had us leaving Brazzaville at 6:30 in the morning, stopping in Libreville, and then on to Yaounde. After a three-hour wait at Yaounde airport, it was onto another plane, back to Libreville, and the same "refuelling" stop in Kinshasa. The plane put down at Kinshasa Airport at 3:00 in the afternoon. After leaving Brazzaville at 6:30 am, we were basically back in almost the same spot eight hours later.

And do you know what? Three people, who were with us for three days at the conference in Brazzaville truly boarded the plane in Kinshasa, rules or no rules. They just came on board, took their seats, and flew on to Nairobi. So this was a "REFUELING" stop after all. These three new passengers "fuelled" the appropriate people in Kinshasa, providing enough "grease" in the right hands to board the aircraft. The "brand" of fuel used was probably either "dollars" or "pounds sterling."

Travelling could easily cause frustrations for those not used to the "rules and regulations." A classic case occurred at Jomo Kenyatta Airport, Nairobi, in 1983. Just before boarding a flight to London, an English gentleman got into a heated argument with security people doing last minute checks. At that time, Kenya also had currency controls and it was prohibited for non-residents to take Kenyan shillings out of the country. A visitor had to re-convert shillings for hard currency before departing.

The security person found the English chap to be in possession of about 500 shillings, which at that time was the equivalent of about £18.

"You cannot take these shillings with you. Go exchange them or leave them with me."

"But if I go back to change them, I will miss the flight," answered the now flustered passenger. "And I am not giving them to you, that is robbery."

Hearing the word "robbery" said in a rather loud voice, the security officer took the English fellow off the line and would not let him board the aircraft. While it might have been an attempt at robbery, the Englishman's first mistake was making a public issue of it.

The two were in a dead standoff. The passenger would not go back outside to convert the shillings for fear of missing the flight, nor would he give them to the policeman. The security officer, to save face, would not let the English chap board the plane.

Finally, as the last boarding call was announced, the passenger, his face completely red with anger, said

"Here you want the shillings, here they are." He proceeded to tear the money into tiny bits of paper.

"Now I do not have any more shillings in my possession and I am leaving."

That was his second and last mistake. Since a President of Kenya's face appears on every currency note and coin, it is a serious offence to deface Kenyan money. The penalty is imprisonment and a stiff fine. The last thing I saw before boarding the flight was a group of policemen taking the poor English fellow away in handcuffs.

A classic case of "travellers' frustration" was observed at the airport in Kigali, Rwanda. Each leaving passenger must fill out a departure card. Besides the regular information that has to be provided, for example, name, nationality, passport number, visa number, date of birth, etc., there was a space labelled "Reason for Departure."

One guy, who must have had an arduous stay in Rwanda, filled out the "Reason for Departure" line with the words,

"Because I hate this f_ _ k_ _g country."

That was another fellow carted off in cuffs.

Even the experienced traveller can get worn out. AMREF started working in Mozambique in the 1990s. On one trip to that country in 1997, my wife came along, never having been to Mozambique before. After a few days in the capital Maputo, we travelled north to Inhambane District where our staff was working with the Provincial Ministry of Health. It was a long, hot, and tiring all-day trip by road. In the evening, with a lot of trouble finding a place to sleep, we eventually located a "hotel" in a small town across the bay from Inhambane. It was the only place that could take us in. Not exactly five-star but our sole option.

The next morning, after being eaten alive by mosquitoes during the night, Ina, who had been all over the world and had slept in some "minus five star hotels," announced "This is my last development trip." That was her way of telling me to travel alone from then on. One does reach a point in one's life where roughing it loses its romantic appeal. Ina had definitely reached that point.

CHAPTER 27

KENYA AND TEA MONEY: CORRUPTION SMALL AND LARGE

Kenya and Tanzania were not without their fair share of "getting around" pain and suffering. Whether the simple act of going to the office each morning, or dropping someone at the airport, it was wise to believe fully in the Boy Scout motto, "Be Prepared."

Each morning, when in Nairobi, I would travel the same route via Langata Road to reach the office. Without traffic, it was about a fifteen-minute trip. However, if one left the house after 7:00 am, the journey might take an hour. To get a jump on most other people, I was always out of the house before 6:30 am.

The short trip was actually quite nice. The journey took me past the western side and main gate of the Nairobi National Park. It was not uncommon to spot a giraffe or two or a herd of impala grazing along the fence at the outer edge of the park. On a rare occasion, an elusive rhino could be seen. Passing the park and then a Kenyan Army Battalion headquarters, one came to the top of a rise before descending along-side Wilson Airport, Africa's busiest in terms of takeoffs and landings. If lucky, as the hill was crested for the drive down toward Wilson, Mt. Kilimanjaro, across the border in Tanzania, could be spotted to the southwest in the far off distance (a little more than 200 kilometres following a straight line). "Kili" as it was commonly called, is Africa's tallest mountain, 19,340 feet high, snow-capped all year round and sitting a few degrees south of the equator. Kilimanjaro is a truly spectacular sight.

One beautiful morning, as I was driving by the game park, a large lorry was in front of me, belching ugly black smoke from its exhaust. Since there was no oncoming traffic in the other lane and not wanting to die of asphyxiation, it was not difficult to pull around and overtake the larger, slow moving vehicle. About ten seconds after going around the lorry, a policeman was on the road in front, signalling for me to move to the side. As a law-abiding individual, I complied.

"Habari za asabuyi, officer, habari yako? (Good morning and how are you?). Beautiful morning, isn't it?"

"Sir, you committed a crime and I have to issue you a summons."

"What crime, officer?"

"You passed a vehicle by crossing a solid white line."

"A what?"

"A solid white line."

The Langata Road, at that time, was a single lane carriageway in each direction. It had not been retarmacked since it was originally constructed. There was not a single marking on the road for kilometres, neither white nor any other colour.

"What white line officer? I don't see anything on the road."

"The white line that used to be there."

"Used to be? When was there a white line there?"

"When the road was built."

"You are giving me a traffic ticket for a white line that used to be there twenty years ago?"

"Yes, you should have known about the old white line."

"O.K, give me the ticket."

"But you can pay the fine right here, only 1,000 shillings (about £10 at the time)."

"No thanks, I'll take the ticket."

"You will have to first drive me to the police station where I can file a report. Take me in your car."

"No, you go ahead to the police station and I will follow you."

After thinking about this exchange, the policeman very politely said:

"Sir, today you are like my father. Because you are like my father, I will let you go."

And so it went at times in Kenya. The poorly paid police, if fortunate, would receive their wages only once a month and sometimes the salary payments were late. They needed "tea money" or "Chai pesa" to survive and invisible white lines were as good a way as any of collecting it. One should have known better than to cross an invisible white line at the end of a month.

The end result was that neither a ticket was received nor a fine of 1,000 shillings paid. After a few more minutes of friendly banter, the policeman realized no money would be forthcoming. If they gave me a summons, perhaps photos of the non-existent white line would have been brought to court. All's well that ended well. The two of us had a good laugh and I had a nice story to tell.

In 1993, our middle son Adam and his girlfriend came to Kenya for a visit. When their holiday ended, Ina drove them to Jomo Kenyatta International Airport for their return trip to the United States. Jomo Kenyatta is about twenty kilometres from downtown Nairobi and can be reached by taking the major Nairobi-Mombasa thoroughfare, which near Nairobi is known as Uhuru (Freedom) Highway.

Not more than five kilometres out of the city, two policemen flagged down Ina and signalled her to move off the road. Obediently, she pulled over.

One of the policemen was holding a black cylinder in his hand. It looked something like a cross between a big searchlight, a torch, and a hair dryer.

"Maam, do you know that this is a 50 kilometre-an-hour speed zone?"

"No," answered Ina. "Isn't the speed limit on all of Uhuru Highway from Nairobi to the airport 80 kilometres?"

"No, here it is 50 kilometres and it is sign-posted. You were travelling at 65 kilometres an hour."

After travelling on this road countless times, Ina could not remember seeing any sign indicating a 50 kilometre speed limit.

"I did not see any sign officers. And how did you know I was going 65?"

"We timed you on this radar gun."

Ina, Adam, and his girlfriend, all looked in amazement at this machine the police officer was calling a "radar gun." Adam peered into the front of the cylindrical contraption for a closer inspection. He still swears to this day that there was nothing inside the so called "radar gun," no bulb, no wires, nothing. It was totally empty, just a hollow tube.

Realizing this was an argument that would most likely not be won, Ina said to the officers, "I have never seen a 50 kilometre sign limit on this road and I do not know how your machine registered my speed at 65 kilometres. But if you have to give me a citation, go ahead and I will go to court."

"Don't you want to pay the fine here and save yourself the trouble of going to court?"

"No, give me the ticket."

Another chai pesa story. But the difference in this situation was the policemen actually gave Ina a summons. She did go to court. But before doing so, she drove up and down Uhuru Highway in both directions looking for a 50 kilometre speed limit sign. Going south, in the direction of the airport, there were no signs at all, not even one denoting 80 kilometres an hour. On the opposite side of the road, however, when travelling from the airport back to Nairobi, there was in fact a sign showing a 50 kilometre speed limit for a short stretch. She was given a citation for a sign that was on the other side of the highway and impossible to see by anyone driving south.

Court turned out to be an eye opener. After her reconnaissance of the road, which proved there were no signs when travelling south, and the phoney radar gun, Ina was prepared to plead not guilty. Everyone warned her it would be a waste of time and she should just pay the fine. But, no, there was principle involved. An innocent victim should not be penalized.

There is no such thing as a separate court in Kenya for traffic cases. All individuals go to the same courtroom. Murders, thieves, rapists, wife beaters, prisoners in manacles, and one falsely accused traffic offender, all thrown together. To help her get through the ordeal, an experienced AMREF driver named Titus accompanied Ina to court. She was told to appear at 7:30 am. By 4 o'clock in the afternoon, after sitting all day and observing case after case, Ina sent Titus home. By five, she had given up the idea of a "not guilty plea" and beseeched a court official to allow her to pay the fine. To do so, Ina had to return to court a second day and only then was she told to send in payment by mail. To this day, our son Adam still talks about the "empty cylinder radar gun."

The search for small tea money was a common occurrence. Sadly, in a number of African countries, in order to transact business, it means providing "big tea money." For the small policeman or lowly bureaucrat, the little payments or bribes really do amount to real tea money, the ability for a family to survive. For big shots, the big tea money, more commonly called corruption, has reached epic proportions.

The best story about big tea money or corruption in Africa was told to me by an Ambassador from a western European country at a dinner party he hosted in Nairobi. This story was frequently told over and over by development workers throughout the continent.

Every other year, the African Ministers of Public Works and Roads hold a conference. Ministries of Public Works and Roads are responsible for large infrastructure development projects such as roads and dams. These have been favourites of large donors because they are highly visible. Sometimes they turn out to be white elephants, with money wasted on projects with little utilitarian value. These are often huge multimillion-dollar projects and not all of the resources go where they should be going.

In the mid 1990s, the Public Works Ministers' Conference was being held in the capital city of an unnamed East African country. At the end of the three day conference, the host Minister of this East African nation held a reception and dinner for his fellow Ministers. One of the Ministers from a West African nation arrived for the reception in his chauffeured Mercedes Benz. As the Mercedes pulled into the driveway of the East African Minister's home, the West African Minister expressed great surprise.

He saw a huge house, with many, many rooms. Next to the house was a four-car garage. In this garage were three brand new Mercedes and one large BMW. The house was surrounded by large, beautifully manicured gardens.

During the cocktail reception, the West African Minister could no longer contain his curiosity. He went over to his host, the East African Minister, and the following discussion took place.

"Tell me, my East African colleague. You are a Government Minister just like me. We are both government servants. The salaries of government servants in Africa are not high. Yet you have a most beautiful house. It is ten times larger than my house. You have four brand new and expensive cars in your garage. And you have acres of beautiful gardens. Please, I can no longer keep my curiosity to myself. Tell me, how can you do all of this on a government salary?"

The East African Minister took his west African colleague by the arm and led him away from the crowd and over to a big picture window.

"Do you see that road over there, just beyond my house?" asked the East African Minister.

"Yes, I see it."

Looking at the road but pointing to himself and tapping his own chest with his right hand, the East African Minister said "10 PER CENT" (meaning 10 per cent of what a donor provided to build that road was pocketed by the Minister).

*   *   *

Two years later, the government Public Works and Roads officials met again, but his time in the country of the above-mentioned curious West African Minister. The East African Minister travelled to the west African capital, attended the three day conference, and on the final evening, went to a reception being hosted by his West African colleague, the same chap who asked him the personal questions at the previous meeting.

Pulling up to the West African Minister's home, the East African Minister was amazed at what he saw. At the end of a long driveway, was a huge house, much larger than his own. There was a ten-car garage and each space was filled with brand new Mercedes, BMWs, and even a Rolls Royce. The grounds surrounding the house were enormous, with many more acres than his own.

During the cocktail reception, the East African Minister, no longer able to contain his curiosity, went over to his old friend and present host, the West African Minister. The following discussion took place.

"Tell me my West African colleague. You are a Government Minister just like me. We are both government servants. The salaries of government servants in Africa are not high. Yet you have a beautiful house. It is even much larger than my own house. You have ten luxury vehicles in your garage, I only have four. And you have many more acres of land than I do. Please, I can no longer keep my inquisitiveness to myself. Tell me, how can you do all this on a government salary?"

The West African Minister took his East African colleague by the elbow and led him away from the crowd, over to a large window taking up the entire wall of the room.

"Do you see that road over there, just beyond my house?" asked the West African Minister.

The East African Minister looked out the window, into the distance and tried to spot the road. But he saw nothing. Not wanting to appear stupid, he looked again. And again nothing. So he looked for the third time and saw the same thing, nothing.

Finally, turning to the West African Minister, the East African replied,

"But I don't see any road out there."

"That's right," answered the West African Minister. Tapping his chest with his right hand and pointing to himself, he said "100 PER CENT."

That was "Chai Pesa" on the grandest scale. When it came to corruption, some had small pockets, some big (or exceptionally big) pockets.

Today, in many countries around the world, recycling has become a major weapon in the struggle to conserve resources and improve the environment. The recycling of glass bottles or tin cans is now common practice. In the eyes of most people, this is a noble effort to make the world a better place to live. If special awards were given to the most innovative ways to recycle, Kenya would win a gold medal. Only Kenya's gold medal would not be for recycled glass bottles or tin cans nor would it be viewed as part of any noble cause.

For the country has perfected the art of recycling, not of things, but of people. And the people who are part of this reusable process are not those who contribute to the making of a better country. Rather, they are those who often actively participate in the corruption game.

The record will show that rarely, if ever, is anyone prosecuted for financial manipulation, outright bribery, or just plain stealing. Oh sure, the little person will get caught and given jail sentences. And yes, the bigger stealers will, from time to time, also be caught. In these cases, though, rather than receive punishment, the crook is simply recycled, to steal from someplace else.

Kenya's labour laws make it almost impossible to fire an employee, especially a senior one, for any reason. Stealing is usually not a good enough reason for outright dismissal. With the difficulties of firing someone, and the unenviable track record of not prosecuting big time thieves, what happens to the upper level crook that is employed in your company? If you are lucky, under the threat of exposure, the person can be convinced to leave on his or her own initiative. A good friend refers to this process as "offloading." There are many cases of "offloaded" ones quietly disappearing from the companies they are employed with, only to turn up later working someplace else. Checking references for senior hires is not common practice – I was called only once in over nine years to provide a reference on a senior ex-staff member. This person in question was one of our "offloaded" ones and after confidentially informing the chief executive who was interested in this person as to the reason he was no longer with us, he was not hired.

This was only a temporary blip. The same individual was eventually employed elsewhere in a very senior position and sure enough, a few years later, was implicated in a financial scandal. But as in the game of American baseball, it takes three strikes to be called out. Even before an investigation of financial impropriety was carried out, Mr. X was already appointed to head another organization through intervention at the highest levels of government. This is an all too frequent occurrence. Hence, Kenya's award for recycling – the recycling of thieves. If some of these Kenyans actually played baseball, there is little doubt the number of strikes for a strikeout would be raised.

CHAPTER 28

AIRPLANES BIG AND NOT SO BIG

When reminiscing about Africa, it seems one always comes back to stories of travel, with airplanes often tending to be the focal point for adventure. Whether it was large planes or small ones, there always seemed to be a story.

About two years after joining AMREF, on a trip from New York to Nairobi in 1981, I was asked to stop over in London in order to interview some candidates who had applied to work with us. A search committee had been formed which included the Vice-Chairman of our Board and myself, among others.

Working for a charitable organization, one looked to save on costs whenever possible. This was the period when Freddie Laker and his Laker Airlines, the precursor of the "no frills" carriers of today like EasyJet and Southwest, were in their heyday. Laker offered the cheapest fares from New York to London.

My flight departed from John F. Kennedy airport about 6:30 pm on Monday, the 4th of May, bound for Gatwick outside of London. This date and time of departure proved to be quite significant. About two hours into the flight, the pilot began speaking on the intercom and announced that there were some problems and he had been advised to make an immediate emergency landing in Gander.

"Gander? Where was that?" everyone asked, "And what are the problems?"

"Gander," we were told, "was in Newfoundland, Canada." But no one told us what the problems were.

That there were issues was in little doubt. The aircraft, a large DC 10 with about 300 passengers on board, made the most rapid drop I have ever experienced while flying on a commercial aircraft. We went down so quickly that just about every passenger developed severe ear aches. As we were dropping, the pilot told us that once the plane was on the ground and came to a complete stop, he wanted everyone off as quickly as possible. There would be no time for stairs to be wheeled up to the doors. Emergency slides would be released and we would go down on our backsides. Orders were given that absolutely nothing should be taken off the plane.

All 300 passengers were in a state of panic when touchdown occurred. Looking out of the plane's windows into the dark night, one saw edged alongside the runway, numerous fire trucks with their lights on. Ambulances and other emergency equipment were also evident. For some reason, the emergency slides were not used. Instead, portable steps were wheeled up to the front and rear doors in a hurry.

Given that it was May, people were dressed for spring. Not being able to take anything with us, all coats and jackets were left on board. We were greeted by a blast of extremely cold Canadian air as the doors were opened. Freezing, everyone quickly boarded buses which then rapidly moved away from the plane. We were taken to an old terminal building that looked as if it had not been used for some time.

Why was the evening of Monday, 4 May 1981 so important for the Freddie Laker flight bound from New York to London? At our departure, it was just after midnight on Tuesday, 5 May in England, or five hours ahead of East Coast time in the United States. At 1:17 am London time on Tuesday, 5 May, Bobbie Sands, the Irish nationalist died in a British jail after sixty-five days on a hunger strike. The time of his death was 8:17 pm Monday on the East Coast in the United States. At that very moment, my Laker flight was somewhere over eastern Canada.

All of this only became known to us after people started calling friends and family to let them know what had happened to our Laker flight and where we were. On the news, it had been reported that as a result of Bobby Sands' death, the Irish Republican Army called every British airline and reported that bombs had been planted on a number of aircraft. Which aircraft, the IRA did not specify. However, the airlines could not take any chances. At about 8:15 pm U.S. East Coast time, all British planes in the air, including our Freddie Laker flight, were probably making emergency landings someplace around the world. Airline officials could only assume there might be a bomb on any plane.

Thus our six hours on the ground in ice-cold Gander. We seemed to be under "house arrest" at an old U.S. military air base while the aircraft and all luggage was subject to a five-hour search. The terminal was definitely not equipped to handle a large DC 10. Some nice local people brought in sandwiches and drinks but there was not enough to go around. Two toilets were totally inadequate for the large crowd. And the one public telephone had a queue over three hours long.

After a thorough check, nothing untoward was found on the DC 10. We eventually reboarded and reached London over six hours behind schedule. Naturally, I missed the interviews and received a harsh tongue lashing from my AMREF colleagues for being late. They could not believe my story at first.

Similar adventures were not limited to large passenger aircraft. Such was the case in 1996, on a small, twin-engine flight from Nairobi to the southwestern part of Tanzania.

With funding from the Canadian Public Health Association, AMREF was implementing a sizeable community based primary health care project in the Rukwa Region of Tanzania. The project office was located in Subawanga, about 125 kilometres west of Lake Tanganyika. Subawanga, a distance of over 1000 kilometres from Nairobi, was about the furthest range we could fly in our own aircraft without refuelling.

When Bethuel Kiplagat became AMREF's Chairman of the Board, we felt it important that he get a first hand look at what the organization was doing on the ground. Hence, a trip to Rukwa Region was organized. Mrs. Eunice Kiereini, another Board member also joined us. Eunice, before her retirement from government service, had been Kenya's Chief Nursing Officer and was quite knowledgeable about health issues throughout Africa. She also served as Chairperson of The Flying Doctors' Society, a fundraising body that helped raise money for our Flying Doctor activities.

Besides the two Board members, someone from AMREF's information department joined to capture the reaction of the visitors to the Tanzanian project. Flying in a twin engine Cessna 402, there was a full planeload on the flight to Sumbawanga.

The first day went smoothly, if rather long. After three hours in the air, upon arriving in Sumbawanga we boarded vehicles and travelled another two hours over rough roads to the shores of Lake Tanganyika. At the tiny village of Kasanga, the party boarded three small boats and sailed another hour and a half north along the lakeshore. Two villages were visited where community health workers had been trained and were now providing primary care. During much of the year, these villages were only accessible by boat. It was essential that some type of health care be available to the villagers on the spot.

The excursion was an excellent but tiring one, travelling by air, road, and boat. Returning late in the evening to Sumbawanga, everyone had a good night's sleep.

The second day was devoted to maternal and childcare, HIV/AIDS prevention, and training activities. The programme for our visitors ended after meetings with Provincial and District Ministry of Health officials. After a second night, we were scheduled to depart for Nairobi the following morning.

Taking off for home the next day, almost all on board fell asleep as soon as the plane was off the grass airstrip. They were exhausted from our previous two days. Luckily, the pilot remained wide-awake.

Flying the Cessna 402 was Captain Bill Hood, an experienced AMREF pilot. Sitting in the right hand seat next to Bill, I observed him tapping some of the indicators on the instrument panel about thirty minutes into the flight. Knowing he was concerned about something, but not wanting to awaken or alarm the other passengers, I quietly asked him,

"Bill, is there a problem?"

"There might be, Mike. I'm getting a lower than normal reading from the left engine's oil pressure gauge. I don't know if it is a fault with the pressure gauge or we are losing oil. I checked the fluid levels before our departure from Sumbawanga and everything was normal."

"What do you want to do?" I whispered.

"I will keep monitoring it carefully and if it does develop that we are seriously losing oil, we can land in either Arusha or Moshi rather than try and make it all the way to Nairobi."

Our policy at AMREF was that when it came to the safety of the aircraft and passengers, it was the pilot who was best prepared to decide on what to do. In over forty years, AMREF's safety record was outstanding, and Bill Hood was an experienced pilot.

About ten minutes later, coming from the left engine was a clear trail of black smoke.

"It doesn't look good, Mike," said Bill quietly. "We are definitely losing oil. We will not make either Arusha or Moshi. I've checked the maps and Tabora is the closest airstrip. We are about ten minutes out. I am going to try and put down in Tabora. I will radio ahead and let them know we have an emergency. Hopefully, they will institute their emergency landing procedures and have the fire fighting equipment on standby. In a few minutes, I am going to shut down the left engine to minimize the risk of fire. We can land on one engine."

"OK, I think we better wake everyone up."

Turning to the back, in as quiet and calm a voice as possible, I announced,

"Folks, there is a slight problem with the aircraft. One engine has an oil leak and Bill feels it best that we land to see how serious the problem really is. We are only a few minutes from Tabora and that is where we are going. Remember the emergency procedures that Bill explained before take off. As soon as we land and the engines are shut down, Bethuel you open the door. Eunice, Bethuel, and Isabel get off the aircraft immediately and walk away from it as quickly as possible. Bill and I will follow you off."

There were definitely some worried faces as I made this announcement. When Bill banked the plane to line up with the airstrip, from the far distance we saw a cloud of dust moving towards the landing spot. On further inspection, it appeared to be one dreadful looking old fire engine coming from the town. Given our descending speed and the snail's pace the fire truck was moving at, we would be on the ground long before the vehicle ever made it to the airport. So much for Tabora's emergency landing capability.

As the Cessna began its descent, the left engine caught fire with flames shooting out toward the rear. Bill shut it down and as we descended, the flames seemed to die out. The landing was now being carried out on one engine.

"To repeat what Mike said," Bill told our passengers, "as soon as we come to a complete stop, evacuate immediately. I am worried about a possible fire so move as far away from the plane as fast as you can."

To his credit, Bill made a perfect landing on the one good engine. Our passengers followed the drill and made an orderly and speedy evacuation. We were all off and away from the plane within seconds of the right engine being shut down. There was still a trail of smoke coming from the left side.

After about ten minutes of standing in ninety-five degree heat, in the middle of Tabora Airport's one runway, an old fire truck entered the airport grounds and came down the runway.

"How can we help?"

"The only thing you can do now is to give us a lift into town. There doesn't seem to be any other vehicles around."

"You can't leave the plane there," declared one of the firemen.

"And why not?" answered Bill.

"It is blocking the runway. It has to be moved off the runway and on to the apron by the terminal building."

Looking in the distance, the terminal building must have been at least 100 metres away. Knowing there was no towing equipment at Tabora Airport, there was only one way that plane was going to be moved. My Chairman, Eunice Kiereini, Bill Hood, our information officer, three firemen, and myself pushed the Cessna for 100 metres, finally moving it off the runway. This proved a great photo opportunity, Bethuel, Eunice, and the rest of us pushing an airplane.

We spent the night in Tabora. The next morning another AMREF aircraft came down carrying our chief engineer and a spare engine. The second plane took us back to Nairobi while the engineer remained behind for a few days and replaced the left engine.

It all ended well. Everyone now had a story to tell his or her children or grandchildren. And I did not even have a tough time in the future convincing my Chairman to visit other projects.

I had the good fortune of knowing, working, and befriending a number of remarkable people in both Asia and Africa. One of the most extraordinary was Dr. Anne Spoerry, a French national, who spent the last forty-nine years of her life in Africa, caring for those most in need in some of the remotest places on the continent. A member of the French Resistance during World War Two, captured and imprisoned by the Gestapo, moving to practice medicine in Aden after the war, and finally settling in Africa in 1950, Anne's life was full and interesting.

In 1963, at the age of forty-five, Anne Spoerry learned how to fly an airplane and joined one of AMREF's founders, Michael Wood, as one of the original Flying Doctors. Her work with nomadic tribes in isolated parts of East Africa earned her world renown. The Samburu, Turkana, Maasai, and Swahili peoples of Kenya's coast referred to Anne in Kiswahili as "Mama Daktari."

The simple literal translation is "Mother Doctor." But as I wrote a number of years ago in the introduction to her book of the same name, "It is almost impossible to convey a true meaning of the Kiswahili term 'Mama Daktari' in English. To appreciate its significance for an African, one must understand a cultural respect attributed to the combined qualities of age, wisdom, education, presence, and an ability to be useful to others." That was Dr. Anne Spoerry.

As a person, she was quite a character. Dynamic, no nonsense, pistol packing when in dangerous areas, she continued piloting her own small single engine aircraft right up until the time of her death in 1999 at the age of 81. To maintain a pilot's license, she had to pass a physical examination, which included an eye test each year. As a medical doctor, unknown to many, Anne would just certify herself fit to fly.

In her later years, she became notorious for "dropping off to sleep" during meetings and then jumping awake with a shout. At times, when flying, she would engage the autopilot and catch a few winks.

Anne owned a home on Lamu Island, a beautiful tropical area about 250 kilometres by air to the north of Mombasa. It is a popular holiday spot for tourists and Kenyan residents alike, with beautiful beaches, sparking blue ocean, and a culture influenced by hundreds of years of contact with the Arab world of Oman and Yemen.

One long weekend, Anne Spoerry invited Ina and myself to join her in Lamu for a bit of relaxation. Taking off from Wilson Airport, Ina was sitting in the right hand seat next to Anne and I was in the back. About thirty minutes into the flight, Ina turned to me with an astonished look on her face and said,

"She's sleeping. What should I do?"

"Talk to her," was my answer, adding "and keep talking to her."

Ina, poking Anne gently in the ribs, said in a loud voice,

"Anne, what is that down there?"

"Down where?" Anne quickly awakened.

"Down there," Ina pointed off to the left side of the aircraft.

"Let's see," said Anne and she immediately banked the plane sharply to the left, rapidly descending from 10,000 feet to 5,000 in a short time. An experienced military fighter pilot could not have executed a better dive. While our stomachs were churning from the quick descent, at least Anne was now wide-awake and pointed out various features of the topography below. We flew just above tree top level for the rest of the journey to Lamu, with Ina asking question after question, and Anne good naturedly answering every one. All of us arrived fully alert.

Committed to the people of the coast, Anne Spoerry did regular rounds, by air and sea to provide medical care in the region. There were sizeable populations not only on Lamu, but also on a number of other islands off the coast. Anne would fly to some of these and others she would visit by boat in the company of Ministry of Health officers. On one of her regular rounds, Anne asked me to spend a week on the coast with her. She wanted to show me exactly what she did.

One of the places she regularly visited was a village called Kizingatani, on the northeastern end of Pate Island. After a short trip of about twenty minutes by air from Manda airstrip across from Lamu, we approached Kizingatani flying low over the village to announce our arrival. The entire village came running out onto the beach to wave greetings and to welcome Anne. It was quite a scene. Brilliant sunshine, a small tropical village surrounded by huge palm trees, a long and spotlessly clean white sand beach, and the sparkling clear blue waters of the Indian Ocean. Lots of kids on the beach excitedly waving at the plane.

While looking like paradise from the air, one knew the problems that existed on the ground. With no regular health services available, Dr. Spoerry's travelling clinics, held three or four times a year, were the only access to care for the people of Kizingatani.

Flying in very low, I noticed only one thing missing from "paradise." There was no place to land the airplane.

"Anne, is my vision bad or is there actually no landing strip down there?"

"Of course there is a landing strip," she said, in a tone of voice that I knew held back the words, "Are you stupid or something?"

"I believe I'm just not seeing too well today. Perhaps it's the heat."

Down we went. The landing strip was the beautiful white sand beach, with kids scrambling out of the way as we touched down. She had it figured perfectly, coming down as close to the ocean's edge as possible, where the sand had packed and was at its hardest. Braking gently, the plane came to a stop and as it did, the nose wheel started sinking into the sand. Unfazed, we climbed down. It seemed she did this all the time. Anne immediately organized a group of kids and everyone gently rocked the plane until the nose wheel became unstuck. The aircraft was then easily pushed a short distance until it rested on a more solid spot.

For two twelve-hour days, Anne saw as many patients as possible. Early on the third morning, when the sand was again packed down hard, we took off for the return to Lamu.

CHAPTER 29

THE FLYING DOCTORS –
EMERGENCY EVACUATIONS

AMREF began in 1957 with a Flying Doctor Service. An important aspect of that service was carrying out medical emergency evacuations. For those who were in need of medical care where it was not available, the Flying Doctors came to the rescue. Averaging between 400 and 500 mercy flights a year, East Africans and visitors alike were provided help on the spot and then transported to the best available hospital. AMREF prided itself in the fact that from the time a call was received in its radio room at Wilson Airport, an aircraft with a specialized flight nurse on board was off the ground in fifteen minutes or less. Countless lives have been saved since this service began fifty years ago.

To generate money for the Flying Doctors and its other health projects, AMREF and its sister fundraising organization, the Flying Doctors Society, sold special memberships, which were in effect, evacuation insurance. A tourist could make a £17 contribution to the Flying Doctors and then become a member for one month. If needed, a member would be entitled to a free evacuation back to Nairobi should there be a serious medical problem while they were on safari. Special annual membership rates for residents also entitled them to free evacuations. The memberships provided important funding for many AMREF health projects.

AMREF's Flying Doctor Service has maintained the highest standards of airborne evacuation care and aircraft safety. This must be viewed in light of highly strenuous conditions in which our pilots and nurses had to operate, situations that took them into unbelievably remote places, often landing on tricky grass or dirt airstrips. Yet they have done a remarkable job. There are hundreds and hundreds of amazing evacuation stories, almost all with happy endings.

One evacuation that received wide spread attention involved Mohammed Amin, the celebrated photographer, and Michael Buerk, prime time news anchor for BBC television. Mohammed Amin called the world's attention to the great famine in Ethiopia with his photos from the northern part of that country in 1984. The Marxist Government of Mengitsu tried to keep the press from finding out what was happening in Ethiopia. Amin's pictures brought the horrific starvation going on to millions of television screens everywhere.

When opposition to the Mengitsu dictatorship, led by the Tigrayan National Liberation Front, captured Addis Ababa in 1991, Mo Amin and Michael Buerk were in the capital covering the story. An ammunition dump exploded a few days after the takeover. The two reporters went to investigate. Caught in a rocket attack, Mohammed Amin was critically injured. Eventually our radio room received a call and an aircraft with medical personnel on board were on their way to Addis. The end result was that while Mo Amin lost an arm, his life was saved. And both he and Michael Buerk became steadfast friends of AMREF.

Sadly, Mohammed Amin was to later die in a plane crash when an Ethiopian Airlines Boeing 767 was hijacked in 1996. After a struggle on board between the crew and highjackers, the plane crashed into the Indian Ocean, close to the Comoros Islands, which lie between Tanzania and Madagascar.

One other example from the many hundreds of special evacuations involved a young boy, about 17 years of age. He was hang gliding off some cliffs at the edge of the Maasai Mara game reserve in Kenya. Something happened, he lost control of the hang glider, and fell quite a distance to the ground. Critically injured and unconscious, he was discovered by some Maasai herdsmen who ran through the bush for about forty-five minutes to the nearest safari camp. The camp manager radioed the Flying Doctors and we were off to a landing strip in the Mara. Upon landing, the nurse and pilot, carrying their equipment and led by the two Maasai herdsmen, trekked back through the bush on foot to where the young man had fallen.

Upon reaching the spot, his condition was quickly assessed as a serious spinal injury. Using the latest mobile emergency equipment to stabilize someone with a spinal injury, he was placed into something best described as an airbag. This was then blown up and pressurized to prevent any movement at all. Placing the patient on a stretcher, with the help of the two Maasai, he was carried for over an hour to the airstrip. Flown back to Nairobi, the boy was hospitalised for over three months. It was a wonderful sight to see him and his grateful father walk into AMREF headquarters one morning to express the family's gratitude. He owed his ability to walk again to those Maasai herders who called for help and to the professional skills of AMREF's emergency evacuation team—the pilot and nurse.

One of the most remarkable evacuations involved a husband and wife who were residents of Kenya. They were on a camping trip in Samburu Park to the north of Nairobi. The couple had set up their own tent in the park when late one afternoon, a large male lion came out of the bush and charged the wife. Lifting her in his mouth, the lion began running out of the camp carrying the woman. The husband, seeing this tragedy unfold before his eyes, had the clarity of mind to jump in his Land Rover, start the engine, and chase after the lion in the vehicle. Gaining ground rapidly on the animal, the lion dropped the wife and disappeared into the underbrush.

The Land Rover was equipped with a two-way radio and the husband called the Flying Doctors radio room. Within fifteen minutes, a plane was on its way to Samburu. The woman was stabilized on site, evacuated to Nairobi, and made a full recovery although she had some serious scars from the lion's teeth. The husband deserved a medal for both bravery and keeping a clear head while his wife was being carried away.

Not all stories involving animal injuries ended so happily. Sometimes our teams were called into situations in which their own lives were at stake. The Maasai Mara game park is probably Kenya's most popular tourist attraction. A number of camps, both luxury and basic, cater to thousands of visitors each year and the park can at times, be inundated with four wheel drive vehicles chasing after the big five: elephant, lion, cheetah, leopard, and rhino.

One such camp is Kitchwa Tembo (literally translated as the "head of the elephant"). It is one of the few resorts that take guests for walks late in the afternoon. Those that desire to walk are led by experienced guides. The first thing that all walkers are told before setting out is to listen to and obey the guide's instructions without question. That is a cardinal rule of safety.

Early one evening, at about 6:00 pm, a small group escorted by a guide left the camp. The guide had, of course, informed the walkers of the cardinal rule. The guides warn the walkers that if they say to stop and get down, the tourists should do so immediately.

Along the path, the guide spotted a grazing herd of Cape Buffalo. These are extremely dangerous animals. He quickly warned the group to be quiet and get down on the ground. One American tourist, a woman in her late fifties, failed to obey his order. Unwisely, she stood in the open with her camera clicking away. The noise spooked the herd and one buffalo charged. The guide courageously jumped between the buffalo and the woman. He was run over and died instantly. The woman was also trampled and critically injured.

It was sometime after 7:30 pm when a call was received in the Flying Doctors radio room. In Kenya and elsewhere close to the equator, nightfall comes rather quickly. There is little variance in daylight throughout the year. By 7:00 pm, it is dark. By rule, we did no evacuations at night because 99 per cent of all the airstrips were unlit and pretty much in the middle of nowhere. It is almost an impossibility to find one of these strips after dark.

Getting the call from Kitchwa Tembo, the staff in charge advised two courses of action. Listening to the camp manager describe the woman's injuries, and because it would not be possible to fly until daylight, he was advised to put her into a vehicle and move her by road to Narok hospital, the nearest such facility to the Mara. Because of the described nature of the injuries, a second but less advisable option would be to wait until daylight. We did emphasize that she should be taken to hospital by road, about a two to three-hour trip.

Thirty minutes later, another call was received from Kitchwa Tembo. The woman's family did not want her to go to Narok hospital and pleaded with the camp manager to have us try and fly in. After consultations with the pilot on call, Joe Moran, he agreed to try and find the Kitchwa Tembo strip. They were advised to have vehicles lined up along the grass landing area with lights on.

Joe and an emergency nurse left about 8:15 pm, just before Wilson Airport closed down for the night. In about forty minutes they were somewhere in the vicinity of Kitchwa Tembo camp. But it was impossible to spot any lights or the landing strip. It was like looking for a needle in a haystack. After about thirty minutes of circling, the plane had to return to Nairobi. The Wilson Airport authorities were kind enough to keep the airport open until our flight came back.

Kitchwa Tembo was contacted by radio and informed that the camp could not be found in the dark. It was now close to 11:00 pm. Again we urged that the woman be immediately moved by road to Narok. Again the urging was to no avail. The woman's family pleaded with the camp manager to convince the Flying Doctors to try again. Joe Moran was reluctant to do so, given not only the problem of finding it at night, but the danger involved in trying such a risky landing in the dark on a rough strip, should he be able to find it. The camp manager had called for help from other camps and now had more vehicles at his disposal. He promised to have these provide much more light.

Joe agreed to give it one more try. With the help of Wilson Airport's authorities who opened and lit the runway, he took off at about 11:30 pm and was able to locate the vehicles' headlamps at Kitchwa Tembo on the second attempt. Risking his own and the nurse's safety, he made a remarkable landing sometime after midnight. The woman was loaded onto the aircraft and flown back, this time to Jomo Kenyatta International Airport, which remains open twenty-four hours a day. Met by ground medical staff, she was rushed to Nairobi Hospital.

With regret, it was too late to save her. She died the next day. In the final analysis, had she been moved by road to Narok Hospital immediately after the accident, it was very likely she would have survived.

Another evacuation, which again put our own staff at risk, also involved some American tourists. A minibus in which they were riding overturned. Most had only minor bruises but one man dislocated his shoulder. We were called to evacuate him back to Nairobi. It had been raining heavily and many airstrips were either covered with water or too soft for a landing. The airstrip closest to the accident site was one that we knew was definitely soft, quite dangerous for both landings and takeoffs.

After a quick discussion, it was decided that a flight would be made to try and evacuate the accident victim. The pilot would do a flyover, assess the area, and then determine whether he would attempt a landing or not. The AMREF pilot did decide to take a risk and a landing was accomplished on a soft strip. The man was placed on board accompanied by his wife. Trying to take off, the pilot had trouble gathering enough speed on the soft runway. After rising only a few feet, the plane came down with a very hard bump, throwing the patient off his stretcher. The wife, who was belted into her seat, was saved from serious injury. Both the pilot and nurse were bruised but not badly hurt. The irony of the story was that when thrown off his stretcher, the man's dislocated shoulder popped back into place. However, he now had a broken leg. They later tried to sue us but were unsuccessful.

CHAPTER 30

A VALUE STRUCTURE FOR AFRICAN MANAGEMENT

As noted previously, AMREF, with its world headquarters in Nairobi, was a non-governmental organization with a full time staff of nearly 700 and an annual budget of about £7.5 million when I was asked to become its Chief Executive in 1989. The staff was primarily African, over 95 per cent. They included Kenyans, Ugandans, Tanzanians, Eritreans, Ethiopians, Sudanese, Somalis, Rwandese, Zairians, Mozambicans, and South Africans. At the head office, Kenyans comprised the largest number, which was natural given its location.

Those who were non-African, less than five per cent, were primarily British. During my tenure, there were never more than three Americans working for the organization at any one time. In effect I was heading an international group of people. We were predominantly an African international NGO.

I had held a variety of previous management positions. These included serving as President of AMREF USA for over ten years, managing Fulbright groups in India, and acting as team leader of a specialized interdepartmental programme at the City University of New York. Spending a great deal of time in Africa for the decade prior to my appointment as Director General helped me somewhat in understanding what my job was to entail. But it did not prepare me completely. From 1989 to retirement towards the end of 1998, I continuously received an on-the-job education.

Many expatriates working overseas, and in particular those working in Africa, do not work for African organizations. Whether employed by bilateral or multilateral aid agencies, the United Nations, NGOs, or for-profit companies, the expats are usually functioning within a work culture similar to that at home, or in an environment that is international rather than African in nature.

165

A British expatriate working for the Department of International Development (DFID) in Nairobi, operates within a British structure, with a British work culture and British rules and regulations. The way the DFID office in Nairobi conducts business is much the same as the head office runs on Victoria Street in London, with one added benefit. The DFID employees in Kenya get to celebrate both Kenyan as well as British holidays.

The same is true for Americans working in Nairobi for USAID. While they would have Kenyan colleagues, the culture of the office is American. The senior most officials would be Americans. Staff would be held accountable based on rules established by the United States Government. American USAID personnel can move from Washington to Nairobi to Manila and feel comfortable because the working atmosphere would be similar.

The United Nations context is somewhat different. Agencies such as the United Nations Development Programme (UNDP), UNICEF, and the United Nations Environmental Programme (UNEP) are more international in nature. They are pretty much governed by UN rules and regulations. This would be similar for UN operations elsewhere in Africa as well as other parts of the world. Sadly, accountability is often not taken seriously within the UN system with a pervading culture that one has a job for life.

Expatriates in private companies in Africa are usually senior staffers working for a subsidiary of some multinational corporation. Glaxo-Welcome Kenya or Del Monte Kenya would most likely have a non-Kenyan as Managing Director. Often, the Chief Financial Officer would also be an expatriate. While the overwhelming majority of staff in these companies would be Kenyan, the operating environment is determined by the culture of the parent company in Europe or North America. The bottom-line and accountability are important motivating factors. The management of such an entity would be based on management theory utilized in the west.

After being on the job for a short time, it was quite obvious that western management theories and organizational structures had little relevance for my situation at AMREF. Over the years, a number of basic African values became evident. These needed to be carefully considered by those in charge, and especially if the Chief Executive was someone from outside, namely an expatriate like myself.

The first of these management values that had to be quickly learned was that "an African Organization in Kenya was really a microcosm of the nation as a whole." I assumed this was only natural. Our NGO was a small-scale replica of the larger Kenya. People brought their culture, their relationships, and their normal interactions into the workplace.

This manifested itself in many ways. Most importantly, it meant that "everyone had access to the Chief." In the village, one did not find complicated hierarchical management structures. The Chief was paramount but all villagers could have access to him. Unlike western companies, with their organizational layers from the top boss down to the deputy bosses down to the assistant deputy bosses and so on down the ladder, the African village structure was pretty flat. If one had a problem that went beyond the family, the Chief was the person to see. Everyone had right of entry. You didn't have to work your way up the ladder and first see the assistant deputy chief, then hope for a referral to see the vice-deputy chief, then the vice-chief, and finally the chief. People went right to the top.

I learned this quite quickly at AMREF and interestingly, also came to appreciate the practice. While the official workday started at 8:00 am, it was a rare day when I was not at my desk before 6:30. Within five minutes, someone would be quietly tapping on my open door. It might be a driver, a messenger, a cleaner, or the Director of Finance. While great deference was shown to the boss, they all expected me to help with some problem or other. People were really acting no differently than they would at home. I was AMREF's Chief.

While such a system was time consuming, it had advantages. As Chief Executive, it gave me direct access to what the staff were thinking—all staff. In the normal course of business, there is frequent contact and interchange with senior people and at times, middle management. But in this African context, I was able to know what was in the minds of the most junior employees. It surely allowed one to have a finger on the pulse of the organization.

I soon learned that "access to the chief" was a custom not only expected in my own organization, but also reflected in many others. To cite one example, a meeting had been scheduled for me to see the Honourable George Saitoti, at that time serving as Kenya's Vice-President and concurrently Minister of Finance. The Vice-President's office was in the Treasury Building and I showed up exactly on time for the appointment. Opening the door to the outer office, before me were over a hundred people packed into the room. These ranged from another Minister to Members of Parliament to local Maasai cattle herders who came to Nairobi from the Vice-President's home district of Kajiado. And I found out that his office was the same every day, whatever the hour. People from all walks of life waiting to see the Chief, myself included. African government offices or non-governmental organizations, they were a mirror of the overall culture.

A third premise one had to understand for effective management was that "first loyalties were to family and tribe and not to the company." Children were acculturated with this concept of loyalty from birth so why should they not reflect the value in the workplace?

In 1989, before a major reorganization and decentralization, AMREF's headquarters was quite large and divided into departments. My goal was, as quickly as possible, to understand how each department functioned. One of our primary activities was the production and publication of health learning materials. AMREF had its own printing department, with high quality German equipment that allowed for turning out prized professional books, magazines, and pamphlets. The head of the Printing Department was from one of Kenya's largest tribal groups found in western Kenya alongside Lake Victoria, the Luo. It was no great surprise to learn that over forty of the fifty full and part time employees in his department were also Luo.

My next stop was to our Environmental Health Department. The lack of access to safe water is a major cause of health problems in Africa. This department was the one most closely involved with water projects. The Department head was a competent and experienced water engineer from Kenya's largest tribal group found in the central part of the country, the Kikuyu. And sure enough, all ten staff members, both professionals and support staff, were Kikuyu.

That's the way it was, department by department. Departments were divided along tribal lines. This spoke volumes about priorities when it came to employment. First loyalties were to those from home. Sadly, it did not make for a well-integrated organization. But, why expect people not to act the way they are brought up from an early age? In order to effect any change and alter behaviours, it was essential to understand why people acted the way they did.

Much has been written and discussed about widespread corruption in Africa, both in government and in the private sector. In North America or Western Europe, it is assumed that people who chose to run for elected office do so out of a sense of service to their country, their entire country, and given the expense necessary to achieve high elected positions, many leading politicians are already persons of means. Neither of the above applies very often in Africa.

Too few African politicians view politics and holding elected office as service professions, nor are they often persons of means at the time of entering into government. Politics is seen as a way of becoming wealthy and at the same time, helping family and friends also become well off. Service to a nation is frequently not the first priority, just as loyalty to an NGO or other organization might not be the first priority of its employees.

A fourth premise was what I came to refer to as the "knock down versus the step up tradition." As an American and someone who participated in competitive sports from a young age, I was raised with the premise that winning was important as long as it was done fairly. Competition, fair competition was a way of life. If someone was a better athlete, you did everything possible to improve your own performance so you could beat that person the next time. The striving to do better permeated all aspects of life, from school, to sports, to a career. This is primarily a "step up tradition," do better than the next person, not by harming him or her, but by improving yourself.

In the Kenya African context, I found the opposite to be true. One tried to get ahead not so much by self-improvement but rather by tearing down the competition. Instead of bettering oneself, energies were spent in the direction of destroying the other person. This took many popular forms. Rumours, innuendo, and sometimes dirty tricks were employed. It was the "knock down culture."

This could make the cultivation of management skills among talented people rather problematic. Many of my African colleagues were recalcitrant in giving praise or rewards to their staff. There was almost an innate jealousy, a view that anyone with talent was a threat. It was alien to my own way of thinking. Win or lose, the other person was always to be complimented. As a manager, praise was always more important for me than criticism. I firmly believed that one's success was achieved through the good works of subordinates and it was essential that they always received recognition. This just did not come easily to my African colleagues.

Therefore, it was no easy task to find strong number two persons at any level within an organization, whether at departmental or sub-departmental levels. Number twos were often there to carry out the wishes of his or her boss. Grooming a number two for leadership was not natural.

With such mitigating factors as tribalism and the perception of capable individuals being perceived as threats, it becomes a real challenge for management to try and develop something that is not normally inherent within a company, namely the "creation of an organizational culture." This proved to be my greatest challenge. For almost a decade, much time and energy was devoted to building an AMREF "ethos," an AMREF "philosophy," an AMREF "unity," an AMREF "family," and an AMREF "culture." Placing AMREF ahead of self was my personnel motto. Whether we succeeded was not for me to judge, that was best left to others. It did often seem like one step forward and two backwards.

CHAPTER 31

THE BURDENS OF A CHIEF

My on-the-job education was a never ending process, learning day by day. Sometimes, people would act in ways that were totally unexpected. While not happening often, a staff member would do something that seemed to internally challenge or question his or her own value structure. You could observe individuals being torn between tradition and change. One such occasion involved an old colleague and good friend, who will be referred to here as Jane.

I first met Jane in Juba, Southern Sudan in 1979. She was working for AMREF on the big USAID funded project. In many ways, Jane was a remarkable person. A Maasai, she trained as a nurse, was recruited by the Kenya Police, and became their Chief Nurse. When Jane joined AMREF, she was still a policewoman, coming to us on a leave of absence.

While President of AMREF USA, I helped her get acceptance into Michigan University where she received a Masters Degree in Public Health. Nurses, along with other health personnel in many African countries, go through medical training programmes that take two to three years. Upon completion of the course, diplomas, not Bachelors Degrees are awarded. American Universities did not recognize these diplomas as being sufficient for entry in graduate programmes. The U.S. schools required a four-year Bachelor's Degree awarded by a college. This meant most East Africans in the health professions could not continue with their studies in the United States after receiving diplomas.

I spoke with some acquaintances at the University of Michigan and convinced them to take a chance on Jane, arguing they should accept her varied African health professional experiences in lieu of an additional year of formal schooling. The arguments worked. Jane was given credit for something called "life experience" and was accepted for a Masters Degree. The end result was that she contributed as much to Michigan's programme as she received from it, graduating as one of the stars of her class. Jane was one of Kenya's first Maasai women to receive a Masters. Her contributions were so well received that Michigan asked us to send others from AMREF. Jane paved the way for a number of our staff entering into American graduate programmes.

At the time I took over as Director General, she was in charge of a Dutch Government funded community health project in South Nyanza, western Kenya. Jane had a number of children, one of whom also worked for AMREF and was based at headquarters in Nairobi. John, her son, was in his mid-twenties, recently married, a member of the Publishing Department, and a personable young man. He was a talented and creative designer. John worked on the designs for a number of AMREF's health manuals.

His only problem was laziness. John could never get to work on time. When he didn't feel like working, John would disappear for days without letting his boss know. It was difficult to depend on him. John's supervisor came to me on a number of occasions, complaining about his work habits. The supervisor knew of my long-standing friendship with John's mother and that was probably why he hadn't fired the young man up to that time. He pleaded with me to try and get John to change his ways. If not, he would have to let him go.

I asked Jane to stop by my office the next time she was at headquarters. After exchanging pleasantries, we came around to the subject of John. I explained the problem. Our long friendship notwithstanding, Jane was told that John's boss had the right to evaluate his performance and to take whatever action necessary if he did not meet standards. Jane realized that I would not interfere with the Department head if John were to be fired. She asked for a couple of days to speak with her son to see if she could straighten him out.

A few days later, Jane came by to see me one morning. I was expecting her to plead John's case, to appeal for him to have another chance, and to implore me to interfere so he would not be fired. My assumption was that Jane's argument would be based on a rationale of appealing to my emotions. I thought she would ask for kindness on the grounds if John were fired, he would probably not be able to find another job and he and his new wife would not have food on the table. In other words, I thought she would use a plea to spare the young people.

As expected, Jane did appeal for John to be given another chance. But her argument took me completely by surprise. It was really not a plea for John. It was a plea to spare her instead.

"Mike, please don't let him get fired. I finally got him out of my house last year and he is currently on his own. He is now one less financial burden on me. If you fire him, not only will he come back home but he will bring his wife as well. I will have the added load of two additional mouths to feed. I have enough as it is and don't need them. Please keep him working. Spare me from having him (and his wife) come back home."

The expected plea but an unexpected rationale. She presented arguments that to me seemed somewhat unAfrican, almost renouncing her responsibility for a family member. There were no "hearts and flowers" for John but rather for herself. It was a valuable lesson for me, proving that cultural traditions can break down and change.

* * *

With a large staff, there was always something going on, both professionally and personally. Births and marriages were joyous occasions. Mourning for deceased employees was never easy. In the last few years of my tenure, we lost a number of individuals through sickness, traffic accidents, and HIV\AIDS.

One death in particular taught me a great deal about how Kenyans, and particularly the Luo, treat adversity. George Okello was someone I had worked with closely for a number of years. A member of the Community Health Department, George was one of the key AMREF people working in our southern Africa programme. He played an important role in our assistance to both Namibia and South Africa.

During the 1960s, 1970s, and 1980s, AMREF had been in contact with a number of southern African health professionals who were in exile from their countries. South African and Namibian doctors and nurses were living and working in countries such as Tanzania, Uganda, and Zimbabwe. During this period, some participated in AMREF training programmes.

When Namibia gained its independence in 1990, most of the country's exiled health professionals returned home. A number were offered senior appointments in the Ministry of Health and Namibia adopted a nationwide primary health care approach. AMREF was asked by the Ministry to help with the development and implementation of the new health strategy. From 1990 until 1994, in collaboration with UNICEF and the Ministry of Health, we provided a group of technical consultants who were specialists in the new primary health care approach. During this period, George Okello was a well-respected member of AMREF´s technical team in Namibia.

Within South Africa, AMREF became involved from the day future President Nelson Mandela was released from prison. Under the old apartheid regime, there was excellent medical care for the white minority. However, the majority of the black population had little or no access to quality health services. Beginning in 1990, with changes apparent, health professionals quickly adopted an equity strategy for health. To achieve and afford health care for all, resources had to be shifted from treatment and hospital support to primary health care.

From 1991 until the first free elections in 1994, AMREF assisted a number of South African NGOs and universities to promote community based primary health care. After the elections of 1994, AMREF provided support to the new South African Department of Health at all levels; national, provincial and district. Our experienced staff became key resource people as the transformation of health services began to take place. George Okello was also one of the best AMREF consultants in South Africa from the beginning of our involvement in that country.

In 1995, at the urging of a number of South African partners in government, NGOs, and universities, we opened a permanent office in Pretoria. The government quickly registered AMREF as an official NGO. Wilson Ondego, an extremely bright and capable Kenyan health educator, was named our first Country Director for South Africa. With a small staff, Wilson requested periodic assistance from technical experts at headquarters in Nairobi and from AMREF's Kenya Country Office. George Okello was a significant technical expert for our South Africa activities, becoming an important resource for Wilson.

In 1996, George was in South Africa conducting a training course for the staff of the Department of Health in Northwest Province. The course, which was scheduled to last a week, was being held at a hotel in the town of Rustenberg. Late one afternoon, at about 5:30 pm, after classes were over, George went into the hotel's sauna room to relax and unwind. When he didn't appear for an appointment later that evening, and was not found in his room, the sauna was checked. George Okello had died while sitting in the steam room.

George was in his 40s at the time of his death. He left behind a wife and two children, all of whom I had met and came to know. George's wife had actually spent time with him in Namibia when he was on assignment there. His death was a great loss, not only to his family but also to all who knew and worked with him.

At about 8:00 pm on the day George passed away, I received a telephone call from Wilson Ondego. He told me the unfortunate news. It was difficult to believe as I had spoken with George about three days before in Nairobi, only minutes before he was about to depart for South Africa. Asking if I should call George's wife, Wilson replied that he had already done so. We then discussed details on how to organize transport of the body back to Kenya. Wilson had not yet had time to check with the South African authorities on what procedures needed to be followed. He promised to do so and get back to me. And just before the phone call ended, our conversation took an unexpected twist.

"Mike, I am really going to need your help."

"No problem Wilson. We will give you whatever logistic support you will need. If you want, I will send someone down from headquarters to assist you with the bureaucratic details."

"That's not the problem, Mike. I can easily handle the logistics. I am going to need your help for another reason."

"What is that, Wilson?"

"Mike, I am going to be blamed for George's death."

"WHAT? Blamed by whom?"

"By George's family. They will never accept that he died from natural causes. They will be looking for a scapegoat and I will be the one accused of killing him."

"But Wilson, at the time of his death you were in Pretoria, more than 200 kilometres away from the place where George died. You hadn't seen him for three days. No one can blame you."

"But they will."

The conversation had turned to the macabre. Had I not known Wilson Ondego well, and had I not been familiar with his professionalism and competence, I might have questioned his sanity. But Wilson was a serious and responsible individual and knew much more about African reactions to death than I did. He was now my teacher.

For all African families, death brings about a special grief and drama. George Okello was a Luo. For the Luos, a death was never accepted easily. Death by natural causes was often viewed with suspicion. Something, or someone had to be blamed for the death. And the burial site was of great significance. The blood family of the deceased, especially if it was a male, would insist that the burial take place at the ancestral home. For the Luos, that meant western Kenya. Stories were plentiful about families fighting over bodies and the right to bury. There were cases that went on for years, with rival factions each claiming a different place for burial. There were situations in which bodies were exhumed after rulings by the courts and moved to different burial sites, with feuds between families continuing long after the person was underground.

In the Luo tradition, with the death of a male, the husband's oldest brother could inherit the deceased's spouse. She would often become her brother-in-law's second or third wife. Should she refuse such a marriage, the woman was often left with absolutely nothing. His family might even try to take away the children.

Wilson Ondego knew what he was talking about and was rightly worried. And being from a different tribe, the Luhuya, he was a plausible target for blame by the Okello family.

The next morning Wilson called again. After speaking to the authorities, he was informed that the body could not be released until an autopsy was performed. That was standard procedure for foreigners who died in South Africa. Hearing this, I felt that an autopsy would be in the best interests of all concerned, especially Wilson. We would have conclusive proof of the cause of George's death. The autopsy would be carried out within two days and Wilson would then be able to sign a form for release of the body to be sent back to Kenya. We agreed that I would contact George's wife and inform her that AMREF would fly her down to South Africa to accompany the body back to Nairobi.

That afternoon, a day after George's death, I spoke with his widow. She was appreciative of the offer to be sent to South Africa and said she would go. But then, for the second time in less than twenty-four hours, the conversation again took a strange twist.

"Dr. Gerber, I really need your help."

Expecting a normal request for financial or logistical assistance, I asked what AMREF might do for her.

"Could you please do everything possible to delay the news of George's death and the release of his body by the South African authorities?"

"Delay the release of the body?"

"Yes."

"Why?

"A few years ago, George and I bought a small plot of land next to his traditional family home. We have slowly been building a house on that land. Everything is completed but the roof. In our culture, if a husband dies before a roof is put on a house, the wife loses the house. It will be taken by his brothers or cousins. I have to quickly go to western Kenya tomorrow and make sure that at least a thatched roof is placed on the house. Then they will not be able to take it away from me and the children."

To say I listened to this in amazement would be an understatement. But I was in complete sympathy with George's wife and told her I would contact Wilson Ondego and figure out a way to keep the news quiet and the body in South Africa for as long as possible.

"Thank you so much. There is one other thing I have to ask you. Within a few days, you will most likely be receiving calls from George's family. They will want to know about his AMREF pension and other benefits. Please don't tell them anything. I and the children could wind up with nothing."

"I will do as much as possible to keep the benefits position confidential."

"Thank you so much."

Wilson Ondego and I discussed ways to keep the body in South Africa for as long as we could. We were actually able to stall its release for about six days, using bureaucracy and paper work as an excuse. George's widow travelled to the plot in South Nyanza and managed to have a thatched roof placed on the house before she proceeded to South Africa to pick up the body. And sure enough, a few days later one of George's uncles called to ask about his pension and benefits. I had spoken to our Personnel Manager and we agreed that anyone making inquiries would receive a patented answer, "That information was only available to the surviving spouse."

The widow and Wilson Ondego accompanied the body back to Nairobi. Before moving on to South Nyanza for burial, a memorial service was organized in the capital. I had been asked by George's wife to speak at both the memorial service and at the burial. One could already sense tension at the Nairobi church where some of George's family hinted at foul play and the need for the Okello clan to claim his land and benefits. The Pastor presiding over the service berated George's family for trying to "steal" what was rightly due to the widow and children. With this as a preliminary, I could hardly wait for the burial service in western Kenya.

Along with Wilson and some other AMREF staff, we attended the funeral where I again spoke about George and his great commitment to helping the needy improve their position in life. One or two of his family members publicly blamed both AMREF and Wilson Ondego for George's death. By implication, as AMREF's chief executive, Mike Gerber was also being blamed. There were strong words about who had rights to his property and possessions. But in the end, cool heads prevailed. George's wife and children gained custody of the land, the house, and his AMREF benefits.

CHAPTER 32

SABOTAGE

There were times when not to be vigilant meant the possibility of finding one of your expatriate employees involuntarily on the way out of Kenya. Or possibly finding yourself on the way out. Foreigners could be at risk if (a) they were perceived to be in competition for a job appointment or promotion, and/or (b) they were a threat to someone engaged in what was not an honest type of livelihood.

In 1989, when taking up residence in Nairobi, I found there was no post for an Internal Auditor within AMREF. That had to change. The organization was too large in terms of staff and financial resources. We therefore created the post, advertised, interviewed, and made an appointment. Our first Internal Auditor was Asmerom Habtom, who would later be promoted to Financial Director.

Asmerom was an Eritrean national living in Nairobi under refugee status. He was highly qualified and experienced. During the Marxist dictatorship in Ethiopia and before Eritrea was independent, Asmerom was a senior auditor for the Ethiopian Government in Addis Ababa. One year he was sent to India by his Ministry with a charge to recruit accountants and auditors for posts with the Ethiopian Government. Life was not easy in Ethiopia for almost all its citizens and particularly so for Eritreans. After completing his assignment in India, instead of returning to Addis he went to Kenya, applied for refugee status, and it was granted. Happily, within a few years his family was able to get out of Ethiopia and join him in Nairobi.

Asmerom Habtom was thorough, competent, and nothing ever slipped by him. He immediately completed an audit of all our internal systems and made recommendations for improvements. His suggestions led to huge cost savings in certain areas, such as controlling vehicle usage and regulating cash advances taken by staff. On a personal level, he was often quite funny and charming when

179

he wanted to be. Professionally, he could really be firm, which was probably important for someone in his position. Staff would complain that he was too demanding of them, which was, in many cases, true. In any case, he was egalitarian. He treated everyone who might not be living up to expectations, including myself, with equal toughness.

Most AMREF employees came to respect what he was doing for the organization. A few, however, were unhappy. Asmerom was able to close the few "back doors" that remained opened. Things stopped disappearing. A few who might have been supplementing their regular salaries now really felt economically threatened.

One afternoon, I received a call from the office of Kenya's Principal Immigration Officer. They wanted to give me advanced warning that Asmerom Habtom's work permit and residence visa was going to be revoked and he would be deported. Upon inquiring as to why, I was told Asmerom Habtom was going to be on the agenda of Parliament the next day.

Sure enough, the following morning during a Parliamentary debate, one MP announced that AMREF was employing foreigners who discriminated against Kenyans. The AMREF Internal Auditor was referred to specifically. The Member called upon Parliament to advise the immigration authorities to take just action.

"Just action?" Asmerom had probably found a staff member lacking in integrity. With that person's supply of supplemental income about to be cut off or even worse, the loss of his or her job, he/she complained to his/her Member of Parliament about the "discriminating AMREF auditor." Without looking into the case, without gathering any evidence, without speaking with management, the MP just went ahead and made it a public issue.

Knowing the immigration people well, we were not going to allow anything to happen without a serious fight. In a private meeting with the Principle Immigration Officer, I explained the facts, pointed out the Auditor was a fellow African, mentioned the name of an AMREF staff person who was under investigation for dishonesty, and told the officer that we preferred not to make all the evidence public, but would, if necessary. This senior government officer responded both professionally and fairly, and promised to look at all the facts before taking any final action. Sure enough, after his investigation and the truth was known, he let the matter just die down. Asmerom was safe to continue ensuring financial integrity remained a priority with our organization.

The "bad guys" did try again a second time. After Asmerom Habtom became our Finance Director, his name was again brought up in Parliament. And again, the source of an MP's accusations was a disgruntled AMREF staff member. The result was the same. Case dismissed because the evidence refuted the claim.

Asmerom was not the only senior manager who faced the "deportation" threat. Dr. Watson Kirube, a Ugandan medical doctor and member of our Health Policy Department, was another victim. We were in the process of recruiting for a Director of his department. Some thought Dr. Kirube was a favoured candidate and would be given the job without even applying. That was far from the truth. As always, we followed standard recruitment procedures. The job was advertised internally and externally, applications received, a shortlist compiled, interviews held, and an appointment made. Dr. Kirube wasn't even on the short list.

Before we had completed the interviews and made an appointment, another call was received from the Immigration Office.

"One of your staff members is a spy."

"A spy?" I replied. "Whom is he spying for?"

"He is spying for Uganda."

"For Uganda? Who is spying for Uganda?"

"Dr. Watson Kirube. He has twenty-four hours to leave Kenya. Make sure he leaves."

At times, as was the case between Kenya and Sudan, there were periodic tensions between Kenya and Uganda. This was one of those periods of tension and Ugandan spies were supposedly everywhere. It was quite easy for one of Watson Kirube's rivals for the Health Policy Director job to let immigration know that AMREF was harbouring a Ugandan spy. One less candidate in the job competition.

Watson was called in and we explained what was going on. Naturally, he was really upset but he was assured that AMREF would fight for his rights and would not accept the deportation order. To give us time to make our case, we asked Watson if he would be willing to go to Somalia and be attached to the AMREF Somalia project for a couple of weeks. That would allow him to remain an AMREF employee and give us time to clear his name. Dr. Kirube went to Lugh the next day and took up his new duties.

I was particularly annoyed with the Immigration office over this situation and we demanded evidence to show that Watson Kirube was a spy. Of course, no evidence was forthcoming because none existed. Behind the scenes, we quietly let the right government people know what was going on and that we strongly believed Dr. Kirube was being sabotaged by an AMREF colleague. Some four weeks later, a letter was received from the Office of the Principal Immigration Officer. It stated that after further investigation, the government now believed that Dr. Watson Kirube was not a Ugandan spy and he could again work for AMREF in Kenya.

It was really a sad state of affairs when an honest, hard working professional could, without any proof, be accused of spying and ordered out of Kenya within twenty-four hours. A person's life could be turned upside down because of a jealous co-worker's complaint to immigration. Watson Kirube did come back to headquarters in Nairobi and was grateful to us for having fought his cause and clearing his name. But the situation really soured him on Kenya in general. Shortly afterward, he left AMREF and returned to Uganda to work there. It was a real loss for our organization. Within a few years, he was hired by one of the international foundations and eventually wound up back in Kenya. I was pleased to see his career prospering.

Not long after the Kirube saga, another Ugandan AMREF staff member faced deportation. Dr. Victor Nsibirwa, also a medical doctor and well respected researcher, was put on the block. It was the same story – probably a jealous Kenyan colleague. And we had little trouble refuting the Immigration Department's charge, reversing it quickly in Dr. Nsibirwa's favour. The only good thing to come out of these battles against "banishment" orders was that our staff quickly came to know that we would take up the case to support anyone falsely accused. All the above mentioned were Africans, namely one Eritrean and two Ugandans. There was now a feeling of both comfort and respect, knowing that senior management would fight hard for Africans unjustly accused.

Unfortunately, we could not win them all. To my great disappointment, we did lose one and it hurt. In this case, our hands were tied right from the beginning.

For many years, an experienced British medical doctor was in-charge of our Flying Doctors Service. Besides his AMREF commitment, this doctor also had a thriving private practice with offices in Nairobi Hospital. In 1995, he left AMREF's employment. Upon doing so, while maintaining his full time private practice, he established a small commercial air evacuation company, modelled after the Flying Doctors. His former AMREF secretary also joined this new company, which in a way was now a competitor, albeit a small one.

We hired a young American, Jerome Lewis, to replace the departed doctor. Jerome, about thirty years old, had been trained as a registered nurse. A veteran of the U.S. Army, he had been given special training in emergency flight medicine and served on an Army air evacuation team. Not only was he familiar with the latest techniques in airborne evacuations, he had many of hours in the air with the military. Jerome had seen service in Africa with his special army group.

The young man was full of energy, dynamic, and a real go-getter. Within a short time, he helped modernize and upgrade AMREF's Flying Doctors, bringing in new emergency equipment and training our Kenyan and Ugandan nurses in the latest evacuation techniques.

While highly professional in his technical area and full of energy and enthusiasm, Jerome suffered from the "young person's disease," and especially from an American young person's disease, namely "impatience." He was not so world-wise and at times could be culturally insensitive. He brought about great improvements but stepped on a lot of toes doing it. The owners of those toes were not amused. They remembered and waited.

Just about a year after he came to work at AMREF, the now familiar call came from the Immigration office. Late one afternoon, I was informed by that office of a newspaper story about to be printed on the front pages of Kenya's English language dailies, "The Nation" and "The Standard." The following morning, these papers were about to report that Jerome Lewis had, in a letter sent outside the country, insulted a senior person in the Kenya Government. With the breaking story imminent, the Immigration office had little choice but to deport Jerome. He had to go immediately and was given twenty-four hours to leave Kenya.

The next day's headlines blared something to the effect "AMREF Foreigner Insults Kenya and the Kenya Government."

What had happened was the following. Shortly after joining AMREF, the Ministry of Health asked to see Jerome's credentials. This was standard procedure for any non-Kenyan who was working in Kenya. The Ministry wanted to ensure that foreigners practicing medicine and health in the country were qualified to do so. It was a fair regulation and the Kenya Government had every right to vet credentials of expats. All of our non-Kenyan professional staff, when hired, were always urged to quickly comply with this regulation.

Jerome, not paying much attention to the request, did not respond at first. A second notice threatened to cancel his work permit. He finally sat down and wrote a letter to the Dean at his former university in the U.S., requesting that his college transcripts be sent as soon as possible. Being young and somewhat foolish, he included in the same letter to the Dean, some disparaging remarks about Kenya, Kenyans, and in particular, one very senior leader. Jonathan referred to "stupid Kenyans bothering him with nonsense" and concluding with the "stupidest Kenyan of all was a certain top government official." Jerome composed the letter in private and mailed it himself, or so he thought. He sent it off over nine months before his deportation order came through.

His transcripts were dutifully sent from his U.S. university to AMREF shortly after the letter. Jerome submitted them to the Ministry of Health, and was given a clean bill of health to work in Kenya. Nothing more was heard about this until the Immigration call and newspaper stories.

Someone whose toes he had stepped on had gone into Jerome's computer and unknown to him, made a copy of the letter soon after he wrote it. That person held on to the letter for nine months, waiting for an opportune time to strike.

By the time of the exposé, Jerome had re-shaped our Flying Doctors and was receiving a lot of favourable attention for the job he was doing. So an AMREF staff person passed on his "personal and private" letter to the former AMREF secretary who was now working for the "competition." She probably gave it to someone in government who then gave it to the press and Immigration.

With the breaking of the news story, and confirmation that Jerome had actually committed his thoughts to writing and sent them abroad, there was little we could do. He had to go. After consultations with our senior staff, it was agreed that this was one battle that, if we chose to fight, would be a loser from the start. All of our chips would be used up in a lost cause. Sadly, Jerome departed.

Shortly after a delegation of staff members came to see me. These were a handful of white, expatriate personnel. A few of them were extremely concerned and fearful for their future in Kenya and their jobs. They viewed Jerome's leaving as an omen and a racial issue. The leader of this group contended that in the past, we had fought hard when African staff were under threat of deportation. She said, "You were willing to put your own neck on the block." And the group cited the cases of Asmerom Habtom, Watson Kirube, and Victor Nsibirwa. Now, the leader maintained, when it came to Jerome Lewis, a white person, nothing was done. Their reading of what happened was that we fought for Africans but not for "muzungus" (whites).

It took some explaining and a revealing of all the details in the letter related to Jerome's departure to make these white staffers understand the situation. In none of the other cases, had any AMREF employee said negative things about Kenya or Kenyans. Nor did they leave behind in writing what would be construed by the government as inflammatory. Falsely accused, they deserved to be defended and we did everything in our power to help.

With Jerome and the negative publicity his letter created, AMREF was left with a position that was indefensible. Once his letter was out in the open, nothing we could have done would have helped. It was explained to the assembled group that if we had undertaken a battle, all chips accumulated would have been used up on a hopeless cause. And we would have had nothing left in the bag to use if any of the people in front of me would be falsely accused in the future.

The staff accepted this explanation and left a little more at ease and somewhat more secure about their positions. However, I had now gained a reputation as being a "reverse racist," favouring blacks over the muzungus. At least, during the remaining years of my tenure as AMREF' Chief Executive, there were no more cases of any staff, black or white, being threatened with deportation.

CHAPTER 33

MANAGEMENT AND TIME

It was sometime during midmorning. People had been hard at work for a number of hours. Throats were getting thirsty. It had to be close to the day's first cup of tea.

"What time is it?" I asked a colleague.

"Almost 4."

Almost 4? The sun was shining too brightly through the window for it to be 4:00 am. And the workday hadn't gone on long enough for it to be 4:00 pm. What time was it really? Well, it was 4 o'clock – 4 o'clock African time. Or for non-Africans, it was more comfortably 10:00 in the morning. But both times were correct. It just depended on where one grew up.

For those countries not far from the equator, day and night were close to being equal in terms of hours. In Kenya, Tanzania, Uganda, or Ethiopia, there was little time variance between day and night at any time of the year. It made a lot of sense to divide one complete cycle of sunrise to sunrise into two equal periods – the part of one day when it was light and the part of the same day when it was dark. Africans in these countries did exactly that.

Sunrise, or what westerners would term 6:00 am in their time reference, was the zero hour for Africans, the hour when a new day was to begin. Then 7:00 am western time would be 1:00 o'clock in the day for an African, meaning one hour had gone by since the day started. 8:00 am western time would equate with 2:00 o'clock for Africans. And it went on that way. 12:00 noon western time would be 6:00 o'clock in the day for Africans. The equation was simple. Either subtract 6 hours from western time to determine African time or add 6 hours to African time for western time.

The second period of the twenty-four hour cycle for an African was nighttime. With a full day broken down into two twelve-hour periods, night began at 6:00 pm western time. Therefore western 6:00 pm was zero hour for Africans, the beginning of the night. 1:00 in the evening for an African was 7:00 pm for westerners. And this continued until 6 am western time the next morning, the African zero hour.

The African system was quite logical, although it could be confusing at times. In most situations, western time was always used but on rare occasions someone would subconsciously revert back to the traditional time. You still had to be prepared for a 6-hour difference.

Ethiopia is an interesting place for visitors. Not only can one come into contact with two different time concepts, but there are also two different calendars. Ethiopians follow the lunar calendar. Because the Ethiopian year is longer than the western year, they are about five years behind our calendar. Instead of a westerner's date of 2005, most Ethiopians would consider the year to be 2000. Their tourist officials are amazingly wise. When advertising the glories of visiting the country, one of their best marketing slogans is "Visit Ethiopia and immediately become five years younger."

For a "foreign" manager, different concepts of time need to be accounted for in weighing options and reaching decisions. If they are not, things usually turn out different from expectations. That happened to me on more than one occasion.

When planning for my own retirement, I wanted to ensure there would be a thorough and professional search for a replacement and a smooth transition. With a "western" thought process, it was assumed that one-year would be a logical time frame for finding and appointing a new chief executive. Operating on this principle, I actually informed AMREF's Board of Directors of my decision to step down fifteen months in advance of the date of departure. The Board was also presented with a plan of action that called for starting the search procedure within a few months. An international job announcement would be made a year in advance, a search firm contacted, resumes screened, short listed candidates interviewed, someone selected, and the post filled by the time I left.

It seemed perfectly obvious that such a time schedule was logical and organized. It also seemed obvious that the advantage of an early retirement announcement was enough lead-time to find a successor. The one disadvantage might have been turning me into a "lame duck" a year before retirement but the advantages appeared stronger than the disadvantage.

All this did seem obvious. But only to me, and perhaps to a few of my western Board members as well. But in the Kenyan context in which I was working, a "lame duck" was simply a fowl with an injured webbed foot, not someone who was known to be leaving a job.

For my African colleagues, time was significant only for the short term or immediate future. Many had a fatalistic outlook toward life, living only for "now" and not for "tomorrow." Historically and culturally, this was actually quite sensible, given the hardships of life for many Africans and the struggle for daily survival. The "now" attitude was often reflected in the way people acted, both professionally and personally. As an outsider, however, it was at first not easy to understand or accept. Regarding any change in leadership, to begin a process one year in advance was incomprehensible to some. A few months were more than sufficient.

When I publicly announced my retirement one year in advance, there was really no need to worry about being a lame duck. Twelve months was so far away in most people's minds that it really had no meaning. I just carried on as always and was considered the boss until the last minute on the job.

My wife would go to the market just about everyday. She usually frequented the same stalls to purchase fruits and vegetables. After living in Kenya for many years, she had a fairly good idea of what the prices were for specific items. Yet every time she went in to buy bananas or mangos, the fruit seller would ask her to pay three times the going rate for these products. Ina would have to go through the routine of bargaining him down to a reasonable price.

At first, in our analysis of what was going on, we thought the duka (shop) owner liked the socialization process of bargaining with Ina, the give and take between two people. But on further thought, our conclusion was only partially corrrect. Socialization was important but it was not the primary reason for the shopkeeper's behaviour. Acculturated to live for today, the merchant was trying to get as much as he could from every encounter with a customer. As a westerner, our first concern might have been to build customer loyalty, to offer a good price so the customer would return on a regular basis. In this case, loyalty was not the stall owner's motivating factor. If Ina was willing to pay three times the going rate today he would take it, even with the risk of her realizing what had happened and never again returning to his place of business. The guiding business principle was "get it today and don't worry about tomorrow."

There were numerous, and often humourous, examples of senior officials leaving or being sacked from jobs on short notice. In Kenya, it was traditional for a Government Minister, Permanent Secretary, or head of a parastatal company to learn of his or her dismissal on the Kenya Broadcasting System's 1:00 pm (western time) news. A Minister might be at a lunchtime function. His driver, waiting in the car, would hear of the Minister's dismissal on the radio. Without hesitation, the driver would then take off. Out would come the Minister (or now the ex-Minister but he did not yet know this) from his official function to find no big Mercedes and no driver. Hopefully, he had some money to take a taxi back to the Ministry. By the time he reached his office, it was locked and all personal possessions out in the corridor. At this point, the message was clear – he was an ex-Minister.

One day, I was having lunch with a friend (I will call him John) who was the Chief Executive and Chairman of a big transportation company. This company was a government parastatal, which meant the government owned at least a 51 per cent share. Heads of parastatals were appointed by the President of Kenya. We were at the Carnivore Restaurant, a popular eating-place on the western side of Nairobi. I was trying to convince John to have his transport company fund one of AMREF's projects.

About two minutes past one, the Carnivore's manager whom we both knew well, came over to the table. John was told he had a telephone call which he could take in the manager's office. Five minutes later, he returned to the table and we just picked up the conversation as before. A little after two, I had to go off to another meeting and we said goodbye. That evening, as I was watching the 7:00 pm news on television at home, it was broadcast that John had been fired from his job that same afternoon. The first announcement had been made on the one o'clock news, while we were actually having lunch. That was what John's phone call was about. He wisely never did commit the transportation company to provide funding for AMREF.

After that, I would always kid John as to how he was able to get home that day, knowing his car and driver would have disappeared. His sacking from the parastatal was only a temporary setback. As was often the case in Kenya, John was soon after made a Government Minister and continued to serve the country and its people.

CHAPTER 34

SWEET TEETH
AND LOOSE BOWELS

Different concepts of time made for different work habits. In much of Asia and Africa, punctuality is not as important as it is in the West. It was often problematic to determine if someone would appear an hour early or an hour late for a meeting. Late was more the norm. But the absence of an obsession with time brought with it distinct advantages when it came to management and work habits. My African colleagues never "watched the clock." Most were highly dedicated and committed to their work. Long hours were a regular routine. Staff could be found in the office late into the evening, long after the official closing hour of 4:30 pm. And some worked on weekends. When away at project sites in the field, the job was a twenty-four hour affair, with time out for sleeping. All this made a supervisor's job easy. You could always depend on people to finish whatever had to be done, no matter how long it would take.

Holiday leave was another matter. AMREF provided each employee with twenty-five days of annual vacation. That amounted to five working weeks, something unheard of in North America. NGOs have a reputation for paying low salaries but offering good benefits. To say the least, five weeks of leave was a good benefit. But the down side for managing an organization was that most of the employees, including senior management, always wanted to take it all in one go.

Valid reasons could be found for such long leave periods but understanding those reasons did not make running AMREF any easier. The British, in their former colonies, left behind a tradition of extended holidays. Former colonial servants would return to England by boat for their leaves from places like India or Kenya. Boat journeys required lots of time. With independence, the new

189

governments maintained extended leaves for civil servants. The benefit was then carried over into the non-profit sector.

A month's annual leave also made sense in a country like Kenya for another reason. Very few of the 400 or so staff that worked for AMREF in Kenya, either in headquarters or in the Country Office, were originally from Nairobi. As in many African and Asian cities, the capital was a magnet that attracted people from predominantly rural areas. With the exception of farming, there was little work opportunity outside of urban centres.

The majority of AMREF's staff did need an extended period of time away. They had to return home as often as they could, to see their families as well as to help tend "shambas" or small farms. But it wasn't helpful for the organization to have employees taking off for lengthy leaves.

As a senior manager, I tried to convince at least the professional staff to break up their vacations so as not to take it all at once. For the sake of professional obligations, my plea was for them to take two weeks at one part of the year and three weeks at a later period. Sometimes negative logic would be used. My hypothetical argument was that if someone left for twenty-five days and AMREF continued to function without that person, perhaps the position he or she occupied was not really necessary. The question was asked, "Do you want to take holidays for five weeks and give us the chance to discover whether we can get along without you?" It became a redundant question. They always answered, "Yes." People would go off and juggling skills would be required to compensate for those who were away.

Friday afternoons held a special significance for a few AMREF employees. It was not quite like the end of the working week at a company in Europe or the U.S. Some interesting phenomena occurred between the end of the working week and the start of the next one.

In any business, controlling costs is always a prime concern for management. Without careful monitoring, personal employee use of a firm's telephones, computers, or vehicles can become abusive. Consumables are difficult to control. How much computer or copying paper is wasted because the company and not the individual purchased them?

At AMREF, there was a close correlation between the "wasting," or rather disappearance of consumables and the end of the working week. The two most precious items that always "walked away" were sugar and toilet paper. Sugar was definitely special. Tea breaks, left over as a British tradition, were an essential part of the day. Everything stopped at about 10 o'clock in the morning and about 3:00 in the afternoon. The organization, as part of its "benefits" package for employees, was responsible for providing tea twice a day. And of course, sugar to go with the tea. Each person was supplied with a small sugar jar that was regularly refilled as the supply dwindled. The sugar jars tended to empty quite rapidly.

The first reason I attributed to high sugar consumption was that AMREF employees all had a "sweet tooth." All except one, that is. I never put sugar in my tea. Yet, without fail, the level of sugar in my personal jar decreased at an alarming rate. Had I been a sugar user, and consumed it at the rate with which my personal supply disappeared, my mouth would have been full of decaying teeth.

After a period of carefully observing my sugar jar, it was obvious that the level had its greatest decline between Friday afternoons and Monday mornings, a period when no tea was being served. Or rather no tea served at work. Tea was, I am sure, being served in many homes and guess where the sugar was coming from?

Now how to deal with the "crisis" of disappearing sugar? After much discussion among senior management, it was decided we could do little to control the problem. Threatening not to serve tea or supply sugar would have been worse then threatening to reduce salaries. So a soft approach was used. Notices were sent around and employees spoken to during staff meetings about sugar consumption, but this had little effect. I just took to locking my own sugar jar away in a secure place, only to be removed when guests were in the office. After doing this for some time, guests in my office must have been using sugar that had aged considerably since my jar seldom needed refilling.

Arriving in the office one Monday morning, as was my habit, I went to use the toilet. And to my great surprise, there was no toilet paper. Naturally, this was disturbing for the personal discomfort I had to suffer. But it was even more upsetting because AMREF was a leading health organization. We should always have been in the forefront of promoting proper sanitary practices and our employees were made aware that AMREF had to set an example as a healthy place in which to work. No toilet paper in the bathrooms was an obvious detraction from a healthy environment.

Out of curiosity, I went up to the third floor, looked in the toilet and found the same condition – no paper. Down to the first floor toilet and the same. Given it was still early in the morning and no staff were around, I knocked on the door of the women's bathroom. With no answer forthcoming, I entered and sure enough—no toilet paper in there either.

At 8:00 am, I asked the Director of Administration to hurry down to my office. He had the responsibility for building supervision in his portfolio. Still somewhat upset over the toilet paper situation, I was prepared to let him know of my displeasure. But my anger quickly turned to amazement as he explained what was going on. It seemed that each weekend, between Friday afternoon and Monday morning, all toilet paper from every bathroom in AMREF disappeared. Like sugar, toilet paper was a precious and for the poor, an expensive commodity. As with the case of the sugar, toilet paper also "went home" for the weekend.

This, however, did present a problem even more serious than a temporary lack of sugar. What happened if we had visitors who came into headquarters on the weekend or some staff who had to work in their offices on Saturday or Sunday? How could they use the toilets? The solution was to have the weekend cleaning staff restock the toilets Saturday morning. The cleaning staff knew that I came in early on Mondays and were now worried that I would inspect the toilets to make sure the paper placed there on Saturday was still available. It was known who worked weekends on the cleaning detail and they knew we would hold them personally responsible. Now visitors on a Saturday or Sunday had access to toilet paper and the few who came in early on Monday could also visit bathrooms with an assurance paper would be available. When accepting the position as Director General at AMREF, never did I imagine that part of my job description would include serving as the organization's "Toilet Paper Inspector."

CHAPTER 35

DEALING WITH GOVERNMENT

At the beginning of 1992, the phone rang in my outer office.

"Mike, it's the Honourable Mr. X on the line," said Margaret, my Administrative Assistant who worked with me for nine years. Mr. X happened to be one of the most senior elected officials in the Kenya Government, and without understatement, a person of considerable importance in the country. He knew AMREF and had, in the past, helped us with a few fundraising campaigns. We met from time to time, either at official functions or receptions.

"Hello Mike. I am calling for some information. Perhaps you can help me?"

"I'll try sir. What do you need to know?"

"I have heard that AMREF is about to begin a water development project in District Y. Is that true?"

"Yes, it is. We recently received a grant from an international donor as well as some funding from a private company located in the district."

"Exactly what will you be doing in the district?"

"We will be working with the local communities to construct shallow wells and at the same time, doing health promotion activity to improve sanitation and prevent malaria."

"When do you expect to begin?" asked the powerful politician.

"Well sir, you know that in any project AMREF undertakes, we always work closely with your government at the district level and with the local leaders as well. Meetings are now underway with the Government's District Officer of Health, the District Development Committee, and tribal chiefs. We want to ensure that the community has a sense of "ownership" of the project before well digging and education programmes start."

The powerful senior politician on the other end of the line happened to be the Member of Parliament from the district where this new project would be implemented. He represented an area that was semi-arid and many of his constituents lacked access to safe water. Naturally he would be interested in this new well construction project.

"Mike, can you give me an idea when your discussions with the Ministry of Health and other officials will be completed? When does the digging begin?"

"We should be ready to start the first wells in about two months if the discussions with your government representatives go well."

The politician's next words left me astounded.

"Mike, forget about the government. It is slow and inefficient. You will do better without them. You do not need them. Just avoid the government and start the project as quickly as possible."

I could hardly believe my ears. Here was one of the most influential members of Kenya's Government telling me to forget about involving in this project that same government which he represented. Slow and inefficient were the words he used.

It took me a few minutes to compose some thoughts and respond diplomatically. Finally, he was told that if we bypassed the District Government offices, this project would have little chance of being sustained when AMREF left. But to keep the politician on our side, it was then offered to have our staff speed up the meetings with district health officials and community leaders, with the promise of getting the project underway as quickly as possible. While we would not produce wells immediately, this solution appeared to be satisfactory.

What brought on this strange conversation? Well, it took place at the start of an election year. Voting was to take place for all members of Parliament as well as for the Presidency later in 1992. It was to be a different type of election than had ever before been experienced in Kenya.

From the time of independence from Britain in 1963 until the beginning of the 1990s, Kenya had one political party. This was KANU, the Kenya African National Union. In almost thirty years, only two men had held the Presidency. Jomo Kenyatta, one of the key leaders of Kenya's struggle for independence, was the first President. Upon his death in office in 1978, the then Vice-President, Daniel arap Moi, succeeded Kenyatta. President Moi, a masterful politician, was able to keep the leaders representing Kenya's divergent tribal groups within the KANU party fold.

But in the early 1990s, Kenya's political landscape changed dramatically. Under pressure from western governments, bilateral donors, and the International Monetary Fund, Kenya was pushed into accepting a multi-party political arrangement. The donors had been seriously questioning KANU's one party rule and the large-scale corruption evident in the country. December 1992 was to be the time for Kenya's first multi-party elections.

Like all KANU politicians, with the newly introduced multi-party system, my caller would be facing real opposition for his parliamentary seat. To have a better chance for re-election and to keep his powerful position within the government, it would be helpful if his constituents saw real activities going on in the district. The voters would appreciate new and improved access to safe water. AMREF's project was likely to be viewed as a feather in the politician's cap. Hence his anxiety to see the project begin as quickly as possible and the telephone call to the office. Government involvement, in his eyes, would only slow things down and perhaps not prove helpful to his re-election prospects.

Interestingly, President Moi was re-elected in 1992 (as was the caller) and KANU emerged as the majority party in Parliament. The new system had resulted in the formation of several parties. Under Moi's leadership, KANU was able to exploit the inability of other factions to come together and form a united opposition. Five years later, the elections of 1997 produced a repeat performance, with Moi again returned to State House. In 2001, he announced he was serving his last term as President and would not stand again in the elections of 2002. In 2002, Mwai Kibaki was chosen as Kenya's third President.

At AMREF, we did work closely with African Governments at all levels, from the national to the provincial and down to the districts. Government Ministries of Health had primary responsibility for providing medical services on the continent. Governments and non-governmental organizations together accounted for over 90 per cent of health care throughout Africa. Given low levels of income, private sector health providers were few. AMREF's strategy recognized the government's importance and we attempted to strengthen its capabilities for providing better care. The governments were viewed as among our most important partners and cooperation was valued. Occasionally, there were some strange dealings with political leaders. And even stranger telephone conversations.

Some months later, another call was received in my office from a different Government Minister. We had met a few times officially but I did not know him well. When he greeted me by my first name, it was an indication that some kind of request was coming.

Like many other people, this Minister had a "sideline." His turned out to be the travel business. He must have been a silent owner or partner in a travel agency. He was interested in AMREF's travel budget, which was considerable given that staff travelled frequently within Africa as well as to Europe and North America for fundraising and donor meetings. The Minister was quite insistent that we give his travel agency some, or preferably all, of our business. By now, such requests and pressure, whether subtle or not so subtle, were common.

My "way out" was always AMREF's Board of Directors and our operating policies.

"Mr. Minister, AMREF would be pleased to consider the travel agency you mentioned for possible business. AMREF's Board has set strict guidelines as to how we consider vendors for services we purchase. I am obligated by the Board to review the performance of each service provider on an annual basis. Then once every two years, all interested parties are invited to submit their capability statements and bid for our business. I strongly urge you to have the travel agency's Managing Director get his material to me as soon as possible. Then we will be able to consider it later in the year when the review of our travel requirements is conducted."

Using the Board and our policies as an excuse almost always relieved the pressure from high places. Rarely was there any action taken on our part or follow-up from the other side.

Being non-Kenyan had its advantages when it came to resisting such requests as the one above. As an outsider, I had no loyalty or obligations to any group in the country. Unlike the situation in some of AMREF's departments where the Directors were under societal obligations to help family and friends first, such was not the case in my situation. It was easier for me to say no. But I did have real empathy for my senior African colleagues, who were always being asked for favours and who, at times, had complications when it came to saying no.

In Kenya and the other countries where we worked, unemployment was a major economic problem. People were desperate for jobs and governments were just as desperate to show economic growth, which would lead to job creation. It was not a problem to understand the hundreds and hundreds of requests we would receive each year for possible positions. It was also understandable to have politicians frequently contact us and apply subtle pressure to employ one of their constituents. These types of requests were endless.

To shelter key management people from constant requests of family, friends, and politicians, we instituted certain policies shortly after my arrival. Our organizational structure consisted of a small headquarters in Nairobi that served as an overall corporate command centre. Headquarters was not operational in the sense that it did not implement programmes. HQ was the overall support group, with responsibilities for strategic planning, financial oversight, resource generation, public relations, and information. All health activities were carried out through operational divisions. These consisted of semi-autonomous Country Offices in Kenya, Uganda, Tanzania, and South Africa. In some countries, where our programmes were not large enough to warrant a full-scale Country Office, there were smaller project offices, as was the case in Somalia, Ethiopia, Rwanda, and Mozambique.

All Country Directors with the exception of one were African. This was consistent with AMREF's approach as an African based and predominantly African staffed NGO. To help these senior managers resist outside pressures, none of them were stationed in their own countries. Our policy prohibited the appointment of a national as Country Director. So the AMREF bosses for the Tanzania and Kenya Country Offices were Ugandans. The South Africa Director was a Kenyan. Uganda had an American head. By avoiding having nationals holding the top positions in their own countries, it did help somewhat in keeping them at arms length from high-level pressure. But not completely, as the telephone calls from various Ministers showed.

Interestingly, at least twice each year I came into contact with the entire Kenya Government in one sitting. All major holidays, such as Kenyatta Day and Moi Day, were celebrated with large rallies and military parades. These were often held in "Nyayo" (National) Stadium, which most often was used for football matches. The climax to these celebrations was a speech by the President. The Cabinet, Diplomatic Corps, all members of Parliament, business, and church leaders were in attendance. Ina and I were always invited and for reasons we could never fathom, our seats were normally in the section occupied by the representatives to Parliament who with one or two exceptions, were black Africans. There we were, within the midst of the government but looking very un-governmental.

An incident, or rather a near incident with an important government figure could have sent us packing only weeks after our landing in Kenya. Upon arrival, we took up residence in a furnished Nairobi flat until a suitable rental house could be found. I was occupied with the job each day so the burden of house hunting fell on Ina's shoulders.

Finding a place to live in Kenya was somewhat different than Ina was used to. Most rentals would either be listed with estate agents or in the newspapers, as was common elsewhere. But in Nairobi, estate agents had no access to transportation. You had to drive into town, locate the right person on the street, pick them up in your car (hopefully the legitimate estate agent), go look at properties, and return them back to town. It was a long and tiring process.

During the 1990s, house rentals in Nairobi were quite expensive. The city was world headquarters for the United Nations Environment Programme (UNEP) and regional headquarters for other U.N. Agencies. This meant there were a great many expatriates living in Nairobi and wherever the U.N was based, prices were always high. Landlords, after observing all the Mercedes with U.N license plates being driven around town, deduced that all foreigners were rich. Besides the U.N., Kenya also had a large diplomatic community. Many international corporations had Kenyan subsidiaries based in Nairobi. Expatriates often headed these. Nairobi was also the East African centre for a number of international NGOs, adding to the foreign population. We would always joke that Nairobi had two sets of prices, one for Kenyans and one for "muzungus," or whites.

Working for a non-profit charitable organization, we were not willing to pay muzungu prices. AMREF provided a limited housing allowance which was quite moderate. Of course the estate agents, hearing the head of AMREF wanted to rent a house and seeing that we were muzungus, always wanted to show Ina properties way beyond our price range. She would go through the same routine each day – pick up the agents, drive out to look at huge properties of five and six bedrooms way beyond our price range, say thanks but no thanks, drop off the agents, and return to the flat tired and frustrated. She had a hard time getting the message across that there was actually a "poorer muzungu tribe," quite different than those who worked for the U.N., and we belonged to the poorer cousins.

One evening the phone rang in the flat. It was an estate agent who had been showing Ina homes.

"Mrs. Gerber, I have the perfect house for you and it is in your price range."

"Are you sure? Every house you have shown me is at least twice what we can afford."

"Don't worry, this one is exactly within the limits you have given. Please pick me up tomorrow morning and I will take you to see the house. You will love it."

So bright and early the next day, Ina drove into Nairobi, picked up the estate agent, and they went out to a section of town called Lavington. Passing through the neighbourhood, Ina began developing doubts as she saw a number of huge houses partly hidden behind high walls.

"Are you sure we will be able to afford what you are going to show me?" said Ina.

"Definitely, don't worry," responded the agent. "This house belongs to a government official who has lots of houses."

The woman directed Ina to what seemed like a considerably large walled property, and they pulled up to a huge gate with a big sign reading "Mbwa Kali" (fierce dog). This was a common warning in Nairobi to ward off intruders. Beeping the horn, a watchman came out through a small door in the gate, holding onto a growling dog. Not a friendly way to greet a prospective new tenant. He started speaking with the woman estate agent in Kiswahili. After a few minutes of discussion, during which Ina could not help but notice a puzzled look on the watchman's face, he opened the gate and they drove in.

In the driveway, were four large Mercedes cars along with another vehicle. And at the end of the driveway was a huge two-story house, better described as a mini-mansion.

"We can't afford this. Why did you bring me here?" said Ina.

"Yes, you can afford it. See, here is the listing with the rental price" said the agent as she showed Ina a paper. And the paper did list a house within our allotted price range.

"Come, let's go inside," said the agent and the two of them knocked on the door. A uniformed servant answered and politely asked the two women what they wanted. The servant, also with a puzzled look on her face, started speaking rapidly in Kiswahili. Again, after about five minutes, the two of them were allowed inside.

The house was grandiose, with the most expensive furnishings and wood-panelling Ina had seen in Nairobi. The estate agent took Ina by the hand and led her through all of the rooms, each one larger than the next. They went upstairs, looked in all the bedrooms, opened all the closets, and inspected the entire house. There were photos all over the place and Ina thought she recognized a woman in many of the photos. But being new in Kenya, she could not quite place the face.

After the house tour ended, Ina and the estate agent thanked the still surprised servant and left. In the car, the conversations continued as before.

"We can't afford a house like that."

"Yes you can. See, here is the listed price."

"Well, even if we can afford it, my husband and I could never live there. He works for a charity and if people see us in a large mansion like that, it would be embarrassing and problematic to explain."

"Think about it," said the agent. "First speak with your husband before making a decision."

Over dinner, Ina told me about the day's house hunting experience. We both agreed that even if the price for that house was right, it would be totally inappropriate for us to live, or even be seen, in a place like that. She would call the estate agent the next morning and say, "Thank you but that house was not suitable for us."

That same evening, the telephone rang about 9:00 pm.

A frantic voice on the line said, "Mrs. Gerber, this is Mrs. (estate agent). I have made a horrible mistake. I showed you the wrong house. That house belongs to Minister Z, an incredibly powerful person. His house is not for rent. I confused the address with another house. If the Minister knew we were walking around his house, looking in all of the rooms and in the closets, very bad things could happen to us. We could be thrown in prison or worse and no one would know about it. Please, please, don't ever tell anyone where we were today. Forget that today ever happened."

By now the poor woman was crying almost hysterically. Ina calmed her down and assured the estate agent that no one would ever know where they were and their secret was safe. Somewhat satisfied, the woman offered profuse thanks and hung up.

After hearing who the house belonged to, Ina put two and two together. She now recalled who the woman was that she saw in the photos. It was the wife of this powerful politician. We both had a good laugh, wondering what the startled servants told the politician and his wife when they returned home. I am sure they said that two crazy women, one African and one white, were walking around the house and looking in your closets.

Eventually, we did find an affordable house, happily through the newspaper and not an estate agent, and lived there for the next nine years. During those years, I would meet that politician on a number of occasions, always wondering if he ever figured out who those ladies were that invaded his house. If he had, we would have been on the next plane out of the country only shortly after arriving.

CHAPTER 36

THROUGH WHOSE EYES?

Having worked first in Asia and then Africa, I was frequently asked to provide a comparison of the two continents. Responding briefly was too large and complicated of a task, so my simple answer was an over-generalized contrast. It was usually something in the order of "Asia was all hustle, bustle, noise, and wall-to-wall people. Africa was miles and miles of wide open spaces, or seemingly uninhabitable bush, where at times one thought there were no people."

While this was often true, it was possible to reverse the above, applying the opposites to Asia and Africa. Rwanda has one of the highest population densities of any country in the world, with too many people living in too small an area. The same applied to the Kisii District of Kenya. Urban settlements like Kibera or Mathare in Nairobi could rival their Asian counterparts such as Tondo in Manila or the bustees of Calcutta when it came to poverty, overpopulation and commotion. Much of Gujerat and Rajasthan in western India is desert where it is a challenge for the populations to subsist. But while the "throw away" answer was grossly overstated, there was still some truth to the response, especially when applied to the parts of Africa where AMREF worked in Somalia, Ethiopia, and Sudan on the horn; Kenya, Tanzania, and Uganda in the east; Mozambique, Namibia, and South Africa in the south. Parts of these countries contained large tracts of desert, scrubland, or forests that few people inhabited.

Flying one time in a small airplane piloted by Dr. Michael Wood, one of AMREF's founders and its first Director General, he used a particularly British expression but one that was often repeated by other pilots. We were on our way to Dareda in the north central part of Tanzania, just south of Lake Manyara. Leaving Nairobi's Wilson Airport, we flew for over an hour above open spaces without seeing a town or any people. I commented to Mike that this was a marked contrast to my experiences in Asia where you could not fly more than five minutes without human activity. "This is Africa," he replied. "It can best be described as MMBA – Miles and Miles of Bloody Africa."

The real comparison between working in Asia and Africa had to be seen in terms of people's needs and economic development, or the lack of such. The countries I was most familiar with in Asia – the Philippines, India, Thailand, Indonesia, Malaysia, and a few others – were on the whole, economically better developed than those in Africa familiar to me. Most Asian countries have old and established written languages. The percentage of people within the Asian nations having completed secondary and higher education is greater than the percentages of those finishing high school or college in Africa. Resources are more plentiful, both financial and human. India and the Philippines, for example, are large exporters of professionals in the health and computer fields to North America and Europe.

Widespread poverty, as reflected not only by low per capita incomes, but also by limited access to basic services such as education and health, is more prevalent in Africa. Unlike Asia, the continent does not suffer from a "brain drain." The opposite is all too true. By the beginning of the 21st century, Africa still does not have enough of the trained human resources it needs. On the whole, it is a much poorer continent. For someone from the outside involved in development work, the challenges are probably greater. When reflecting on where the needs are greatest, Africa always comes first.

The continent, however, has suffered from an unbalanced portrayal in the west with regard to reporting by both the television and print media. Africa is usually referred to in one of two ways, a place that is either an unmitigated disaster or one that is overly romanticized. Both do Africa an injustice. The first presents the constant catastrophe syndrome; wars, famines, droughts, and refugees. This type of reporting too often ignores real progress that is being made. The second, usually reflected by a few whites that have settled there, imparts a starry-eyed view of a land with glorious scenery, wide-open spaces, solitude, and magnificent animal life. The romantics, who have a keen love for the mountains, the valleys, the plains, the beaches, and most importantly, the elephant, lion, rhinoceros, and other wildlife, do not seem to have as sharp an eye for the African people, for their problems, their struggles, and their achievements.

Many who visit Africa come for a single purpose, be it to report an event, for business, or as tourists, and do not see the "larger world" around them. Never was this truer than in Kenya during the years 1984 and 1985. Drought was widespread throughout the Rift Valley, with famine conditions ranging from Ethiopia to Kenya, Tanzania, Zambia, and Zimbabwe. While Ethiopia was front-page news throughout the world, with starving children on news magazine covers, few took notice of serious food shortages in the other countries.

Kenya, with its famous Maasai Mara and other game parks, with Mt. Kenya and the green highlands in the north, with the Indian Ocean and beautiful white sand beaches on the coast, attracts hundreds of thousands of tourists each year. And they came in 1984 and 1985, in the midst of a severe drought and famine. Food shortages were so severe in those years that AMREF, which was not a relief organization, began feeding Kenyans through its health programmes for the first time since its founding in 1957. Particularly hard hit was the Kibwezi Division of Machakos District. But tourists rarely saw any of this.

Kibwezi lies about 200 kilometres from Nairobi along the main road to Tsavo National Park and the coastal city of Mombasa, a route heavily travelled by visitors. Yet the thousands who passed were focused intently on their holidays and the animals. It was as if outsiders were wearing blinders, seeing only what they came to see. Sadly, the same is often true for those who come to Africa to report on wars and other crises, providing westerners with limited perceptions. And it is not different with the romantics, who most often view everything around them as an African paradise.

To be able to see things through the eyes of others is essential for understanding what is happening in Africa today. While not easy to do, it allows for a more balanced perspective. Taking off the blinders permits an ability to see not only disorder and scarcity but also great changes and advancements taking place at the same time. And these changes often occur at a pace that seems amazing when compared to similar transformations in the western world.

At AMREF, we were always trying to get a number of European and North American Board members and western friends to understand why things in Africa were often done differently from the way they were used to functioning in the west. Only with a greater understanding of an "African rationale" would our important contributors appreciate constraints and problems that had to be overcome. They could then observe and value real progress. But to succeed in trying to have people see the world through someone else's eyes was never easy and often frustrating.

A case in point involved a Board member from AMREF Spain. At the time, the Spanish organization was our newest, founded in 1994. It was started by a dedicated and committed plastic and reconstructive surgeon, Dr. Javier Beut who practiced in Majorca. For many years prior to his involvement with AMREF, Javier would spend three to four weeks of his vacation time in Kenya, serving as a volunteer surgeon at an Italian mission hospital, Wamba, in the north central part of the country. After opening AMREF in Spain, he recruited a friend and colleague, Dr. Alfonso Villalonga, to serve as the first Chairman. Also a prominent plastic and reconstructive surgeon, Alfonso was based in Madrid and had many contacts in Government and the business community. The two surgeons put together a dynamic Board of Directors for AMREF Spain, and within a short period, were successful in raising funds for our activities in Mozambique and Kenya.

In mid-1998, Alfonso Villalonga called me in Nairobi. He wanted to organize a trip to Africa for two people, the first a newly appointed Board member and the second a leading personality from the Spanish entertainment world. Alfonso wanted the new Board member, Paulo, to see first hand AMREF's health programmes. Paulo was a successful businessman and the Chairman hoped to get him more closely involved with our work. Maria, through her contacts in television and the media, would be an important ally in helping AMREF gain wider recognition in Spain.

The three came to East Africa in July for a two-week visit. Alfonso and I discussed their programme and decided on a couple of field trips. The first was to northern Kenya, specifically to Lokichogio and Lodwar where AMREF was working with a nomadic tribe, the Turkana. Hydatid disease was endemic among the Turkana. It is caused by a parasite transmitted from dogs to humans. The life cycle of the parasite involves the Turkana's camels and goats whose faeces and offal are ingested by dogs and the parasite is then passed on to humans. The Turkana are animal herders and keep large numbers of dogs to help with tending the animals.

Besides helping to keep the livestock together, dogs played an important part in the everyday life of the people. The region where they lived was semi-desert, hot, and arid. Water was a scarce and precious commodity. It therefore had to be used only for drinking, by animals and humans. All other functions that we normally take for granted, such as bathing or sanitation in the toilet, were superfluous activities for the Turkana. In any case, toilets were non-existent with the exception of an odd pit latrine. This was only natural given the nomadic nature of life.

Thus dogs often performed certain "hygienic" functions. After a child defecated, a dog would lick the youngster's bottom, performing a sort of cleaning service. With little water and no paper available, this practice did make sense. Regrettably, it constantly exposed the children to the dogs' infested fur and faeces.

Initially, AMREF's Flying Doctor surgeons would remove hydatid cysts caused by the parasites that could grow appallingly large, usually in a human's abdominal cavity. If not removed or reduced, the cysts could rupture and enormous numbers of daughter cysts spread throughout the body. Serious cases often resulted in death. Surgery alone was not the answer because of a high incidence of re-infestation of the parasite. It was obvious that other approaches besides operating were necessary. AMREF began to do research into drug treatment for the cysts. This proved to be more effective than surgery, but expensive. The number of individuals who received such treatment was relatively small in relation to the total population. Even though the drugs reduced cysts, re-infestation was still common.

We realized that the only long-term solution was changing the Turkana's behaviour in relation to their animals, and in particular, to their dogs. By changing the relationship to animals, it would be possible to break the transmission cycle of the parasite. By 1998, we had been implementing a significant health education project centred in Lokichokio and Lodwar for close to ten years. It was producing positive results.

*   *   *

Paulo and Maria would find a trip to the Turkana region both educational and interesting.

The second part of their programme was a scheduled visit to Kibwezi in central Kenya. AMREF had been involved in a large community based health care project in that area for many years. One component of this project was to implement a community focused approach to the rehabilitation of disabled children. Our staff worked with parents and the youngsters right in the villages where there were significant numbers of both physically and mentally handicapped children. Before immunization campaigns were begun, polio cases were common. Kibwezi had its fair share of youngsters who had been crippled by the disease. For some reason, which was not as yet determined, the Kamba people living in this region had an unusually large number of children born with Down's Syndrome.

Because any type of government or private service for the disabled was totally lacking in rural areas, our approach was to work with the parents and get them to be the key actors in the rehabilitation of their own children. Classes for both fathers and mothers were held and extensive training given. Low-cost exercise apparatus were constructed using locally available free materials such as wood and bamboo. These were used within and outside the homes, as the parents assisted their children in learning how to move about. The mothers of Down's Syndrome youngsters were taught to understand that the children could be a part of community life and did not have to be shunted off and hidden. Anyone visiting our Kibwezi project could not help but be touched by the bonding observed between parents and the disabled kids. The community-based programme for the disabled was a remarkable story and we felt that Paulo and Maria would appreciate the efforts being undertaken in Kibwezi.

AMREF flew Alfonso, Paulo, and Maria to Lokichogio and Lodwar in the Turkana District. They were scheduled to be in the Turkana region for four days and return to Nairobi for the weekend. On the Monday of the second week, they would be driven down to Kibwezi. Ina and I invited the Spanish group to dinner at a Nairobi restaurant on the Friday evening between their visits to Turkana and Kibwezi.

All three guests were wonderful people and we truly enjoyed their company. But Paulo, who had never visited Africa before nor, any other part of the developing world, came back from his trip to the north in a somewhat "shell shocked" state. He had been totally unprepared for what he saw. That was not the case with the other two. Alfonso, as Chairman of AMREF Spain, came to Africa often and knew our programmes well. Maria had also travelled frequently as her job took her to many parts of the world.

Alfonso and Maria spoke English quite well. Paulo spoke only Spanish. So Ina, Alfonso, Maria, and myself would carry on a discussion and then Maria would translate for Paulo. He would respond and she would pass along his words to us. Not being able to speak directly with Paulo contributed to the confusing and often frustrating nature of the discussion, frustrating for both Paulo and myself.

He had been totally surprised by what he termed "the level of poverty" found among the Turkana people. It affected him greatly. Paulo was a caring person and still saddened by his Turkana experience when we met for dinner. The numbers of children and the conditions in which they lived had greatly disturbed him.

In the restaurant, all he could speak about was the "poverty children" and doing something for them. Paulo felt the Turkana had few pleasures in life, comparing the way children were treated in Spain to those in northern Kenya. He spoke of a large-scale "handout" solution that would give Turkana youngsters things that Paolo felt all children should have.

I not only listened closely while Maria translated what Paulo was saying but also watched him while he said it. There was no doubt he was emotionally upset. His response was to try and deliver instant help, relief, and happiness to the kids. I expressed empathy for his feelings and at the same time, tried to diplomatically explain that the answers to the problems he encountered were not to be found in giving out things that Spanish children enjoyed.

The conversation was steered to comparisons between how things were done in Europe versus how they were done in Africa. How could Paulo be made to understand that that "European solutions" were not always the best way to solve problems here? How could he be convinced that there were no quick answers? The Turkana themselves would need to be involved in finding solutions to how their lives could be made better.

Paulo was torn between the rationale of these questions and his emotions. In the end, he could not separate himself from his feelings to look at issues from a broader perspective. The rest of us were now worried about how the upcoming trip to Kibewzi would affect Paulo. He was about to see many more children and be exposed to large numbers of handicapped youngsters. If the kids in Turkana had such an effect on his psyche, it was not difficult to imagine what would happen during the next week. I was already dreading a meeting with the Spanish group after they returned to Nairobi next Friday for the journey back to Europe.

Since we were not yet finished with dinner, there was still an opportunity to set the stage and prepare Paulo for what he would experience the following week in Kibwezi. We had to try and get him to understand some of the things he would experience from the viewpoint of the region's Kamba people. Without any meeting of the minds on quick, or not so quick, solutions to problems in Turkana, the discussion was steered toward conditions in Kibwezi and some of the cultural practices that were important to appreciating our programme for disabled children.

It was explained that what Paulo would see represented tremendous progress from ten or twenty years ago. He would observe cases of parents showing love and tenderness to disabled children when in the past, those children would have, at best, been hidden from sight, or at worst, abandoned at birth. Some tribal groups, especially those that had nomadic roots, abandoned handicapped newborn infants, leaving them to perish in the bush. Some groups also had superstitions about twins and these too would be abandoned when born.

While seeming cruel to those of us in the west, for nomadic peoples such practices were related to reasons of survival. It was crucial for every man, woman, and child to keep up with the group as it moved from place to place seeking grazing lands for animals and water for the livestock and humans. Those that could not keep up or who would hinder the able bodied were a danger to the entire group. In such a harsh environment, it was basically the survival of the fittest.

Looking at Paulo, we explained that while such customs were strange for us to accept, it was still important to understand why they were practiced in Africa. But seeing Paulo's facial expressions, it was evident that we were making matters worse instead of better. If astonished by what he saw in Turkana, our description of certain tribal practices was now causing him to withdraw further into himself, instead of trying to understand the beliefs of others. Abandoning a newborn was such an abhorrent idea that Paulo didn't even want to make an effort to comprehend.

He turned to us and replied in rapid Spanish, with Maria translating as best she could.

"I cannot believe you are telling me that people would put their babies in the bush to be eaten by animals. It doesn't matter if the babies were handicapped or that twins were born. It is not the fault of the babies. How can those people be so inhuman and do such savage things? I am a father. I would die myself before allowing anything to happen to my children. Nothing comes before my children. You are asking me to understand about these people having to move around. I can never accept or understand such cruel behaviour toward children."

He continued for another five minutes with more of the same. By now, we were convinced the evening was an unmitigated disaster. Here was a Board member with means and instead of getting him to appreciate Africa, it seemed with each explanation, he was being driven further away from any kind of understanding.

Not wanting to give up, we were prepared to make one last try. Turning the conversation to Nigeria's civil war from 1967–1971, I asked the Spanish trio if they remembered Biafra's struggle to break away and the hardships and starvation that took place as a result. Children were the primary sufferers during that conflict. Biafra was one of the first African crises to make the television screens and front pages of newspapers in the west. Scenes of starving children left a big impression on North Americans and Europeans. NGOs collected large amounts of money for relief efforts.

Those groups involved with bringing relief to Biafra reported an interesting phenomena that contrasted sharply with practices we were familiar with. It was discovered that when food was distributed to a family, the parents would feed the oldest children first. Then, and only if there was still enough to go around, were the smaller ones given a share. In the west, our priorities were reversed. The biggest fuss is made over the youngest, the most vulnerable child. Had the famine occurred in England or Spain, parents would have made sure the youngest children ate first, and then the older ones.

Our dinner partners agreed that as Europeans, they would have responded to a food crisis as we had hypothesized. Therefore, an explanation as to why Biafran parents had different priorities was in order. Poverty was widespread and life expectancy in Nigeria at that time much lower than in the west. Infant mortality rates (under one year of age) were very high as were those for child mortality (under five's). If a child made it past twelve or thirteen years of age, their chances of reaching adulthood were greatly improved. With food in short supply, decisions had to be made as to how it would be distributed. A sort of "triage" decision was made. Resources were first being invested in those that had the greatest chance of survival. While none of us at the table would ever want to be making those kind of decisions, under the circumstances in Biafra there was a great deal of logic being employed. At least we felt that way. But with Paulo, there was still the look of puzzlement.

Then, it was on to a concluding presentation. We had to come up with some kind of analogy that would be comfortable for Paulo and get him to appreciate the viewpoint of others.

"Paulo, may I tell you something about the Maasai?"

"Si."

"They are a nomadic tribal group here in Kenya who treasure their livestock, especially cattle. Wealth is measured by the number of animals that a man owns. The Maasai diet is dependent on the milk produced by the animals. And for dietary iron, they would bleed an animal and mix blood with the milk. The Maasai are skilled at such bleeding and it is not harmful to the cow.

There is a story that the Maasai believe every cow in the world belongs to them. They have often tried to take away the cows of other people, which have led to serious battles. The Maasai truly love their cattle. Every Maasai boy, before he is initiated into manhood, will spend all day taking care of his father's animals. There might be fifty cows in the herd but that boy will have an individual name for every single cow. He will be able to easily distinguish one cow from another. The Maasai boy knows that should anything happen to the cattle or should one become lost while herding, he would be in for a difficult time.

Now Paulo, suppose we find a Maasai man willing to travel and accompany you back to Madrid. Then next Sunday afternoon, you can take the Maasai to the Plaza de Toros to see the bullfights. We all know how much many Spanish people love the spectacle of bullfighting. I understand that each Sunday it is the most popular programme on television.

What do you think will be the reaction of the Maasai man as he watches the bullfight with you? What will he think when the matador finally kills the bull? And what will be his reaction when the appreciative audience awards the matador with an ear or two for his performance? Let me tell you what I think the Maasai would say.

'These Spanish are crazy,' would be the reaction of the Maasai. 'They are barbarians. Why would any people in their right minds torture and kill such a beautiful animal as that bull? I love all my animals. I would never think of treating any of them so cruelly. And we would never kill an animal for so called sport. Animals are to be cherished and loved. These Spanish are truly a barbaric and uncivilized people.'"

We do not know how much of the above was lost in translation but there was a great deal of explaining back and forth in two languages. We could think of no other way to show Paulo that diverse people see things differently, depending on their culture and their conditions. And with this, the evening came to a close.

Paulo went to Kibwezi, returned home to Spain, and continued to serve on the AMREF Board. Unfortunately I retired a few months after his visit. Unfortunate because it would have been interesting to see his reactions to any subsequent visits he made to Africa.

CHAPTER 37

MAKING A DIFFERENCE

"More than any other time in history, mankind faces
a crossroads. One path leads to despair and utter
hopelessness. The other to total extinction. Let us
pray we have the wisdom to choose correctly."

Woody Allen

Too often what is heard or read about Africa might seem as if selecting one of the
above two paths have been the only options. Fortunately, there are other roads to
follow, roads which offer hope and promise rather than pessimism and despair.

African news too frequently relates accounts of external wars, internal
conflicts, and people forced to flee their homes. Refugees and displaced people
make for sensationalist stories. Yet there is another side to Africa, one that hardly
ever receives attention. When people hurriedly flee from a place, they must
relocate somewhere else. That somewhere else has to have, if not a "welcome
mat," then at least a mat that says "come in, you can stay for a while." By
tradition, African countries have always kept their doors open, allowing outsiders
to come in as temporary, or at times, long-term guests.

The contrast between refugee policies of western countries and African
nations has been striking. The United States and Europe have too often placed
serious obstacles in the way of people legitimately in danger looking for asylum.
The period from 1933 to the end of World War Two has been the most criticized.
Individuals not being able to find safe havens from Nazi persecution in Germany
because of religious or political beliefs brought about a shameful evaluation of
the western democracies' immigration policies. With the break-up of the Soviet
Union and troubles in the Balkans, much of Western Europe is uneasy about
migrations of people into their countries. And when the U.S. accepts a handful of

young men from Southern Sudan for resettlement in the States, boys who had been child soldiers and then refugees in Kenya for many years, it warrants banner headlines and a self-serving patting on the back by Americans involved.

But the fact that a poor country like Kenya has always opened its borders to hundreds of thousands of refugees should definitely merit the recognition it deserves. Africans as individuals, and by extension African states, have always been hospitable to strangers. When civil war erupted in Somalia in the early 1990s, within days over half a million Somalis crossed into Kenya. By the year 2000, it was still host to over 250,000 refugees from Sudan, Ethiopia, Uganda, Rwanda, Burundi, Republic of the Congo, and Somalia.

When the Rwandan Popular Front (RPF) marched toward Kigali in 1994 and the Hutu led Interahame began its mass slaughter of Tutsi and moderate Hutus, perhaps as may as one million Rwandans moved into Zaire. Another 300,000 to 400,000 thousand settled in Tanzania. None of Africa's recipient countries were prepared or in an economic position to accept and support such large numbers of refugees. Yet there were no bars to entry. Numerous other examples of "open doors" in southern and western Africa can be cited. The African tradition does not turn people away.

What is true in Africa on the global scale, the willingness to help those from other countries, is an ingrained part of local customs. Africans in general are always willing to lend a hand in grim or emergency situations that involve their own families, communities, or nation. There is a natural tendency to rally around those who need assistance. This can be seen over and over, whether it is a crowd rushing to aid people hurt in a road or rail accident, a village coming together to support a family in need of funds, or large numbers of people responding to a nationwide campaign to help groups suffering from drought or food shortages.

In Kenya, this instinct to help is reflected in the "harambee" spirit. Harambee or "pulling together" is a tradition that is seen everywhere. Rallies to collect money for various purposes are an everyday part of life. And Kenyans give generously based on what they can afford, poor as well as rich. As with refugees, they do not turn their backs and walk away from local or internal problems. In many African countries, time and again, I have witnessed total strangers or groups of people quickly responding to local emergencies. Africans seem to react instinctively with their eagerness to be of assistance. And they do so in a manner that is quite unruffled. Why do these qualities fail to be recognized by so many who send their reports on Africa back to their western readers or television audiences?

What we often do not recognize or understand is the pace at which change has, and is, taking place on the African continent over the past forty years. In some ways, this change not only rivals but also surpasses what has occurred in the west over the same time period. That has been true even when recent developments in both space and computers are taken into account. Africa has undergone its own transition. While not as well known as the exploration of the moon or development of the Internet, the changes have been just as important to millions of Africans whose lives have been affected.

* * *

In late 1990 and the beginning of 1991, as the winds of change were blowing over South Africa and the release of Nelson Mandela was imminent, AMREF hosted a number of prominent visitors from that country. The old leadership in South Africa recognized that great changes were about to take place. The country had been isolated for so long and viewed as a pariah State by the rest of Africa and much of the world.

The political changes about to happen in South Africa opened up doors to the outside world. There was a great desire to know what was happening elsewhere. Health professionals had only limited exposure to the latest trends and policies. While much of Africa had adopted a community based primary health care approach for reaching large numbers of people, South Africa had been committed to an inequitable hospital based health scheme, delivering high quality care only for the minority whites. Health services for the majority of the black population were far inferior, or at times, almost non-existent in remote rural areas.

By 1991, a number of more forward thinking leaders from the government, universities, and research institutions wanted to find out what was happening on the rest of the continent with regard to health delivery innovations. As part of the white establishment, they hoped to play some role in the transformation that was about to take place, at least during any transition period.

That year, AMREF hosted visits in Nairobi for South Africa's National Director General of Health (the Chief Executive of the Department of Health who reported to the Minister); the President of the Medical Research Council or MRC, South Africa's most important research institute, and the Dean of the Medical School at the University of Pretoria. All were interested in our programmes and in particular, the community based approaches we had been implementing since the early 1960s.

As AMREF began its work in South Africa in 1991, first with the University of the Western Cape and NGOs such as the National Progressive Primary Health Care Coalition, the South African Red Cross, and the Southern African Catholic Bishops' Conference, I would visit the country frequently. And as the Department of Health began to change even before the first free universal elections held in 1994, I would, from time to time, meet with some of the people who had visited AMREF in Kenya. One such person was Dr. C. Slabber, the Director General of Health.

Dr. Slabber was a pragmatist. He was realistic enough to appreciate that his term of service would end with elections in South Africa. Most of those appointed by and associated with the apartheid government felt they would play little or no role in the new South Africa. Dr. Slabber, while aware that his days of service were coming to an end, was a sincere and caring person. He would have very much wanted to be of service but was sensitive enough to realize it was not likely to happen. This was understandable. After so many years of repressive rule by the minority white regime, a new South African government and the majority of people would want nothing to do with the old leadership. In the changes that took place, some valuable professional resources that could have been utilized were not availed of.

In 1991, I was asked to visit the University of Western Cape, located not far outside of Capetown. Western Cape was committed to making its health related courses relevant to the needs of the underserved poor in surrounding communities and adopted a community based curriculum for its students. The university had a large nursing programme. AMREF was invited by Dr. Caroline Ntoane and others from the University's administration to help with changing the curriculum to a primary health care approach. Our two key Kenyan staff assisting the university were Penina Ochola, one of the most effective and dynamic trainers ever employed by AMREF and George Okello, who as described earlier, was to die during a training course in South Africa. Penina and George requested that I come and meet with the University's Vice-Chancellor and other senior officials.

During that trip, I was invited to address the staff at the MRC where I was introduced to Dr. Olive Shisana. Olive held a joint appointment at both MRC and the University of Western Cape, where she was involved with AMREF's staff and the new community based curriculum. Since Parliament was in session in Capetown, Dr. Slabber was there advising the Minister and invited Penina Ochola and myself to dinner one evening. He also asked Olive Shisana and Caroline Ntoane to join us.

This occurred at a time when there was great excitement in South Africa. Nelson Mandela had just been released from prison. There was a realization that within a short time, South Africa would be a new country. In the restaurant, our dinner discussion centred on what would have to happen over the next few years to bring about the necessary changes in health policy and the health infrastructure.

In looking back, I realize how fortunate I was to have participated in that discussion. There I was, with three of the brightest and most capable African women I had ever met, one Kenyan and two South Africans, invited by a dedicated health professional who was so excited about the changes to come but saddened by the fact he would not be part of them. Those three hours proved to be insightful into what had been and what was to come.

Unknown to any of us at that time, after the 1994 elections in South Africa resulting in Nelson Mandela being chosen as President, Dr. Olive Shisana was to become the first black South African National Director General of Health, replacing Dr. Slabber. She later joined the World Health Organization as a senior advisor to Dr. Bro Harlem Gruntland, WHO's Director General. As South Africa was reorganized into nine provinces and health services were decentralized, Dr.Caroline Ntoane was named the first Director of Health for Northwest Province. Sadly for us but with a large increase in salary for her, Penina Ochola eventually left AMREF in 1994 and took her talent to USAID, and later to senior positions in other NGOs. My African dinner mates at that 1991 gathering were to play influential roles on both the national and international scenes.

Changes were taking place so rapidly that it was impossible not to experience them on a personal level, even for the sometime visitor to South Africa like myself. In 1992, I was in Western Cape Province with two colleagues from AMREF's headquarters in Nairobi. Dr. David Nyamwaya, a Kenyan, was a Cambridge University trained medical anthropologist and one of Africa's leading health behaviour specialists. Dr. Pat Youri, from Ghana, was a paediatrician by profession, and a health policy expert with special emphasis on community based care. After the conclusion of our meetings at the University of Western Cape, we were taken to visit the beautiful Stellenbosch Valley, home of South Africa's major wine growing region.

The area was also the site of Stellenbosch University, which historically had been the hotbed of Afrikaner conservatism and apartheid rationalisation. We asked if it would be possible to visit the university and were taken there. Stepping onto the campus, it was as if the year was 1965 rather than 1992. Besides David and Pat, there was not another black African to be seen. Going through the modern and well-stocked library, the silence was deafening as hundreds of eyes followed us. It was not difficult to interpret those looks – not too many appeared either friendly or welcoming. I was most interested in the reactions and feelings of David and Pat. But they were totally professional and unaffected. Three years later, in 1995, there was an opportunity to return to Stellenbosch University. The changes and reception were quite different. There were quite a few black students on campus. Accompanied again by a Kenyan colleague, we were warmly received by the faculty and administration with whom we met. Quite a change within a few years.

Transformation was and still is evident everywhere on the continent. Only by stepping back to view time and change in Africa from a distance, can one appreciate the pace at which transformation is occurring. For me, the classic story of rapid change is one of a former associate and friend, Dr. Nimrod Bwibo.

Nimrod Bwibo grew up near Busia in Kenya, close to the border with Uganda. He came from a large and poor rural family. During our frequent evening chats while away from Nairobi visiting AMREF projects, Nimrod related stories from his youth. He told me that he never owned or wore shoes until entering high school at the age of fourteen. Nimrod was the first in his family to attend secondary school, which was quite far from the village where he grew up. Shoes were then needed because he had to travel the long distances to school on foot, primarily because he could not afford the bus fare even had the buses not been scarce or irregular. Nimrod did not wear long pants on a daily basis until he was nineteen years old and entering into university.

As a top student, he was among the best and brightest of Kenya's youth to be accepted into Makerere University. During the time before independence for Kenya, Uganda, and Tanzania, the three countries were administered as British East Africa. Makerere, located in Kampala, Uganda, was the best university in Africa and served the three colonies. Only the best students from the region were admitted. Its medical school was judged equal to those in Europe. After independence, Makerere remained among the best until the late 1970s and the era of Idi Amin's dictatorship. Amin caused many of the faculty to flee. Others were locked up or even killed. The university was turned into a shell of its old self. By 1980, it had basically collapsed. With the overthrow of Amin and under the current Presidency of Yoweri Museveni, Makerere was rehabilitated but has yet to return to its former standards.

Nimrod Bwibo graduated from Makerere University with a degree in medicine and achieved top honours. Interested in children's health, he went on to specialize in paediatrics, doing his residency at the University of Washington in Seattle and later also studying at the University of California in Los Angeles. He was the first in his family to travel outside of Kenya and Africa.

Dr. Bwibo's career carried him from one success to another. He was invited back to Makerere University and became a Professor of Medicine, teaching an entire generation of present day East African doctors. It was impossible to travel anywhere with Nimrod without some former medical student coming forth to greet him and offer thanks, always with awe and reverence. His reputation was second to none.

After independence, universities had been chartered in both Kenya and Tanzania. Professor Bwibo was invited to become Dean of the College of

Medicine at the University of Nairobi. From his position as Dean, Nimrod moved on to become the first Principal of the College of Health Sciences when the University of Nairobi restructured its faculties into constituent colleges. He was subsequently promoted to Deputy Vice-Chancellor in charge of academic affairs. Under the British influenced system of higher education, a university's Chancellor is normally the President of the country. This is basically a figurehead position. The Vice-Chancellor is the real university head. The title is equivalent to a university President in the United States. A Deputy Vice-Chancellor could be compared to an Executive Vice-President within the university setting. Nimrod Bwibo was the number two person at the University of Nairobi. All of these achievements were accomplished by an individual who did not own or wear shoes, or long pants, until he was fourteen and nineteen years respectively.

When he was about to retire from the University of Nairobi, we recruited Nimrod to join AMREF as Deputy Director General with overall responsibility for the health and medical side of our organization. He was a great addition to the staff and provided instant credibility with health professionals, Ministries of Health, and donors. Nimrod became a mentor to me on how best to act within the African context and his wisdom and advice were always invaluable.

In reflecting on his career, I would frequently compare Nimrod Bwibo's path to his professional development with my own. In my family, neither set of grandparents received any formal education beyond primary school. The next generation, namely my own mother and father, both went to secondary school. And as the third generation, I was the first to attend university. It took three generations or about seventy-five years for my family to produce its first college graduate.

In comparison, Nimrod Bwibo's achievements seem extraordinary. He went from never leaving his village to being the first in his family to attend secondary school, to graduating from university as a medical doctor, to specializing in paediatrics in the United States, to becoming a Professor at Makerere University's Medical School, to taking the position as Dean of the Medical School at the University of Nairobi, to finally becoming its Deputy Vice-Chancellor. He did all that in one professional lifetime. For Nimrod, it was as if time was compressed and three generations merged together.

Nimrod Bwibo's story is extraordinary. But it is not the only remarkable tale. Many Africans have overcome restraints and economic hardships to achieve a great deal. Among the current leadership, whether in government or in the private sector, few were born wealthy. Most of today's leaders were born before independence, in the 1950s or earlier, when prosperous Africans were few and far between. People pulling themselves up by their own bootstraps is most appropriate when describing achievements of individuals on the continent during colonial rule. So much has been accomplished in so short a time period. Sadly, this is hardly recognized in the reporting we see about Africa. It is essential to keep a proper time perspective in drawing conclusions and making judgments.

With high fertility rates, large population growth increases, and life expectancy much lower than in Europe and North America, Africa is a continent of young people. And the young represent the real hope and future. One story can best illustrate that hope.

 AMREF's Kibwezi project in Kenya was a long-term commitment. It was viewed as a field laboratory, a place where innovative approaches to integrated rural development could be tested. My own involvement with the site dated back to 1979. An arid area with a population of approximately 250,000 at that time, it had few health facilities or trained personnel. Many of the people were recent arrivals to Kibwezi Division, having migrated from other parts of Machakos District. They moved in to try and improve their living standards, but the area proved to be a gruelling one for producing crops. Farmers were growing barely enough for subsistence. Cotton had been unsuccessfully tried as a cash crop. There were a few large tracts of land given over to sisal production for export but this had little impact on the local economy.

In the late 1970s, the closest health centre for the people of Kibwezi District was at Makindu, hours away by public transport. For many, making the trip was either impractical or unaffordable. In consultation with the Kenya Government and external donors, AMREF was involved in the construction of a health centre at Kibwezi that was eventually opened in 1979. The Ministry of Health provided staff for the centre and AMREF conducted primary health care activities out in the villages. Kibwezi Health Centre became a model for using a static facility as the focal point for training village selected volunteer community health workers. While providing basic first aid, the primary role of the community health worker was health promotion, preventing disease before it struck. They were basically health educators. Problem patients that could not be dealt with at village level were referred to the health centre.

*   *   *

From this beginning of establishing a health centre and training primary health care workers, the Kibwezi project began to add various components, all geared to improving the community's health. In 1980, NASA, the American space agency, selected our Kibwezi project to test the application of photovoltaic energy in developing countries. Solar energy had been used in NASA's various space missions. Since electricity to generate power in most rural areas was nonexistent, NASA made the technology available and AMREF was selected as one of the initial recipients. Kibwezi was the first health facility in Kenya to pump water and light a small operating theatre using solar energy.

Providing water through boreholes and shallow wells, so essential in the region, was a second component added to this project. And, as previously described, with large numbers of disabled youngsters in the area, AMREF instituted community based rehabilitation activities. By the 1990s, the Kibwezi project was a good example of an integrated primary health care programme, linking various activities in the villages and rural areas with services provided at a health centre. It received a lot of attention from government, donors, and NGOs.

My work frequently brought me to Kibwezi. On one visit to the health centre in late 1989, I noticed a young boy hanging around. He was quite small and looked about three years of age, but it was not easy to tell exactly. He had a beautiful face that was always lit up with a big smile. And he was disabled. Both of his legs were badly misshapen. On his left he was wearing a specially built up shoe with a brace attached. It appeared that part of his foot must have been missing. The right was also strangely bent and longer than the left. But this did not stop him from doing everything.

The young man in question was as active as any of the other children who were attending the health centre with their mothers. He would sort of run and hobble around in his own unique way, but was able to do so quite quickly. He would disappear for a time and then return. During a quick trip into Kibwezi town, about a kilometre from the health centre, I found him there. The child appeared totally independent which was amazing for someone so young, small, and disabled. The boy was friendly to everyone and seemed to be known by all. The one difference I noticed between him and the other children was he did not appear to be at the centre with his mother.

The person he was most attached to was Shaya Asindua, AMREF's coordinator for our community rehabilitation of the disabled project. On my next visit to Kibwezi a few months later, I could not help but talking to the boy and playing with him. His smile and personality were infectious. I asked Shaya who he was and why he was at the health centre on both of my trips.

The story she told was heart wrenching. A few years back, a young child was found abandoned on the front doorstep of the health centre. It was this little boy. But sadly, that was only the best part of the story. The child's legs were horribly burned and shrivelled, with part of one foot missing. The burns were recent and on careful examination, it could only be surmised that the cause was either hot scalding water or oil. The only conclusion that could be drawn from the extent of the burns was that the child had been deliberately kept in the scalding liquid for some time. Who could do such a thing to a child? Why someone would do it, no one could understand. Who he was, no one knew. Exactly how old he was could not be determined. Residents of Kibwezi town had never seen him before. The child spoke only a few words of the Kamba language and a few words of Kikuku. Perhaps he was the offspring of a mixed tribal union.

The boy was given immediate treatment for the burns. His rehabilitation was slow and long but eventually he was able to move around and then walk on his crippled legs. Through the AMREF workshop, special shoes and braces were made. Not knowing whether he had a family, the youngster was unofficially "adopted" by the Kibwezi health centre staff and given a name. They called him Wambua. And Wambua's story is one of true courage.

He was a permanent fixture at Kibwezi. Wambua belonged to no one while at the same time, belonging to everyone. He was just there, eating and living with the staff. And nothing could dampen his spirit of independence. Wambua would hobble off when he wanted, go into town or someplace else, and return on his own schedule. He could not have been more than four or five years old at the most when I observed him doing this for the first time. Being small of stature, he appeared younger than he probably was.

Wambua was a lovable child but a free spirit. He never sat still and was always on the move, either playing or wandering off. He had an especially keen sense of observation and missed nothing that went on around him. To see him running and fooling around with other children was a sight to behold. Despite his handicap, he was always in the midst of the action. In a way, it was only those observing Wambua who considered him disabled. Wambua never gave his physical limitations a second thought. Nothing would hold him back.

While Shaya Asinduya worked on the disabled project in Kibwezi, her husband and children lived in Nairobi. Whenever possible, she would return home for weekends and holidays. Shaya frequently took Wambua to Nairobi on those trips. On one occasion, she brought Wambua and her children over to our house. He liked animals and was torn between fascination and caution when he saw our three large Rhodesian Ridgeback dogs. He also liked visiting our head office at Wilson Airport and seeing the airplanes.

While Wambua was extremely happy with his "independent" lifestyle at Kibwezi, Ina and I would often wonder what would eventually become of him later in life. Shaya had discussed the possibility of him going to school while recognizing the complexities involved. First of all, there were no special education facilities for disabled youngsters and having him accepted by a school would not be easy. Secondly, there would be the problem of getting him to sit still in a classroom for six hours a day. He had never been confined to one place before. But difficulties notwithstanding, we agreed that he would need some kind of formal education to be able to support himself as an adult.

I offered to explore the possibility of a school for Wambua. After visiting two in Nairobi, it was evident that they did not want the responsibility of accepting and providing special care for a disabled youngster. No amount of persuasion on my part could convince the headmasters that Wambua needed no special attention given the child's independent and self-sufficient nature.

The third try brought positive results. A wonderful combination of home and school in Nairobi, the S.O.S. Children's Village, agreed to take Wambua on a trial basis. S.O.S. provides homes for orphaned children in an uninstitutionalized way. A group of youngsters, anywhere from eight to twelve of them, live together as a "family" in the same house with one "mother" and a "mother's helper." The "village" might have as many as ten houses with a total of over 100 youngsters living on campus. The kids in each house grow up together and become a close-knit family, with the older ones helping to take care of the younger children. Originally founded in Austria, S.O.S. has Children's Villages in many of the developing countries in Africa, Asia, and Latin America.

S.O.S primary schools are found right on the village grounds. Older children who pass the entrance exams either go to S.O.S secondary schools, if one exists on campus, or to the local government school. As a charitable organization, S.O.S. is dependent on sponsorships for the children and general contributions.

After a short stay at the Nairobi S.O.S. Children's Village, Wambua was transferred to a new facility that was established in Eldoret, to the northwest of the capital. This became Wambua's permanent home and his "mama" and housemates, his first real family. That is where Wambua is today. He has completed his primary education and is now in secondary school. He had absolutely no trouble adapting to his new environment and family. Being outgoing and personable, he was immediately accepted by all the children. Those in his own age group looked to him for leadership. When it came to school, the beginning was somewhat unsettling for Wambua. As expected, he was not used to being confined in one place and having his freedom curtailed. But with time, his schoolwork began to improve and he settled in.

Wambua's story is a tale of courage. The boy is an inspiration to all who know him. With young people like Wambua, it is not far fetched to anticipate Africa's future as one of great promise.

CHAPTER 38

A VIOLENT AND
SAD GOODBYE

It was a typical August "winter's" day in Nairobi. Being south of the equator, the seasons are reversed. The mild temperature and usual grey sky were normal for that time of year. I was in my office at Wilson Airport on this Friday morning in 1998. For me, it was an especially busy time, both personally and professionally. Scheduled to retire on 30 September and to leave Kenya shortly afterwards, less than two months were left to organize the end phase of our current life and prepare for the next. I was busy tying up loose ends at AMREF and arranging for a smooth transition while Ina was dealing with the many details for our move to Portugal.

Sometime just after 10:30 am, there was a thunderous sound accompanied by the rattling of windows in our building. The noise was loud enough that I assumed it had come from close by. Since our offices were located on the airport grounds, my first reaction was that a plane had either crashed or blown up. Staff members came out of their buildings, wondering what had happened. We called over to our Flying Doctors hangar located adjacent to the Wilson Airport runway. The pilots and mechanics, while hearing what sounded like an explosion, reported nothing had happened at the airfield.

Within minutes, I was told there had been an explosion at the Kenya Cooperative Bank building. The bank was a tall, modern, glass-encased multi-storied building on Haile Salassie Avenue in downtown Nairobi, about five kilometres from the AMREF office. There was some panic in our corridors because about thirty minutes before the reported explosion, two AMREF staff had left for the bank to transact business. But moments later we found out what really happened. While the bank building was severely damaged, it was not the primary target of suicide bombers. Their object was a building close by. The date was Friday, 7 August 1998 and the structure attacked, very close to the bank, on the corners of Haile Salassie and Moi Avenues, was the United States Embassy.

Islamic terrorists, reportedly belonging to al Queda, a group supported by the exiled Saudi Osama bin Laden living in Afghanistan, planted bombs that exploded simultaneously at 10:40 am at the United States Embassies in Nairobi and Dar es Salaam. In Nairobi, a car driven into the U.S compound contained the bombs that destroyed the Embassy building, the Ufindi Cooperative offices right next door, and did extensive damage to the large Kenya Cooperative Bank structure not far away. The first reports at AMREF, while mistakenly claiming the bank building had exploded, were close enough to the exact location. The strength of the bomb was such that much of the surrounding area was extensively damaged, with many killed or injured, not only in the Embassy itself but also in Ufindi House and the bank building. The two AMREF staff who had gone to the bank were later located in one of the local hospitals, injured but thankfully alive.

Traffic that Friday morning, as always, was heavy with the Embassy being located at a busy intersection not far from Nairobi's central train station. Large numbers of those injured or killed were either pedestrians or passengers riding in public buses or matatus (mini buses) along Haile Selassie Avenue. In total, 258 people died, of which 246 were Kenyans. Over 5,000 were injured, many seriously. In Tanzania, the death toll at the Dar es Salaam Embassy was 11 people killed and 72 wounded. The Embassy in Dar was located in a less populated area than the one in Nairobi.

Less than ten minutes after the explosion, we were in the AMREF Information Centre watching the news, on both Kenya National Television and CNN. It was reported the two Embassies had been bombed, resulting in extensive damage with loss of life and many injuries. Immediately, I thought of my wife. Every Friday morning, Ina took dance classes in a downtown studio adjacent to the Nairobi National Theatre and across the street from the Norfolk Hotel. She was less than a kilometre as the crow flies from the Embassy. If we could feel the blast out at Wilson Airport, and hearing of extensive damage in downtown Nairobi, my concern for Ina was only natural. With no way of getting in contact, there was little I could do in the aftermath. My focus turned to what AMREF could immediately do to help those injured.

Everyone at our headquarters was rushing about with countless ideas about the type of help we could offer. Some made sense, others didn't. What became evident was that a logical plan needed to be quickly devised for our response, one that would maximize AMREF's resources to the fullest extent. By 11:00 o'clock, we had rounded up fifteen doctors and a number of nurses for a short meeting in the conference room.

After a few minutes, a three-phased plan of action was agreed upon (a fourth component was later added but that was for a less immediate need). The first step was to get our Flying Doctors Emergency Evacuation teams down to the bombsite as quickly as possible to assist with the injured. Fortunately, they were way ahead of us. At the first report of an explosion, our highly capable and experienced Emergency Evacuation Coordinator, Dr. Bettina Vadera, had mobilized her teams and they were already on site. So within fifteen minutes of the blast, the AMREF evacuation team was there.

And for the next three days, that team worked day and night. Initially, they worked alongside a number of Kenyan organizations. By the next day, emergency teams had flown in from Israel, Europe, and the United States. When bumping into Bettina late that Friday afternoon as she came back to AMREF to pick up more supplies, I had never observed her so shaken and pale. With all her experience, nothing had prepared her for the type of devastation brought about by the bombing. But when asked if she needed to rest for a while, her response was "We'll rest when all the injured are cared for."

In our quick analysis, the next great need after on-site care and evacuation of the injured was to assist nearby hospitals. Within a short time, the local hospitals would be inundated with emergency patients and few, if any, had the human resources to cope with such a disaster. The AMREF group of doctors and nurses were divided into three teams and dispatched to Kenyatta National, Mater Miseracordia, and Nairobi Hospital. They worked continuously at those three facilities throughout the weekend and into the first part of the next week, assisting each hospital's in-house staff.

It was anticipated that blood would be in short supply and we agreed that as our third course of action, a blood drive was crucial. Some of our laboratory staff wanted to go out and help the hospitals in the collection of blood. But after discussion, we agreed that the best course of action would be to set up a blood collection centre right at AMREF's headquarters at Wilson Airport. With high rates of HIV\AIDS in Kenya, blood collections and transfusions were often looked upon by potential donors with suspicion, whether deserved or not. AMREF's reputation was of a high standing and it was felt that if we ourselves set up and controlled the blood drive, people would respond quickly and without fear. This proved to be totally accurate.

Under the direction of Dr. Jane Carter, head of AMREF's laboratory programme and assisted by Dr. Vinand Nantulya, the entire first floor of the headquarters building was turned into a blood screening and collection centre. As a blood bank specialist, my wife, who by 12:00 noon had been able to make her way to AMREF (uninjured), assisted Jane and Vinand.

Just before 12:30 pm, the first donor had been screened and was on a table giving blood. Word spread rapidly on television, over the radio, and by word of mouth that AMREF had become a blood collection point. The response was remarkable. By 2:00 pm, the lines were long, with people coming from everywhere in the Nairobi environs, young and old, from every walk of life. From the Moi Secondary School across Langata Road from Wilson Airport, the entire senior class came to donate. There were Africans, Asians, and Europeans. The lines became so long that prospective donors waited for hours. But they waited. Our assessment had been correct. The confidence factor in AMREF played an important part in the massive response. People trusted us and it was at our headquarters where they wanted to donate.

By 10:00 pm on Friday evening, over 150 pints of blood had been taken from donors, all typed and safely screened. As soon as ten to fifteen pints were collected, a regular courier service was organized to get the blood to various hospitals. By the early hours of Saturday morning, most hospitals had an adequate supply on hand. Because of limited storage facilities, they asked that we stop collecting for a while. But how could all those people who responded and wanted to help be turned away? They were not.

We decided that while collections could stop for the time being, potential donors could by typed and screened. Then when the hospitals needed more blood, individuals could be contacted and come in to AMREF to donate. A donor base would also help to identify individuals with rare blood types. By mid-day on Saturday, well over 600 people had been accommodated. In the following few days, as requests came to AMREF from the hospitals for specific or rare blood types, we were quickly able to locate such donors. No one contacted failed to come in and donate.

As people around the world witnessed on their television screens the loss of life and injuries, they too responded with great generosity. The AMREF offices in North America and Europe, and in particular the U.S. Office in New York, began to receive large numbers of contributions. Anticipating that funds would be donated, the fourth phase of our plan involved using the money where it would be most helpful. We decided that in the immediate emergency period, hospitals caring for the injured would quickly run out of medical supplies. The AMREF strategy was to use contributions from overseas to help restock the hospitals. By Tuesday, we had raised over £260,000 and more was to be received in the weeks ahead. Within a day, supplies were located and purchased, first locally and then from abroad. These were dispersed to various hospitals. In all, AMREF helped restock fourteen hospitals that treated bomb victims in Nairobi and Dar es

Salaam.

With these four responses organized and implemented to deal with the shorter-term emergency, there was then time to prioritise longer-term needs. Our staff quickly recognized that many of the injured would need plastic reconstructive surgery after the initial wounds had healed. Many of those hurt suffered serious facial and eye damage caused by flying glass. Given AMREF's long tradition with reconstructive surgery, a plan was organized in concert with Kenya's Ministry of Health and a number of hospitals. Within six months, as the wounds healed, AMREF would provide a team of reconstructive surgeons to operate on the most serious cases. And if evaluating that more than one operation on a patient might be necessary, the AMREF surgeons would do a second operation when necessary about a year after the first. While retiring before the first group of surgeons carried out more then 200 operations in the first half of 1999, I left with some sense of comfort knowing that action would continue to help the most serious of the bomb blast victims.

Those few weeks in August and September of 1998 will never be forgotten by anyone even remotely affected by the bombing of the American Embassies in East Africa. In hindsight, it was the real precursor of al Qaeda terrorist activities that culminated with 9/11. Outside of Africa, television screens brought the death and destruction into the homes of millions. For those living in Kenya and Tanzania, many of us came away with personal memories that will keep those days always in the forefront of our minds for years to come. Some of these memories involve acts of courage and selflessness, others of a less heroic nature.

Two days prior to the bombings, on 5 August, Ina and I attended a farewell reception at the home of the Dutch Ambassador to Kenya. He was about to leave for another posting. At the evening's end, after saying goodbye to our hosts, we met the American Ambassador, Prudence Bushnell, waiting on the veranda for her car to be brought around. Saying hello and making some small talk, the conversation then somehow turned to America as the land of opportunity, and specifically opportunities for women. The Ambassador proudly spoke of her diplomatic appointment and career. Ina, whose family came to the United States as displaced persons after World War Two, mentioned that she was fortunate to have become a naturalized American Citizen and the fact that America provided her, as a poor immigrant, with free education right through her graduation from the City University of New York. Listening to the two of them, one could easily sense each had similar feelings of gratitude towards the country of their citizenship.

It was ironic that so shortly after this discussion with the Ambassador highlighting the advantages of being an American, the bombings took place.

Flying glass injured Ambassador Bushnell, who was at a meeting in the nearby Kenya Cooperative Bank building that Friday morning. With luck, her facial wounds were not serious. But as the United States Ambassador to Kenya, I safely predicted she was to undergo in the weeks and months to come, the most trying period in her life. In the immediate aftermath of the Embassy bombing, there was some serious political and public relations fallout. While this was partly caused by insensitive U.S. State Department policies and to a certain extent by bad advice from her advisors, Ambassador Bushnell held up incredibly well and did an admirable job in the most trying of circumstances.

Reactions by the Kenyan public cannot be forgotten and were a testament to the true "harambee" spirit of pulling together. Directly following the bombings, those uninjured near the site rushed to help. Private cars and matatus became ambulances for getting the injured to hospitals. For days afterwards, volunteers worked around the clock with professional teams to find bodies buried under the rubble and, on a few occasions, to free a few who miraculously were still alive. People gave, whether it was donating blood, money, or services.

To many in Kenya, the official American response appeared less than "harambee" like. Kenyans viewed everything the Americans did in the context of the 258 people killed and the more than 5,000 injured. Of the 258 who died, 246 were Kenyans. Of the more than 5,000 injured, 99 per cent were Kenyans. The Kenyans were all innocent bystanders of an action directed not against Kenya, but against America.

As they were trained, American marines assigned to the Embassy sealed off what remained of the building following the blast. As people in the vicinity rushed to help at the three buildings most seriously damaged, the Bank, Ufindi, and the Embassy, the U.S. Marines kept them away from the latter at gunpoint. Of course, in the chaos of the situation, Kenyans could not understand why the Marines acted the way they did when they were trying to help, as they helped at the other two buildings.

When the Marines' action caused a public outcry, the U.S. Embassy issued a statement to the effect that they were only trying to keep looters away. This incensed Kenyans even further. The Embassy was now referring to people trying to be of help as looters. It was pointed out that if looting were a primary concern of those trying to be helpful, the Kenya Cooperative Bank building would have been a more likely choice to be targeted. It appeared the U.S. Embassy statement was a slap in the face to Kenyans.

The Embassy spokespeople made a serious mistake. Instead of explaining that the Marines were acting as they were trained to do and that there were possibilities of further explosions and more injuries, they described the actions as protecting U.S. property from looters. It was a bad error in judgment that the Embassy tried to rectify in the days to come. But the harm had been done. For Kenyans, the initial explanation was like adding insult to injury. And this was not the only insensitive action on the part of the U.S. Government.

In the early hours of Saturday morning, the day after the bombing, it was reported that two injured American Embassy staff were air evacuated to Johannesburg, South Africa. The State Department had chartered a large South African transport plane in Johannesburg. It flew from there to Nairobi, picked up the two Americans, immediately turned around, and flew back to South Africa. The patients were taken to a South African hospital for emergency surgery.

The two Embassy staff members were indeed fortunate. They were given the best medical treatment available on the African continent. But the episode looked somewhat different when viewed through Kenyan eyes.

The Kenyan press and population were quick to point out that most of the dead and injured were not Americans but Kenyans. The bombing had targeted American interests, not Kenyan ones. So how did it look when a huge airplane, capable of carrying well over a hundred people, flies back to Johannesburg with only two wounded Americans on board? Another public relations disaster for the U.S. Government. With any common sense, it would have been a tremendous good will gesture to evacuate or at least offer to evacuate, a hundred of the most seriously injured Kenyans along with the two Americans. The second instance of insensitivity within twenty-four hours. And a third was to take place a few days later.

In the following week, the United States' State Department issued a travel advisory for American citizens. It warned Americans that because of the dangers that exist in Kenya, they should stay away. Tourism has always been among the three most important earners of foreign exchange in Kenya, along with exports of tea and coffee. The tourist industry was crucial to the Kenyan economy. In 1998, it had just started to see an upturn after suffering a setback due to internal political problems and tribal clashes the year before.

A travel advisory would definitely have had serious economic repercussions for Kenya. It appeared to many that the U.S. Government was unduly punishing the country since it had only been an innocent victim of political terrorism. The official American response was viewed in Kenya as the third phase of insensitive actions, given the large numbers of blameless Africans killed and injured. It took some time and a large public outcry, but the travel advisory was eventually lifted. To many Africans, the overall American response to the Embassy bombings, both in the immediate aftermath and in the longer term, did not reflect well on the United States Government.

Many in Nairobi had a personal connection to those injured or killed in the bombing, either as family members, friends, or casual acquaintances. I was personally saddened by the deaths of two Embassy staff members, one American and one Kenyan. Julian Bartlett was the U.S. Consul General at the Embassy in Nairobi. While only having met him once, and briefly at that, Mr. Bartlett and his teen-aged son were killed on 7 August. The Consul General's position is often the most demanding in any U.S. Embassy located in a developing country, often more demanding than that of the Ambassador. Each day, hundreds of people will be lined up at the Embassy from opening to closing, hoping for a visa to enter the United States. They come for various reasons, looking to get to America as tourists, as students, as business people, or as immigrants. The Consul General has the ultimate responsibility for the Visa Section, often acting as the "court of last resort" for those trying to leave. It is a job that entails constant pressure.

During our time in Kenya, the various U.S. Consul Generals proved very helpful. Often, we would have a need for an African staff member to travel to the United States for professional meetings, or to accompany an American tourist back home on an emergency medical evacuation. The latter was always a rushed event, never knowing when such an evacuation would occur. On more than one occasion, I would be reached at home over a weekend and told of the need for one of AMREF's African nurses to travel to the U.S. with a patient. The emergency number at the U.S. Embassy would be called and the Consul General contacted. A short-term visa would be quickly issued for the AMREF nurse and the evacuation would take place as scheduled. The nurse would accompany the patient to a U.S. airport, hand over the individual to American medical personnel, and return to Kenya on the next flight. All this was made possible through the quick action of the Consul General's office at the Embassy. On learning of Julian Bartlett's death, I was reminded of all the people helped through the years by the office he represented.

*   *   *

My work actually brought me into frequent contact with the Consular section at the U.S. Embassy in Nairobi. As an American travelling repeatedly throughout Africa, visas were a major headache. Just about every country visited required U.S. passport holders to have a valid visa for entry. At times, some countries such as Sudan and Somalia, even required exit visas. On rare occasions, it was possible to acquire multiple entry visas. But these became harder to receive, as African countries preferred issuing single entry visas and collecting a visa fee for each entrance. Since an American passport was valid for ten years, within six months the pages in mine were often completely filled with stamps from various countries.

Until the mid 1990s, the U.S. Embassy in Nairobi would just add additional pages to a passport with no trouble. Then the U.S. State Department directed Embassies to discourage the addition of more pages to a passport. When pages were used up, the only alternative was to pay £27 and obtain a new passport. With the amount of travelling and all the visas required, I would have been buying new passports twice a year. Not only was this to be expensive but also a great inconvenience. The few multiple entry visas and Kenya work permit stamped in my passport would have become invalid with the constant purchasing of new passports.

To resolve this problem, I went down to the Embassy to speak with someone in the consular office. An American woman in charge that day politely informed me that the Secretary of State had issued an order to all Embassies not to provide additional pages for American passports. Explaining my problem about the need for many visas and in particular multiple entry visas, I showed her my current passport, which was the size of a small bible. Her unimpressed bureaucratic response was "Buy another passport," and away she went.

Furious, I was about to march upstairs to see the Ambassador or Consul General when a kind Kenyan woman employed at the Embassy came to the counter and asked,

"Are you Dr. Gerber from AMREF?"

"Yes, I replied.

"Is Ina Gerber your wife?"

"Yes."

"I know Mrs. Gerber. She is a nice lady. She is really trying to help Kenyans."

The United States Information Service (USIS) had an excellent library in Nairobi. Until 1995, it was open to all at no charge. Then the policy was changed and anyone wanting to use the library had to pay. For Kenyan students, the fees requested were significant and the new policy was discouraging their use of the library. Ina needed some reference material from time to time and on one visit to the library, learned of the new charges. She felt the fees were unfair to Kenyan users and went to the U.S. Embassy to present a case for reversing the charging policy.

On one of those visits, she met the Kenyan woman in the Visa Section who was now across the counter from me. Evidently, this woman was impressed with Ina's arguments on behalf of Kenyan users of the USIS Library. When hearing of my unsuccessful plea to her American colleague for additional passport pages, she quietly asked for my passport and a few minutes later, returned it with a new leaf stuck inside. Quietly, she told me to come see her in the future when more pages were required, which I always did. When relating the story of my Embassy visit to Ina, she immediately knew the woman I was talking about and concurred that she was both kind and helpful.

On 7 August, the Visa Section at the U.S. Embassy was one of the most seriously damaged in the bomb blast. Besides the Consul General, at least three other staff members were killed. On hearing this news, Ina and I immediately thought of the kind Kenyan woman who had been so helpful and hoped she was still alive. Our first thoughts turned to making inquiries as to her condition but we realized that neither of us knew her name. So when things quieted down a little, we did follow up and after describing her to some of the surviving embassy staff, it was learned that the woman had been killed.

Both of us wanted to do something for her family. A general fund had been set up to receive contributions for those killed and injured. However, we discovered that she had no family. There was only a boy she had adopted who lived with her. We tracked him down at her flat. He was a secondary school student. To ensure he could continue his education, we made a special contribution through the Embassy. It continues to sadden me that we never learned the name of our kind Kenyan friend until after her death.

Within two months after the bombings, we departed Kenya to begin the next phase of our lives. Going away was not easy as our home, many friends, wonderful memories, and the beauty of the continent were all left behind. But I knew it was not to be the end of my relationship with Africa. There were job offers that could have been considered, both full time and on a consulting basis which would have kept us there. I had no interest in taking on further paid employment at this time. Being "retired" had a rather nice ring to it. Yet, it was obvious that professionally, my life would continue to have some connection with both Africa and Asia. And it did. But in a voluntary capacity as a non-paid Advisor, Trustee, or member of the Board of Directors of Non-Governmental Organizations.

In re-living my "journey" from Fulbright awardee, to family Peace Corp volunteer, to a working career in the NGO world, from India to the Philippines, to Kenya and many other African countries, it was evident that I had formed impressions and opinions – impressions about the types of people working in the development field, opinions about what works and what doesn't work to help poor people, primarily in Africa. And there are views about the large government and non-governmental organizations that feel they are making valuable contributions towards alleviating poverty.

Now, in my second career as a "volunteer" Trustee, I have come to see the inner workings of an NGO from the other side of the fence. In serving as Chief

Executive of a non-profit agency and reporting to a Board of Directors, much time was taken up receiving advice (often unsolicited) from, catering to, and battling with, the volunteer Trustees. In reality, many were wonderful people, dedicated and committed. A few, though, were real pains. Now as a volunteer Trustee, I could only hope that I am not in the "pain in the rear " category. But serving in this capacity provided additional valuable insights into the world of non-profit organizations working in developing countries.

What are these insights, views, opinions, and potential solutions that have evolved from both a working and voluntary perspective over the past three plus decades?

BOOK THREE

THE "BUSINESS" OF DEVELOPMENT: THE ACTORS AND THE ISSUES

CHAPTER 39

THE CAST OF CHARACTERS

In the summer of 1995, an NGO undertook a job search to replace its recently departed Executive Director. The charity had its offices in a large metropolitan city but only implemented projects overseas in developing countries. Generating financial resources to support the projects was the Executive Director's primary responsibility. The Board of Directors hired a young man in his early thirties. Roger Smyth was bright, aggressive, thorough, domineering, self-confident, persistent like a bulldog, and best of all, knew everything. And Roger was definitely not shy about telling others that he knew everything. All in all, a number of the above qualities were actually not detrimental for someone whose main task was to raise money.

Roger had graduated with honours from a prestigious university and then went on to take employment with a company in the private sector. Never having lived or worked in Asia, Africa, or Latin America, he was nevertheless hired to head this charity. Lack of any experience abroad was not going to prove a handicap for Roger.

Within a few weeks on the job, he undertook a review of all donors who were contributing or had contributed to the charity. As a fundraising endeavour, each year Board members were asked to do a mailing to friends and acquaintances. In reviewing the mailing lists, Roger noticed that a former donor was a prominent member of an extremely famous and wealthy family. This multi-multi millionairess had been on the mailing list of an ex-Trustee who left the charity's Board a few years before Roger was appointed. The rich woman had not made a contribution to the charity in the previous two years.

Excited by the past association of this prominent wealthy family with his charity, Roger had no hesitation in attempting to solicit additional contributions. He was determined to do so even though contact with the woman had always been made by the former Board member. Roger had never met and did not know this ex-Trustee.

So one day, he addressed a letter to the Foundation that had been established many years ago by the wealthy family:

"Dear Mrs. Millionairess:

My name is Roger Smyth and I am the new Executive Director of the charity you have generously supported in the past. In reviewing the files, I have noticed that in the last two years, your foundation has not made a contribution. Our efforts in the developing countries have only been possible through the generous support of individuals such as yourself. I sincerely hope you will again see fit to support our work.

Enclosed you will find our latest annual report. Thanking you in advance for your continued support.

> Sincerely,
> Roger Smyth
> Executive Director

P.S. Charles Shadduck sends his warmest regards."

As one can probably surmise, Charles Shadduck was the charity's former Board member who knew and solicited contributions from the multi-millionairess. Just because Roger did not know Mr. Shadduck or ever had any contact with him did not prove to be an obstacle in passing on Mr. Shadduck's warmest regards to the very wealthy woman.

About two weeks later, a letter was received from the office of the wealthy family's Foundation.

"Dear Mr. Smyth:

Thank you for your recent solicitation letter addressed to Mrs. Millionairess. I regret to inform you that Mrs. Millionairess passed away two years ago.

> Sincerely,
> Faith Smart
> President
> Wealthy Family Foundation.

P.S. By the way, thank you for Charles Shadduck's regards. You might like to know that Charles was a prominent guest at Mrs. Millionairess' funeral."

True to character, this setback left Roger undaunted. His career lasted three years with the charity, during which time he never hesitated to exhibit his aggressive tactics or impart knowledge based on little experience to highly trained developing country professionals. Not unlike the FAO expert used to the niceties of Rome and five star hotels, Roger's trips to the developing world were centred around his creature comforts at Hilton-like hotels in capital cities. Visits to remote field projects were abhorred. Roger represented a special breed of NGO worker, *the Dilettante Development Expert.*

Although "Rogers" are not unknown in the NGO world, fortunately they are the exception rather than the rule. But the milieu of charitable organizations does tend to attract some interesting people, especially among those who volunteer their time. These are often Board Directors or Trustees. Many can often be described as "characters."

A friend who served as President of another international NGO told me about a "special" Board member he had to deal with. His characterization of this particular person was summed up as *The Mysterious Contributor.* This type of person, in some cases a Trustee, in others a loyal supporter, usually well liked and popular, is someone who never quite reveals the whole story about themselves. He or she has a knack for allowing questions to be raised about their motives and actions, which can at times, appear to straddle the fence between being helpful, unhelpful, or both.

The NGO in question was an international NGO, headquartered in North America and with affiliated chapters in Europe. Its "Mysterious Contributor" referred to here as Trustee X was involved with one of the NGO's chapters in Europe. Travelling frequently, from time to time he would show up at the NGO's headquarters carrying a brown paper bag stuffed with money.

"I have raised some money for you," Trustee X said to the NGO's President.

"Thank you but I have not yet heard from the Finance Director about your contribution."

"No, here it is," as Trustee X handed over a brown paper bag filled with cash.

"Thank you. We better count it together so you can be issued with an official receipt."

After an hour of counting small bills, most of which were in denominations of twenties, tens, fives, and ones, the President said,

"We'll have the Finance Director present you with a receipt immediately."

It could have been worse. The £5,000 could have come in sacks full of coins. The explanation for the cash in this case was that it had been raised at a charity concert in Trustee X's country. But with international bank wires an easy and safe way to transfer money, why deliver it in cash in a paper bag?

My friend was never able to get a logical answer to this last question. And yes, a few more brown paper bags were still delivered. It was not rare for other NGOs to have their own "Mysterious Contributors."

In fact, there are "Less Mysterious, Mysterious Contributors." It is not uncommon for a charitable organization to receive a gift from an anonymous donor, usually received through the donor's attorney. An important reason for an anonymous gift is that the donor does not want his or her name in the public domain. This prevents other charities from soliciting the person. Another possibility, believe it or not, is that some individuals have small egos and do not seek recognition. These types are rare. Anonymous gifts open up one other avenue for thought. Not knowing who the donor is does not allow for determining if the source of the donation is legitimate or not. Could someone actually want to "launder money" by giving it to an NGO? Nah!

For every "sinner" there is always a *Saint*. Many charitable organizations have one. This person is either a member of staff or serves as a volunteer on the Board of Directors. She/he often comes from a well to do and/or a well-connected family and seems to know everybody. If the person does work for the charity, salary is never an issue. Personal gain and comforts are not important to her/him.

The Saint is like Mother Teresa without the vows but even better. Mother Teresa took strong stands against certain things and was quite outspoken about issues she was against, like birth control. The charity's Saint takes no position on anything, or at least never openly expresses an opinion. She/he publicly never has a bad word against anybody or anything. For her/him, the sun is always shining and everything is always rosy.

Totally dedicated, committed and with boundless energy, the Saint works long hours, weekends, and holidays without complaint. As a matter of fact, working for the charity is like an addiction for this person. She/he can never get enough.

Having a Saint on board can be a blessing for any charity. There is still a downside. Loving everyone equally and never being able to say no, the Saint takes on endless tasks and creates a great deal of work, only some of which is constructive. Because of the person's good nature and always wanting to please, the charity at times finds itself involved with things that can be tangential or unessential. It then becomes necessary for someone to clean up after the person. But who can reprimand a Saint? Perhaps only God. Cleaning up was just a small price to pay for all the good she/he does.

One easily recognizable "character" is the charity's *Old Timer*. She or he can trace their roots back to the beginning days of the NGO, often right to the birth. The founder or founders might have been their friends but it was more likely she/he would have been the young disciple of a charismatic leader. Now in their 70s or 80s, she/he is the last of the original volunteers. Keen of mind, prominent, well connected, respected, and regal in bearing, the Old Timer is the repository of an NGO's history. Younger Board members (basically all Board members are younger) treat her/him with deference.

The Old Timer can take one of two forms. The first is *The Royal Personage*. This form of Old Timer is often soft spoken, reserved, remaining more in the background than in the forefront. She/he exercises influence quietly, allowing her/his reputation and years of experience with the charity to speak for her/him. Without deliberately calling attention to herself/himself, she/he has a presence that is obvious.

The second form of Old Timer is *The Star of the Show*. Staying in the background is not for this person. She/he wants everyone to know and understand that she/he is the center of the universe. Personal appearance is very important. While taking on the mantle of humility and equality, it is obvious that in this person's mind there are different levels of equals. The Star of the Show's ego can be large and she/he loves to be fawned over by people.

For both the Royal Personage and Star of the Show, the charity is often synonymous with their lives. As volunteers, they have devoted long years to its service. Their commitment and dedication are to be admired.

The Star of the Show tends to highly personalize her/his relationship with the organization. In some ways, she/he feels that because of her/his lengthy service and connections to its beginning, she/he actually owns it. It is "her or his" NGO and she/he often describes it that way. Her/his relationship to many of the staff is a "motherly or fatherly" one. The staff are their children, especially those individuals who have worked for the organization for a long time. The Star of the Show has a special concern for the long serving staff.

And projects are "their projects." If she/he raises the money (and the Star of the Show does raise a lot of money) for a specific project, it is hers/his. She/he has proprietary rights and without hesitation, gets deeply involved. This involvement creates headaches for the professionals and management. The Star of the Show is not a professional. Her/his involvement often borders on interference. But how can you tell this person that she/he is causing problems for the professionals? Only with a lot of tact. The Chief Executive of the charity needs patience and great diplomatic skills to handle the Star of the Show. It is often a job unto itself.

Not being a professional, the Star of the Show is often intractable when it comes to change. In her/his eyes, the charity is exactly as it was when it was founded many years ago. Never mind that it might have grown a hundred fold in terms of employees, budget, and areas of operation, to her/him it is still the small little family group that she/he knew at the start. The Star of the Show becomes uncomfortable as the environment changes although she/he doesn't admit to being so. Rather than deal with reality, she/he just continues functioning as if nothing has changed.

But no matter how exasperating the Star of the Show can make life for professional staff members, you cannot help but love her/him. Because beneath the flamboyance, bravado, and ego, there is a person who really cares about helping others. And their caring is genuine. She/he has dedicated their life to the charity without ever wavering. And in a time of crises, they will always be there. It is almost impossible not to have admiration for both The Royal Personage and the Star of the Show.

* * *

Because the nature of a charitable organization lends itself to a mix of paid professional staff and volunteers, the line of responsibility between the two groups sometimes becomes clouded. Volunteer involvement with a charity is not unlike certain imposed interventions by some parents in western countries in the affairs of their childrens' schools. Teachers are often challenged by parents (if not challenged directly by the kids they teach) and told how to do their jobs. It seems as if everyone is an expert teacher, with or without a teaching license. Few people without a medical degree would claim to know how to practice medicine and patients rarely question what their doctors tell them, or do to them.

A charitable organization is more like a school setting than a doctor's office or hospital. It is often the case that certain volunteers who have a lot of time and energy to devote to the organization, without hesitation get heavily caught up in the day-to-day running of the NGO, much to the chagrin of its professional staff. The extreme case of such involvement is represented by *The Dominator*.

The Dominator is a person who might have retired from his or her professional career at a fairly young age (mid-fifties). She/he would have enjoyed a senior position and a lot of responsibility within her/his company. The Dominator would have been successful at what she/he did and in retirement, well off financially. With time on her/his hands, she/he looks for new interests and serving as a volunteer Board Trustee on a charity is one way to stay active.

Starting off slowly at first, the Dominator gets more and more involved and often becomes an officer of the charity, perhaps serving as Chairperson or Vice-Chairperson of the Board or heading a Board committee. Because she/he has free time on her/his hands, the Dominator tends to frequently show up at the charity's offices.

At first, the Chief Executive Officer of the charity is encouraged with the assistance offered by this Board Trustee. Over time, however, the Dominator becomes more and more involved with staff functions and in essence, operates as a non-paid staff person. The line separating responsibilities for volunteer trustees and the paid senior staff seems to disappear.

It makes for both a delicate and difficult relationship. It is not easy for the Chief Executive to tell her/his Chairperson or Board Trustee that she/he is stepping over the line and interfering where she/he should not. The relationship usually deteriorates and one or the other leaves, more often than not the paid Chief Executive after letting the Dominator know what he or she really thinks of the Trustee.

Many charities have similar characters to the ones described above associated with their organizations. But it is not unusual to find a character within an NGO that is one of a kind, a unique individual. AMREF had such a person affiliated with it, code named *The Red Baroness*. Had the person been a male, he would have been the *Red Baron*.

From a noble family, the Baroness was on the Board of Directors of one of AMREF's European affiliates in the early 1980s. Besides serving AMREF as a volunteer Board member, the Baroness had a full time job. She worked for her government's official organization for overseas development. This organization was a European equivalent of the U.S. Agency for International Development or the Canadian International Development Agency (CIDA). These official aid agencies provide public funding to developing country governments, universities, and NGOs for projects in Asia, Africa, and Latin America. The Baroness' government was heavily involved in a number of African countries.

In true liberal fashion, the Baroness' agency supported a number of causes that more conservative governments at the time, such as the United States, did not openly support. She was in charge of providing quiet and sometimes not so quiet funding to national liberation movements in Africa. A number of African countries had revolutionary groups fighting against the established governments. These included the Sudanese Liberation People's Army (SPLA) in Sudan, FRELIMO in Mozambique, the African National Congress (ANC) in South Africa, and SWAPO in Namibia. The goals of these revolutionary movements were to overthrow the established governments in their countries and take over power. During the cold war period, many of these movements were associated with the Soviet Bloc.

In the 1970s and early 1980s, most western government aid agencies provided funding to established governments for infrastructure development, health, education, water, refugees, and disaster relief. Supporting and fomenting revolutions was not within the mandate of USAID or CIDA. That was left to clandestine agencies like the CIA. But in this European country, there were no covert policies. Everything was out in the open and official. AMREF's Board member, the Baroness, proudly and publicly gave away money to the revolutionaries. Hence, she was dubbed *The Red Baroness*.

CHAPTER 40

GOD WILL PROVIDE OR IF NOT, THEN MARIE ANTOINETTE

During the mid-1980s, many countries along the Rift Valley in Africa were suffering from serious drought. For a few years, there had been little rainfall and countries from Ethiopia to Zimbabwe experienced severe food shortages. In Kenya, its Eastern Province was acutely affected.

Like most poor subsistence farmers, Emmanuel Musyoka had great problems coping during the years when the rains failed. Emmanuel had a wife and five children. He was hardworking, honest, religious, and devoted to his family. While the Musyokas had very little and seemed to scrape by year after year, Emmanuel was always able to ensure the children had food on the table. And while he and his wife were both illiterate, Emmanuel saved every shilling he could to ensure that school fees were always paid for the five kids.

But the drought of the mid-1980s posed great problems. Crops in Eastern Province had failed for two years. Not only was there little to eat, nothing was left over to sell. Emmanuel was distraught at the thought of his children being turned away from school because he could not pay the tuition. The situation became so desperate that the family was forced to eat the seeds that would have been planted for the following year's crop.

Being a devoutly religious person, in desperation and as a last resort Emmanuel turned to God. Deciding to appeal directly for divine intervention, Emmanuel called over his oldest son, who was eleven.

"I want you to get your school notepad and a pencil and bring them here," he told the boy.

Being respectful and obedient, the son went and fetched what his father required.

245

"Sit down," said Emmanuel. "I want to send a letter to God and you will write it for me. I will tell you what to write."

While the boy was puzzled at what his father was asking of him, he nevertheless sat down at a small table with his pencil in hand.

"Address the letter 'Dear God in Heaven:' and write the following," dictated Emmanuel.

"Dear God. This is your faithful servant Emmanuel appealing to you as a last resort. My family goes to church every Sunday and we pray to you faithfully. We have brought up our children in a religious way. God, there has been no rain for two years. My crops have withered in the field. We have had to eat the seeds and now there is nothing to prepare for the next planting. My children will soon have nothing at all to eat and they will not be able to go to school. Dear God, please listen to my plea. I do not know what else to do. I urgently need 100 shillings to buy new seeds to plant and some food for my children. Please, please God, with your love for all mankind and generosity, please send me 100 shillings. I will anxiously be waiting for your response."

After dictating these words to his son, Emmanuel told the boy to sign the letter,

"Your faithful servant, Emmanuel Musyoka"

"Now go get an envelope," Emmanuel told the boy. When the child returned, Emmanuel asked him to address the letter "To God in Heaven" and to put the family's farm as the return address. He then told the boy to take the letter to the post office in Machakos town and mail it.

The boy walked more than six kilometres to Machakos town, bought a stamp, posted the letter and returned home.

The next morning, one of the post office workers was sorting the mail. In the large stack of letters, he came across one that was addressed "To God in Heaven." Never having seen such an address before and therefore puzzled, he called over his fellow workers. They were as perplexed as he was but their curiosity got the better of them. Everyone was urging that the letter be opened so they could see what was inside.

One of the postal workers opened the envelope and read the contents to his fellow employees. After hearing what Emmanuel had written, they all burst out laughing.

"What a stupid farmer," the workers exclaimed. "Can you image that man believing he could write a letter to 'God in Heaven' asking for money and expecting God to send it to him? That farmer is a complete idiot." And they all continued to laugh hysterically at the letter.

At that moment, the post office supervisor walked in. He saw all the workers standing around in various states of amusement. No one was working; everyone was just laughing.

Curious as to what was going on, the supervisor went over to the workers. "Why are you all laughing so hard?" he asked.

"Look at this letter," they replied. "Have you ever seen anything so stupid? Can you imagine a farmer actually writing a letter to God asking for money?"

The supervisor took the letter and read it. When he finished, there was a solemn look on his face.

"You all should be ashamed of yourselves," the supervisor told his workers. "You are enjoying yourselves at the expense of this poor farmer who in his desperation, has written to God as a last resort. The man is only concerned about his wife and children. And all of you are standing around laughing and making fun of him. You are heartless."

Hearing these words from their supervisor had an immediate effect on the men. They stopped laughing and began to realize they had been foolish. The supervisor was right, this poor farmer was desperate and was asking for money as a last resort.

"I have an idea," said one of the men. "Why don't we take up a collection and send some money to Emmanuel?" Reaching into his pocket, he found sixteen shillings. "I will contribute all I have today. Here is my sixteen shillings to start the collection."

"I have twenty shillings to donate," proclaimed another. "Here are my fifteen shillings said a third." And on it went, with each worker and the supervisor contributing everything they had with them. At the end of the collection, the post office workers had come up with an amount of eighty-nine shillings.

"Get an envelope," said one of the men. When it was brought over, he put the money into the envelope, addressed it to "Emmanuel Musyoka, Farmer" and listed the return address as "God in Heaven." They put a stamp on it and gave it to the postal delivery person. The next day, the envelope was delivered to Emmanuel's farm.

Upon receiving the envelope but not being able to read what was on it, he again called over his son.

"What is on this envelope?" asked Emmanuel.

"It is addressed to you," said the boy "and the return address is from 'God in Heaven'."

Emmanuel was now extremely happy and excited and urged his son to open the envelope. The boy did so and poured the contents out onto the table. Seeing the shilling notes, Emmanuel was amazed and immediately started counting the money. After completing his count, a startled and confused look came over his face. He counted the money again, but his puzzlement remained. Then he asked his son to again fetch his school notepad and another envelope.

"I want you to write a second letter for me" said Emmanuel. "Again address the letter 'To God in Heaven:' and I will tell you what to write."

Emmanuel now dictated a second letter.

"Dear God in Heaven:

This is your faithful servant Emmanuel writing to you once more. God, I really hate to bother you a second time after you have been so generous to me. I knew you would listen to the pleas of a poor desperate farmer. My family is so happy that you have graced us with your benevolence. But there is a problem, God, that you should know about and that is the only reason I am bothering you once more.

You are all knowing and powerful and it is not the place of a poor farmer like myself to give God advice. But I must share something with you to avoid any mistakes in the future. God, the next time you want to help me and send me money, please do not send it through the post office. I know you sent me the 100 shillings I had requested but only eight-nine came. Those post office guys are GOD DAMN ROBBERS.

Your faithful servant, Emmanuel Musyoka"

A Filipino version of this often repeated story was told to me for the first time by Dr. Juan Flavier, who was serving as President of an NGO, the International Institute of Rural Reconstruction. In 1993, Juan was named by Fidel Ramos, the then President of the Philippines, as the country's Secretary of Health. He was later elected to the Philippine Senate where he now serves. Juan was a great fundraiser and he used the above story to illustrate the old mentality of some charities wherein "God will provide."

*   *   *

Even in the year 2006, there are a few involved in the "charity world" who would like to believe that you just look to the heavens for support and the money drops down. Unfortunately, it doesn't work that way. Today, while the hundreds of western NGOs working around the world are non-profit organizations, they are run more like business enterprises than the old volunteer charities. Overseas development work has become a very big business – with hundreds of millions of dollars generated annually by NGOs from governments, international organizations, foundations, corporations, and individuals. It is big business indeed.

Still, every so often, the charitable saviour does seem to reappear. In the

Daily Nation, one of Kenya's leading English language newspapers, a headline on 31 January 2006 read **"For Starving Children of Kenya, 42 Tons of Dog Food...."** It seemed as if the modern day version of Marie Antoinette was coming to the rescue.

For the past two years, Kenya (as well as a number of other countries in Africa) has been suffering its worst drought since the previously described period of 1982 to 1985. There had been no serious rains until a few months ago and the nomadic pastoralists who inhabit the remote semi-arid regions in the north and northeast of the country have been most adversely affected. To help alleviate the shortage of food, enter the reincarnation of Marie Antoinette.

Marie Antoinette, wife of King Louis XVI of France, at a time just prior to the French Revolution, when informed that the people of Paris were starving because there was no bread, supposedly responded to this news by saying **"Let them eat cake."**

In January 2006, a New Zealand woman, when hearing of starving children in northern Kenya, responded by saying **"Let them eat dog food."**

The founder of a New Zealand dog food company seriously wanted to come to the aid of Kenyan children by sending them 42 tons of dog food. When hearing about the drought from the daughter of a friend who had just visited Kenya, she proposed shipping the dog food in powdered form, which could then be mixed with water. The woman claimed that the powder was full of nutrients and was quoted in the Daily Nation as saying "it tastes yummy" and stated she sprinkled some on her porridge every morning as a pick-me-up.

Reaction to the charitable offer from Kenyans was swift. The next day, the newspaper reported one Minister in charge of relief operations saying "It was an insult for somebody to think that Kenya can accept food meant for animals." There was a public outcry and outrage as to what was regarded as an insult to Kenya.

An official from an international aid agency summed up the essence of this strange offer in a few words. He said, "Kenyans are dignified and proud people and we are concerned at the message it sends if they do find out that children are being fed the same ingredients as dog food. While it is a well-meaning impulse, we are concerned it is sending the wrong message." I believe that the words "well meaning impulse" succinctly capture the honest but poorly thought out solutions of many who see a quick fix to serious development problems.

What is the real message here? Perhaps none? Or, maybe handouts do not work? These were two stories – one possibly funny, one strange. Charity doesn't help the poor climb out of poverty. From whatever source (God, New Zealand, or other donors) or in whatever form (money or food but hopefully not dog food), giving out and creating dependency is no answer. To alleviate poverty, people must participate in a process that allows them to help themselves. How many times have we heard the old adage "Give a man a fish and he will have one meal; help him learn how to fish and he can eat for life."? No matter how often it is repeated, some in the "aid industry" are slow learners.

CHAPTER 41

THE VULTURE CULTURE

Nothing appeals to the sentiments and pocketbooks of an average westerner more than an emotional picture of a hungry African or Asian child, except perhaps, saving the elephant, or saving whales. We are bombarded daily with thirty second television sound bites, usually aired pro-bono, showing the latest victims of famines, earthquakes, landmines, volcanic eruptions, or wars. Millions of dollars, pounds sterling, and euros are raised from countless individuals in North America and Europe in response to the latest disaster publicized by the NGOs.

Aid to the developing world has often been characterized in two ways – relief and/or development. Many of the international non-governmental organizations working overseas today, especially the older ones, began as relief operations. They were usually involved with feeding hungry people or sponsoring needy children. Only a handful of NGOs began their "lives" as true development agencies – not responding to disasters and crises but taking up activities that would lead to long-term change for the poor. As aid experts began to realize that responding only to emergencies was not the best approach to alleviating poverty, development became the vogue. Many NGOs solely involved in relief type activities realized they had better get on the development bandwagon if they were to have access to official government aid funding. So these NGOs re-evaluated their original missions and started to incorporate longer-term development projects into their portfolios along-side their traditional relief work.

The result has been a profusion of organizations that now try to do everything. They tend to become what a lawyer friend of mine jokingly referred to as "ambulance chasing NGOs," following the latest "hot issue" and running after whatever the donors are favouring at the moment. While in the past they might have built up a professional expertise in food distribution or child welfare, today they become instant experts in HIV/AIDS, or water and sanitation, or malaria eradication, or urban decay, or refugees, or microcredit, or whatever else the World Bank or USAID or the European Union deems the problem of the year. Sadly, too many of these organizations, in their quest to "cash in" on available funding, try to do too many things and the quality of what they do can be seriously questioned.

While the major share of development funding comes from such groups as the World Bank, the Asian Development Bank, or government bilateral donors, individuals remain the major contributors to appeals in response to catastrophes around the world. Although many NGOs have focused on moving into development, they have not abandoned their enthusiasm for responding to emergencies.

"Enthusiasm for emergencies" might sound harsh but many organizations are only too aware of how much money can be raised from the general public in times of crises. The worse the disaster, the easier the effort to appeal to millions of individuals for contributions. "Only £5 (or $5 or €5) can feed a starving child for a month," blares the quick spot on our television sets as an emaciated child stares at us from the screen. Large NGOs have their fundraising machinery geared to taking advantage of human disasters and at the first sign of problems, they spring into action. Without too much imagination, we can picture the fundraisers and publicity staff waiting around, almost hoping for the next large-scale tragedy. As a friend who worked for one of the large relief type NGOs once told me, "It is the poor and the suffering who create jobs for us."

Over the past twenty-five years, a number of NGOs have perfected their techniques for mobilizing support from individual contributors. They appeal to our emotions and our willingness to help the unfortunate. Africa provided the perfect backdrop for building fundraising machines. A case can be made that Ethiopia, with the horrific famine in that country during the early 1980s, a disaster that captured the attention of the entire world through television exposure, provided the first global opportunity to raise huge amounts of money for disaster relief. Fundraising techniques had ample opportunity to be fine-tuned when clan warfare in Somalia led to the dissolution of that country in the 1990s. Hundreds of thousands of Somalis had to flee and settle in squalid refugee camps in Kenya. Probably the greatest tragedy of all in the past two decades was the genocide in Rwanda, which began in the mid-1990s and resulted in the slaughter of up to 1 million Tutsis and moderate Hutus by the Hutu fanatics, the "Interahamwe" (translated as "those who attack together"). As the RPF, Rwanda Patriotic Front, militarily took control of the country, the Interahamwe forced millions of Hutus to flee the country with them and to settle in refugee camps in what was then the eastern part of Zaire (today the Democratic Republic of the

Congo) and western Tanzania. Tragedies such as these provided ample opportunities for NGOs to raise millions and millions of dollars.

Though the intentions of these NGOs are often noble and the generosity of individuals who contribute cannot be questioned, the responses of some organizations to emergencies can be queried. They can be queried on both political as well as financial grounds. The Rwanda crisis provided a sorry example of NGOs allowing themselves to be used as foils for those that committed the genocide in Rwanda. The NGOs became involved in the refugee camps in Zaire and Tanzania and collected millions of dollars in contributions to help many of the mass murderers that fled Rwanda.

There have been too many examples of well-meaning NGOs rushing into a crisis situation and providing relief, which is either unnecessary or unusable. How many examples do we have of foodstuff bought and transported thousands of miles and then rejected by those in need because they do not eat the wheat or the rice that has been delivered? How much of the funding is wasted because of a rush to assist without understanding what is actually needed?

The Rwanda crisis was the one example of a wrong type of rush to help that stands out in my mind above all others. When hundreds of thousands of Hutus began fleeing Rwanda in 1994, the initial influx into eastern Zaire was chaotic. The United Nations High Commissioner for Refugees and the NGOs were ill prepared to deal with the mass of humanity that came across the border from Rwanda. Huge refugee camps sprang up around the Zairian town of Goma. As in most early stages of a refugee exodus, there were very high death rates in the camps, especially among young children. This was quickly brought to the attention of the world in most part by professional appeals of NGOs appearing on television and in the press.

While in Nairobi, I remember watching CNN's coverage of the Goma situation. On the screen was a young man from Ireland, in his mid-twenties, wearing a T-shirt with the logo of the Irish NGO that he worked for on the front.[2]

---

[2] T-shirts with NGO logos are now a must, sort of the mandatory "aid worker" costume. In the old days, NGOs produced such shirts and other merchandise for the primary purpose of generating income through sales of these items to the general public. Today the T-shirts and logos are standard attire for NGO workers in refugee camps or other emergency situations. The shirts now have the primary purposes of public relations and fundraising – extra credit is given to the NGO worker for getting onto the television screen wearing a shirt with his/her NGO's logo. If one looked closely at the television war coverage of U.S. Marines landing on the beach in Mogadishu, Somalia in 1992, there appeared to have been some people wearing NGO T-shirts standing right next to the CNN cameraman.

What struck me about the Irish NGO worker being interviewed on CNN were the tears streaming down his cheeks. He was visibly upset and shaken. The tears were real. When asked what kind of work he and his colleagues were doing in the camps, his reply was "we are burying the dead." That task had taken a terrible emotional toll on the Irish relief worker.

After seeing this news brief and sympathizing with the young man, I could not help but ask myself, "What is an Irish guy doing thousands of miles away from Ireland burying dead in Zaire?" It seems that his NGO's immediate response to the humanitarian crisis in Rwanda was to fly planeloads of young Irish people to help bury dead in Goma. Were there not enough Africans to bury the dead? Could that Irish agency not have used its resources in a more productive manner? The answer to both of these questions was, of course, "Yes." But I am sure that the picture of the young Irish worker on television with tears streaming down his face and dead bodies in the background was worth millions of pounds when used for fundraising purposes back in Ireland.

The previously mentioned maxim of "giving a man a fish means he has one meal; teaching him to fish allows him to continuously feed himself" really points out the difference between relief and development. The first is a quick fix. The latter, a slower process taking much more time and commitment. For NGOs, the first is easier to sell. Feeding a child tugs at our emotions; it makes for a good television spot. The latter is less dramatic, takes time, and presents more challenges for raising money.

The laws of nature, with continuous cycles of life and death, ensure that the vulture will never lack for its next meal. They are patient birds, sitting and waiting for something bad to happen to some poor creature. And then they eat. For the fundraisers in those NGOs that are in business to respond to catastrophes – natural or manmade – the "laws of human nature" basically guarantee that something bad will happen sooner or later. Then money-raising machines can spring into life.

CHAPTER 42

THE DEVELOPMENT BUSINESS

There are a number of avenues open to those who want to volunteer their services in the developing countries. Just about all of the western industrialized nations, as well as Japan, have organizations that recruit people willing to work without a salary. The United States Peace Corps is one of the most well known of these agencies but Britain's VSO, Canada's CUSO, the Netherlands' Voluntary Service, and Japan's Overseas Volunteers all run programmes similar to the Peace Corps. Even the United Nations has a voluntary service.

Most of the above tend to cater to younger people, in their twenties and thirties with limited work experience. In reality, there are no age limits and from time to time, older volunteers will be enlisted. But to take advantage of experienced, retired professionals, specialized NGOs were created in Great Britain, Canada, and the United States. These NGOs were set up primarily with funding from official government aid agencies in the above countries – namely DFID, CIDA, and USAID. Established as retired executive voluntary services, they also solicit contributions from private companies to supplement government funding. Taking advantage of a pool of retired executives who want to do more than just play golf, these NGOs usually recruit people for short-term contracts, anywhere from one to six months. The NGO organizes the consultancy assignment in a developing country and provides transport for the volunteer and his/her spouse. The host establishment, be it a private company, educational institution, or non-profit organization then provides a moderate stipend to cover the cost of the consultant's accommodation and local transport. There is no salary involved.

A good friend of mine named Sean had an interesting experience when he signed up as a volunteer with one of these retired executive service NGOs. An extremely bright and capable individual, he had been the Chief Executive of a thriving company and after making a great deal of money by his mid-forties, was able to hand the business over to someone else and retire. An active person with a private pilot's license, Sean and his wife travelled the world. Wanting to get involved with development activities primarily in Africa, he joined the Board of Directors of an NGO. However, desiring even more hands-on involvement, Sean signed on as a volunteer with his own country's retired executive service NGO.

With his qualifications and experience, the NGO welcomed Sean with open arms. In initial discussions, it was explained to Sean that there was an interesting opportunity in Romania. A factory in Bucharest with a great deal of potential was underachieving and had requested a specialist to help with reorganization and modernization. Sean accepted the assignment and was off to Romania with his wife for two months.

Six weeks later we had an interesting email from him, the gist of which went something like this:

"The project here has involved me trying to help a Romanian Gypsy with connections to both the Gypsy and Russian mafias. Both are strong in Romania. What my government is doing supporting this kind of activity remains a mystery. I have rationalized my presence here by the fact that we are building up a company that is creating new jobs for Romanians who are desperately poor and I suppose that's what it is all about. But the owner has six Mercedes and lives like an African dictator. I really think my Aid career is coming to a close and I am going to return to the nice, clean, uncomplicated world of capitalist money making."

Thus went Sean's welcome to hands-on involvement in the development business.

There is no doubt that over the past twenty-five years we have seen the emergence of a new industry – the development industry. Years ago, expatriates working overseas in the developing world happened to be engineers, or doctors, or teachers assigned abroad. Today read any article or watch television coverage about western NGOs actively working in Asia, Africa, or Latin America and it will quickly be noticed that the individuals involved with those NGOs are now commonly referred to as "Aid Workers." They are workers in the Aid Industry. No matter that the Irish lad burying bodies in a refugee camp in the former Zaire had never been outside of Ireland before. Once he was hired by his Irish NGO and shipped off to Africa in his NGO T-shirt with the "company logo," he was an instant aid worker. When asked his profession, his answer would most likely have been "aid worker." Asked for qualifications and experience, the reply would likely have been, "I am a university graduate."

It has been argued by some that western foreign aid is basically a domestic subsidy for their own country's aid industry. With the exception of the Scandinavian countries that have committed to a certain percentage of their national GNP's going towards foreign support, getting Congresses and Parliaments to obligate funds for overseas assistance is a hard sell. The argument politicians can use for not supporting an increase in foreign aid is that there is no voting constituency in their home countries to support it so they do not have to worry about taking an anti-position.

I remember in the late 1970s and early 1980s, when USAID provided large funding for projects in Sudan and Somali, some critics of the United States' aid programme argued that 90 cents of every U.S. dollar committed to foreign aid was actually spent on Americans or American products. That's right – ninety cents of each dollar went for paying American salaries, buying American vehicles that were then shipped overseas, buying American pharmaceuticals, and other U.S. products.

Working in the southern part of Sudan in 1979 with funding from the previously noted USAID grant, the stipulations in the agreement mandated that we could only purchase U.S. manufactured vehicles. As described, the southern Sudan was one of the poorest, isolated regions in all of Africa and it had been further devastated by years of civil war (the first civil war), which only came to an end in 1973. What passed for Sudanese roads was something not seen in the United States in the 20th century. Our argument was that no American vehicle manufactured for commercial use would last six months in southern Sudan. And the nearest service facility for an American vehicle was probably located in Cairo. After expressing our concerns, some wiser heads listened in Washington but the USAID officials had to go to Congress for a special waiver allowing us to purchase non-U.S. vehicles. A good argument must have been made because Congress granted the waiver and we bought European and Japanese vehicles that could survive in the Sudanese environment and at substantial cost savings. This was one occasion when less than 90 cents on the dollar from official U.S. foreign aid went for American goods and services.

Critics of U.S. foreign aid policy argued that not enough of the assistance was going to the poor who needed it. They saw that such a high percentage of U.S. investment was actually bypassing the economies of developing countries. In an ironic twist, supporters of the aid programme used the same arguments as the critics to defend American policy. They argued that rather than reform the aid programme, it should be kept as it was but with increased budgets. After all, their argument went, only ten cents on the dollar is going overseas. Ninety cents goes right into the American market. So foreign aid was really a good thing – it was a domestic subsidy for the American economy.

What a business!

CHAPTER 43

WORKING ONESELF OUT OF EXISTENCE

In the good old days, before development became a big business and the "charity mindset" still prevailed, there was a basic difference between missionaries and NGOs. If a missionary were asked what he was doing in India, or Tanzania, or Brazil, the answer would be, "I am doing God's work." And since God's work would need to go on for a very long time, if not indefinitely, missionaries always assumed they and their future generations would be overseas forever.

Thirty or forty years ago, if NGOs were asked what they were doing in India, or Tanzania, or Brazil, their answer would be somewhat different from the missionaries. The NGO answer would most likely have been, "We are here to work ourselves out of a job." The basic tenet of all NGOs was that they were working in partnership with local people to alleviate poverty and disease and improve the standard of living. Once that was accomplished, the NGO would no longer be needed and would disappear, leaving behind much improved conditions and a group of people who would be self-sufficient. Unlike the missionary vision, this was a finite mindset. Here today, hopefully gone tomorrow.

In 2007, we might ask ourselves "How many NGOs that were active in the 1960s and 1970s are no longer in existence because they worked themselves out of a job?" I would hypothesize that the answer is not too many, if any. As a matter of fact, with the growth of development as an industry, rather than a decrease, there has been a tremendous profusion of NGOs working in development, not only international ones based in the developed countries but indigenous ones in the less-developed nations as well. It could be argued that the problems are so great that "working oneself out of a job" cannot happen for the foreseeable future. The new NGO rationale for existence is now more in line with the missionary vision of an indefinite timeline.

There is too much invested in the "development business" for most NGOs, or for that matter The World Bank, or United Nations agencies such as UNDP, UNICEF, and WHO, or bilateral government donors like USAID, DFID, CIDA, DANIDA, SIDA, NORAD, JICA, etc., to willingly work themselves out of existence. While admittedly there are unlimited problems to solve in the developing world, there are also bureaucracies to sustain and jobs to maintain for all of the above institutions.

The established international NGOs that have been around for some time have gone through an evolutionary process to reach the institutionalised stages they are at today. A number were created through the vision and charisma of dynamic individuals or small groups of people. These founders had a missionary zeal (religious or non-religious) often based on the concept of voluntarism to do good and bring about change for those most in need. Their strong personalities attracted supporters and money and their organizations did commendable work from a charitable viewpoint. What they were doing at the beginning was often neither systematic nor professional but this was offset by the strong motivation to help.

It was after the passing of the first generation founders that NGOs began to evolve into the structures they are today. For many, it was a struggle. The charismatic first generation of committed individuals was interested in the activities of the NGO (the programme) but were much less concerned with how the organization was being managed. As more and more funding came in and the NGO became larger, the lack of proper systems began causing problems. Without systems there can be little accountability and when an NGO is receiving contributions from both public and private donors, accountability is crucial to its survival. The NGOs began to improve systems and hire competent professionals to manage both its programmes and systems. It would take time during this stage for the systems to catch up to the programmes. But eventually they did. And that led to the third stage – the consolidation and institutionalisation of the NGO, which is where most of the older, established ones are at present.

Without doubt the original founders were serious about helping the less fortunate to help themselves and honestly believed that the organizations they established would hopefully not be needed sometime in the future. But how do you maintain this same belief in the 3rd stage when an NGO has a staff of hundreds of employees all over the world and an annual budget of £80-£110 million? Now there needs to be as much effort devoted to maintaining what has been built as there is to implementing a programme.

If we consider many NGOs as well-established institutions, the same but even more so can be said about the international, bilateral, and U.N. agencies. While varying in size regarding the numbers of employees and resources available, most are large, entrenched bureaucracies staffed by international or national civil servants. Some have well deserved reputations for being easier to work with, having fewer bureaucratic regulations, and being able to respond fairly quickly. These are usually the favourite partners of NGOs and include the Scandinavian donors (Sweden's SIDA, Denmark's DANIDA, Norway's NORAD), Canada's CIDA, and the United Nations Children's Fund (UNICEF). At the opposite end of the scale are such organizations as the European Union (EU) and the Italian government's aid department.[3] Working in partnership with either often turns out to be an NGO's nightmare. Somewhere in the middle are agencies such as the Britain's DFID and the United States' USAID.

Even as these large funding agencies expect the NGO recipients of their money to maintain the old vision of working oneself out of a job, the likelihood of them doing the same is as far fetched as it is for the NGOs. This does not, however, stop the donors from preaching such a mantra to the NGOs. The hypocrisy is not something easy to understand.

Large international and government funders do not seem to work on the same rules of accountability as do for-profit or not-for-profit businesses in the private sector. Private companies are successful because non-performance means going out of business. NGOs are usually held to high standards and public scrutiny by those that provide them with funds. Non-performance results in less or no funding and an inability to function. But can the same be said for The World Bank, some United Nations agencies, or the European Union?

While laying claim to many success stories, the failures of these large development agencies are just as renowned, highlighted by the billions of dollars often wasted on ill-conceived or ill-planned schemes. Outright corruption is another cause of wasteful projects. Development history is rife with stories about multi-million dollar roads that go nowhere or large dams that produce little hydroelectric power or airports in places that serve no purpose. But despite the

---

[3]For an NGO dealing with the EU, the problems are legendary and the inefficiency of that organization is something to behold. The lack of accountability at the EU is easily recognized. NGOs entering into partnerships with the Italian Government do so at their own peril. There are cases where a grant agreement was signed and the NGO started activities using its own funds to initiate work because the government was slow to pay. After large sums were spent, the government realized it didn't have enough money and tried to change or cancel the agreement. However, the NGO had already advanced large amounts under the assumption the money was to be forthcoming. It is difficult for NGOs to remain solvent under this kind of arrangement.

failures and losses of huge amounts of money, none of the above-mentioned organizations suffer the ignominy of going bankrupt from a lack of recapitalization. There does not seem to be a strong culture that either condemns lack of success or holds these institutions accountable. They just go on doing business as usual.

One of my first introductions as to how these multi-million pound agencies are held to different accountability standards came on a trip to India in 1969. I spent part of this visit looking at agricultural projects in the northern part of the country and visited many poor rural villages. Water, either the lack of, or poor access to it, was a major problem. The Indian university hosting the visit was especially keen to have me see a scheme that had been funded by one of the major development banks. I thought my hosts were pushing such a field visit because it was an example of a great success. Sadly, they wanted it seen for the opposite reason.

In the district we visited, each of the villages was comprised of two or three different groups of people. The dominant group in each village were landowners. The others were either tenant farmers or performers of menial tasks. In much of India, group interactions are clearly defined as to what contacts can or cannot take place between groups. The sharing of food and water between the groups is one of those things that rarely, if ever, takes place.

In one village, it was noticed that an old well was strategically situated near the centre of a group of larger homes. It was easily accessible to the villagers living in those dwellings and there was a lot of activity around it. My hosts explained that this central well was only for the landowners. The lower caste group was denied access to it. About two kilometres from the village was a river. That was the water source for the second group.

The fetching of water has traditionally been a woman's role, thus women of the lower caste had to make at least two round trips each day to the river carrying their heavy water jars for eight kilometres. The development bank decided that to make life easier for the lower caste women, they would sink boreholes and provide wells much closer to where the women lived. When we visited this one village, my university colleagues took me a few hundred metres outside the centre to what looked like a newly constructed well. But this well had only little activity.

In discussions with women of the lower caste, they explained that the new well was hardly used. The women were still walking two kilometres down to the river and two kilometres back – twice daily. When asked why, they described the problems brought about by the new well. It seemed that the river, while far from the village, was an important meeting and socialization point for the lower caste women. It was actually a place they could legitimately go to get away from their husbands and children and have some privacy. The new well was too close to the village and took away their privacy. Not long after the well was constructed, the lower caste women became extremely unhappy and quickly abandoned it for the old water source at the river.

Since wells were being funded by the donor throughout the district, one could only surmise that there were a lot of other new wells not being used. This was a typical big donor solution to a problem. Just throw in money, dig boreholes and construct wells and the problem is solved. Only it wasn't. No one at this donor agency thought to look at the social and psychological impact on people that the new wells would have. You had to wonder if the designers of this project still had their jobs. I am sure they did.

To perpetuate their own existence, these large international or multinational organizations need to keep reinventing themselves. One might expect them to do so through major reorganizations or innovative programmes. More often than not they stay in business by doing neither. Rather they keep on going by proclaiming ten to twenty year grandiose campaigns or by carrying on with business as usual but inventing new jargon to give the "more of the same" a new twist.

The United Nations most often takes the lead in broadcasting goals for the next "decade" or the "millennium." The current "big push" is to "Make Poverty History" with the cancellation of debt owed by the world's poorest nations as the key component of this campaign (see next chapter). Over fifteen years ago, in 1990, a U.N. conference established a decade long target of universal primary school enrolment by the year 2000. The year 2000 came and went without every eligible child starting school. Did the U.N. promoters of the program stand up and announce failure? No! Instead, that year, the U.N. announced another set of idealistic but probably unachievable targets with the issuance of its Millennium Development Goals for the year 2015. Very quietly, the idea of universal primary school enrolment was incorporated into the new proclamation for 2015. I can hardly wait for 2015 to come around.

These grandiose schemes have little chance of achieving their targets. They are so theoretical and broad that here again, it is impossible to hold anyone or any organization accountable when the so-called "decade" comes to an end and the goals have not been achieved. In addition, everyone jumps on the bandwagon to support these extravagantly large plans. If proposed by the United Nations, it is then just about guaranteed that the other major lenders and donors will support the "millennium goals." Singing the same song will be the World Bank, the International Monetary Fund, the U.K.'s Department for International Development, the United States' Agency for International Development, and most of the other wealthy nations' foreign assistance agencies. With everyone on board, it makes it easy to diffuse the accountability question when the grand plans do not come to fruition. Just blame the other guy for the failures.

Taking what others have done and repackaging it is another "strength" of these international aid agencies. Forty to fifty years ago, the few NGOs that were primarily interested in long-term development realized that the solution to alleviating poverty was not easy. But they also knew it was not too complicated. The NGOs followed the strategy of "helping people to help themselves". The principles of their approach encompassed people participating in and taking responsibility for improving their own lives. This was the only way to bring about positive and prolonged change. The NGO partners coming in from outside could not really help people if they just "gave them what was needed" and then disappeared. The roots of this kind of approach were laid down in the 1920s and 1930s in Asia and by the 1960s, this type of developmental strategy was practiced by a number of NGOs in Asia, Africa, and Latin America.

Towards the end of the 1990s, UNDP, the United Nations Development Programme, came out with what they claimed was a "revolutionary" approach to improving conditions for the less fortunate around the world. With great fanfare and publicity, the gurus at UNDP, including the number one person called the Administrator, announced that the panacea for change was "Sustainable Development." Now what exactly is sustainable development? Well, it seemed the principles were: not giving handouts to the poor by those with money (the aid agencies and NGOs); a commitment for the long-term by those from the outside trying to help; getting those who were to be recipients of outside help to take part in planning the solutions to their problems; having those being helped assume responsibility for improving their own lives.

Sound familiar? It sure did to those NGOs who understood this was the only way to bring about real change and who had been practicing such an approach for decades. But now it was as if UNDP had discovered a miracle, as if the Administrator of this UN agency went up to the top of a high mountain and came down with stone tablets on which were engraved the ten commandments for helping people, summed up by the term SUSTAINABLE DEVELOPMENT. This term became the focal point for the large agencies, including the World Bank. Voluminous papers and treatises have been produced and the culmination of this "new" method was a massive U.N. sponsored conference on Sustainable Development held in Durban, South African in mid-2002. Following the customary pattern of such large U.N. sponsored meetings, millions of pounds were spent to hold the gathering and most knowledgeable observers agreed there was little to show for it.

Interestingly enough, in 2005 UNDP claimed another "coup," another great discovery that will help alleviate poverty around the world. It is as if they have someone in the agency that periodically climbs the mountain, has a revelation, and comes down with a new way to save mankind. They were calling their latest wonderful innovation "Community Conversations."

To those who have long worked in the development field, "Community Conversations" sounds an awful lot like "talking to the poor people whom you are trying to help and listening to what they say." It was back in the 1920s when Dr. Y.C. James Yen, who started the rural reconstruction movement in China, established a credo for working with communities. The credo went like this:

"Go to the people."

"Live among them."

"Learn from them."

"Plan with them."

"Work with them."

"Start with what they know."

"Build on what they have."

The above sounds as if eighty years ago, someone already realized that speaking with and listening to the poor was the way to go about helping them uplift themselves. But perhaps Dr. Yen did not have the same public relations staff available to him that UNDP has today. If he did, the credo could have been repackaged as "Community Conversations" and he would then have raised millions of dollars for his efforts.

In 1997, the World Bank thought up another revolutionary strategy for bringing about change. It coined the phrases "Commitment to Human Capital" or the "Development of Human Capital." Someone at the World Bank must have realized that people were valuable commodities, definitely worth something, and perhaps the donor community should invest in this human capital. I received an invitation to a meeting in Nairobi for leaders from the donor agencies, universities, and a few NGOs to hear about and discuss the World Bank strategy of Commitment to Human Capital.

As we sat in a plush Nairobi hotel for a day listening to speaker after speaker, it became clearer and clearer that they were talking about something that was more than vaguely familiar. It sounded very much like this new principle of Committing to Human Capital was a complicated way of stating the same thing that in simple terms could be presented as an investment in "training people." Training people had been the backbone of NGO activities since the time the first NGO was founded. There is probably not an NGO in existence that does not do training.

At that time as Chief Executive of AMREF, I had been struggling for a few years to raise £1.7 million we desperately needed to build a new training centre. Widely recognized as one of the leading health training NGOs in Africa, we had outgrown the physical space needed to carry out our work. Up to this time, we had presented our proposal to all the leading donor agencies, including the World Bank and UNDP, with little response and no success. Now I was sitting in a room with leading figures from these agencies and listening to them preach about what they were now calling human capital investments, or translated into layman's terms, training people.

During the discussion period, I just could not resist the urge to address the World Bank and UN representatives at the conference.

"Ladies and Gentleman, I have listened with fascination to this wonderful new development strategy you have proposed today, namely the commitment to human capital. I think every organization involved in development should, if they have not already done so, adopt this approach. I would hope that since you are promoting such an approach, your institutions would be generous and provide the funding necessary for those of us who want to implement it.

As a matter of fact, I have in my pocket a proposal that I would like to give to the World Bank people here today. I revised this proposal during our lunch break. It used to be called 'A Proposal to Build a New AMREF Training Centre.' But after listening to you today, the proposal has been revised and is now entitled 'Building an AMREF House for Investing in Human Capital.' While it may sound like the name of a brothel, I can assure you it is not and look forward to receiving a grant of £1.7 million so we can continue to train health professionals and volunteers throughout Africa."

My NGO and university colleagues in the audience greeted this little speech with much appreciation – the World Bank and other donor representatives with less than enthusiasm. Not unexpectedly, AMREF did not go home that day with £1.7 million in its project portfolio.

* * *

No one is better than the large development donor organizations at staying in business by reinventing themselves through the recycling of old ideas and presenting them wrapped in glossy new packaging. This recycling keeps countless people in jobs inventing new jargon, which leads to the production of massive amounts of paper used for producing policy documents, books, and manifestos. It can be argued that "recycling" is an important element in bringing about Sustainable Development – but not the above type of bureaucratic recycling.

CHAPTER 44

MR BONO AND MR GELDOF – GOOD TRY BUT...

How can we alleviate poverty and make life better for the millions and millions around the world who need help?

How can we especially help those in Africa where the needs of the poor are the greatest?

Does anyone have the answers to these questions?

By the year 2006, sadly no one had yet come up with a precise solution that would fix the problem of world poverty. In helping to focus on the issues, of all international leaders, Britain's Prime Minister, Tony Blair and his Chancellor of the Exchequer, Gordon Brown, get the highest marks. Their efforts to bring Africa's predicaments onto television screens and the front pages of newspapers are commendable. Mr. Blair's leadership recently mobilized the G8, the world's richest nations, to initially cancel debts owed by eighteen of the poorest countries. Over the past few years, debt relief has become the latest high profile panacea for dealing with poverty alleviation. In the United Kingdom, millions of people walked around wearing white rubber bands on their wrists, which supported the campaign slogan "Make Poverty History." Promoted by highly recognized celebrities such as Bono and Bob Geldof of rock music fame, and endorsed by business leaders such as Bill Gates, the advocates of debt relief seemed assured they now had, if not the total solution to ending poverty, at least the best and most important way to go forward. Will this turn out to be another in the previously mentioned long line of great schemes to save the world?

Over the past few decades, both poor and middle-income countries have been suffering from external debt burdens in relation to their capacity to service such debt. Of the external debt, the largest share is owed to bilateral donors (rich country governments) and multinational lending agencies, such as the International Monetary Fund (IMF) and the World Bank.

In short, the simple argument of the debt relief advocates is that countries have had to channel a larger percentage of their overall budgets to debt repayments than they have been able to allocate to health, education, and economic development, all three sectors crucial to helping the poor. They argue the debt burden on interest alone has taken money away from where it is needed most, and this still leaves the principal to be paid. The Make Poverty History campaign has been pushing a three part programme: (1) canceling all debt; (2) increasing foreign aid from donor nations, and; (3) better trade terms for developing countries.

While the debt relief advocates have made their case loud and clear (the G8 listened), the critics of such an approach have also been vocal. There are some sound arguments as to why the cancellation of debt will not be the real answer to reducing poverty.

First, most debt owed by the Heavily Indebted Poor Countries (HIPC) would not have been repaid anyway. Second, the G8 proposals will only apply to those countries that have followed conditions that have been set down by the World Bank and the IMF. There is little proof that these conditions have led to increased per capita growth or a reduction of poverty. Third, looking at the history of many countries included in the HIPC list, it might be unrealistic to expect that tax revenues freed up because of debt relief will be applied to health and education programmes. Fourth, there are over sixty countries that need immediate debt cancellation and the G8 proposal only covered eighteen. Fifth, there is a possibility that writing off the debt will enable some of the HIPC countries to begin borrowing again. Sixth, the net flow of financial resources to poor countries has been positive throughout the past few decades. New lending in the form of aid has been larger than the repayments on debt. The impression given in the G8 documents and other sources is that poor countries are being financially drained and that is not true. These are only some of the critics' arguments – they have put forth a number of others.

Clearly, there is no unanimous agreement that debt relief is the answer to the problems of world poverty. It is the current hot topic of the moment, like "sustainable development" was a few years back. Debt forgiveness might be part of the answer but more is needed. As yet, we do not know the other pertinent factors.

It is not inconceivable that in the near future, the answer or answers might be forthcoming. I can envision turning on our television sets one Sunday afternoon and tuning in to one of CNN's talk shows. What we will see on this future programme is a CNN interviewer speaking to a Radical Development Expert who claims to have the answers. What we might see and hear is the following:

"Good Afternoon: This is the CNN Sunday afternoon talk show. Today we have in the studio Mr. Radical Development Expert who claims he has the answers for alleviating poverty in Africa. Welcome Mr. Radical Development Expert to the show."

"Thank you. It is a pleasure to be here."

CNN Interviewer: "We have recently heard a great deal about debt cancellation being the solution to alleviating poverty. You have been one of its critics. It is easy to be a critic. Do you have any of the answers?"

Radical Development Expert: "Yes I do. Firstly, didn't I read in *Newsweek* that the recent debt relief plan of £21 billion for the eighteen poorest countries in the world is already in trouble? It has been reported that only four out of the eighteen might benefit. The other countries are now back into debt because of corruption and poor management. I have a two-tiered strategy that will definitely help to end poverty in Africa."

CNN Interviewer: "Could you please enlighten us?"

Development Expert: "The first thing I would do is to ask Bono and Bob Geldof and Bill Gates to actively promote my campaign to raise money for human cloning."

CNN Interviewer: "Human cloning? What does that have to do with alleviating poverty?"

Development Expert: "I would start with one African country. We need to clone Lee Kwan Yew, create an African version of him, and make the clone the absolute ruler of that country."

CNN Interviewer: "Lee Kwan Yew? Do you mean the former autocratic ruler of Singapore?"

Development Expert: "Yes. You see, the first thing we have to do for Africa is not build western types of democracy and not concentrate on economic development as a start. We have to find a Benevolent Dictator, a strong man who will rule with an iron fist but who will put the good of his country first. Initially, what he will have to do is put an end to corruption because corruption is the biggest hindrance to economic growth and poverty alleviation. It will take a strong but honest dictator to end corruption. Putting such a benevolent dictator in place will allow him to then concentrate on education for all in his country and to improve other social services such as health. When there is no longer corruption and good programmes are in place to educate people and improve their health, then conditions will be ripe for economic growth. With economic growth, there will be improvements in living standards and a decrease in poverty."

CNN Interviewer: "Are you saying Dictatorship is the answer to alleviating poverty?"

Development Expert: "Yes, Benevolent Dictatorship. That is why I want to clone an African Lee Kwan Yew. Look at what he did in Singapore. In Singapore you could be jailed for spitting your chewing gum on the floor. But no one can argue with the economic development and improvements in the standard of living. I know you will criticize me because this will put 'human rights' on the backburner. However, the western countries have made their first priorities for Africa issues such as creating democracy and canceling the debt. As I said, before you can have democracy you first need to eliminate corruption. And only a strong benevolent dictator in the mold of the former Singapore ruler can do that. Africa has had its fair share of dictators. But they have always had themselves and their friends as the primary beneficiaries of their rule. Perhaps the person who comes closest to the model I am presenting is President Yoweri Museveni of Uganda."

CNN Interviewer: "I have never heard anyone beside yourself advocate dictatorship as the solution to Africa's problems. You said you had a two-fold programme. Now I am almost afraid to ask what is the second part of your plan."

Development Expert: "That's OK. I will tell you. The second part of my plan is to cancel any ideas of debt relief."

CNN Interviewer: "You want to do away with the cancellation of debt? Then what do you propose?"

Development Expert: "I propose that instead of canceling HIPC debt, the western governments holding the debt should sell it to NGOs."

CNN Interviewer: "You want the debt sold to NGOs? How will that reduce poverty?"

Development Expert: "Allow me to present an example. Let us suppose that the Tanzanian Government owes the British Government £100 million. Instead of canceling the debt, I propose that the British Government sell the £100 million debt to an NGO it has confidence in for £1 million. The NGO will now hold the £100 million I.O.U. from the Tanzanian Government."

CNN Interviewer: "What good will that do for the NGO? Tanzania cannot afford to pay even £1 million of the £100 million debt so why would an NGO pay out the £1 million for it?"

Development Expert: "The NGO will go to the Tanzanian Government as it is now the owner of the £100 million debt. It will also state that it is not necessary for Tanzania to pay back £100 million. All the NGO wants paid off the debt is £2 million. One of the best things about this plan is the Tanzanian Government can pay the NGO the £2 million equivalent in Tanzanian shillings rather then in Sterling. Since Tanzanian shillings are worthless outside of Tanzania, the NGO must now spend the £2 million worth of shillings in Tanzania. The NGO will promise to spend the money on development programmes in health and education for the poorest people in Tanzania."

CNN Interviewer: "Slow down a moment. Please again explain for our viewers who will benefit from such an arrangement?"

Development Expert: "Everyone benefits. The British Government, who would never have been paid anything by Tanzania, will at least receive £1 million from the NGO. The NGO, who works in Tanzania anyway, will double the £1 million it would have spent in Tanzania. While it bought the £100 million debt from the British Government for £1 million, it will sell the entire £100 million debt back to the Tanzanian Government for the equivalent of £2 million in Tanzanian shillings. The Tanzanian Government will have reduced its debt by £98 million and will only have to pay the remainder in shillings, not hard currency. The poor in Tanzania will benefit because the NGO will spend double the amount it originally had on health and education. This is a better development model than just canceling the debt. Giving away something for free is not nearly as effective as having someone or some country pay at least a minimal price. Paying for something makes it appreciated more. A programme to sell the debt to NGOs who will then sell it back to the African countries at minimal cost is not a handout. And by entrusting the NGOs to spend the local currency payments on social sector projects, western donors who sell the debt for very little can be assured that the repayment will be well spent."

CNN Interviewer: "Most interesting. Isn't your proposal similar to a number of examples that took place in the late 1980s and 1990s in an NGO programme called 'Debt for Development?' I thought some NGOs did buy debt and used it the way you have described."

Development Expert: "You are correct. There was a Debt for Development programme whereby some NGOs did buy debt at largely discounted rates, paid the debt holder in hard currency, and collected almost face value from the host governments in local currency. There were a number of successful examples. Most of the purchased debt at the time involved private debt. It worked. It can work now with public debt."

CNN Interview: "Our time is up. Thank you for some interesting and perhaps controversial proposals. Goodbye."

I am not sure who this Radical Development Expert will be but he is likely to make a lot of sense.

CHAPTER 45

THE END

Towards the latter part of 2002, after retiring from AMREF, I had an opportunity to spend some time in Kenya reviewing the work of an NGO involved with grass roots community development activities. A trip was organized to visit one village close to Vihiga town in Western Province, about 350 kilometres from the capital of Nairobi and about forty kilometres from the city of Kisumu on Lake Victoria. This NGO had devised a microcredit scheme for granting small loans to village community groups who then used the money for income generating enterprises. Microcredit has become an important strategy in development. It is an important mechanism for making capital available to the poor. The poor rarely have access to borrowing from commercial banks because they lack credit ratings and the amounts of the desired loans are too small for the banks to consider commercially viable. In successful microcredit scenarios, small amounts of funds are made available to community groups rather than individuals. The groups take responsibility for ensuring repayment by their members and past experience has shown that such schemes have low default rates on the part of the borrowers.

There was really nothing exceptional about the microcredit programme this NGO was implementing in western Kenya. It followed a model that many others are putting into practice. What was out of the ordinary in this case was the composition of the village group that had borrowed the money. It was no ordinary assemblage of village people. The group consisted of twenty women and three men – the youngest of whom was seventy-two and the oldest, a woman of about eighty-six (the villagers claimed the latter had stopped counting a few years before).

These elderly folk had conceived a plan to make cooking oil from pressed sunflower seeds. With a loan from the NGOs microcredit scheme, they bought a pressing machine, hired a young man to work the machine, which required some level of strength, found a steady supply of sunflowers, developed a strong local market for the finished product, and became quite successful in selling an exceptionally healthy cooking oil. The elderly group, close to paying off the original loan, were already planning to apply for a second one. They intended to start growing their own supply of sunflowers on leased land so as to ensure a guaranteed future supply of seeds. The group was also looking to expand their market. Kisumu City was the first new market priority and they spoke ambitiously of selling to retailers in Nairobi.

Interestingly enough, the financial success of this project was not the most exciting result of what the NGO was implementing. In much of Kenya, as in all traditional rural societies, extended families have always been the social security blanket for older people. The elderly had a built-in family support system. But over the past twenty-five or so years, the extended family system has been breaking down not only in Kenya but also in many countries of Africa. Children and grandchildren have been migrating from rural areas to urban centres in order to find work. The elderly today are more and more being left alone to care for themselves. In this village group near Vihiga, just about all the older people lived alone with only periodic visits from family.

The NGO microcredit scheme provided a wonderful boost for the elderly sunflower oil group. It gave them a new lease on life. They were busy working hard to clean the seeds, ensuring the seeds were pressed properly, selling the oil, and meeting regularly to keep proper accounts and plan for expansion. And they loved every minute of what they were doing. It was wonderful to see the joy on their faces. There was a vibrancy and excitement not usually associated with older people in their 70s and 80s. They were inspiring and made one feel that there was much to look forward to as we advance in years. As an offshoot of a typical microcredit activity, this NGO had latched on to an important discovery – an innovative approach to dealing with the problems being encountered by the elderly as the traditional family structure continues to dissolve.

These pages have been filled with what at times probably appeared to the reader as cynicism towards organizations that are involved in trying to bring about a better life for many millions of people in Africa, Asia, and Latin America. Singled out have been The World Bank, parts of the United Nations system, the European Union, certain bilateral government donors, and some relief oriented NGOs. However, the same cynicism must be applied to myself. In a way, I am one of those who can be held up to the same criteria that I have subjected others to. It is true that at times, I wore one of those publicity seeking NGO T-shirts, made my living "off the poor," did not work my organization or myself out of jobs (having retired gracefully from an NGO still in existence), and have been part of the development "recycling" process. For in retirement, I have been recycled as a volunteer – having served on an Advisory Board of a large international NGO consortium and as Chairman of the Board of Trustees for another old and well-established charitable agency.

In reality, time spent as a volunteer is not so much different from the work one did in an earlier lifetime. The difference is that when you were formerly employed, there was remuneration attached to the job. As a volunteer, just as much work is often done but no income is associated with it. There are definite rewards attached to staying involved, sharing experiences and trying to offer whatever small contributions relevant past experiences will allow. But I can assure the reader that I am committed to never becoming an "FAO chicken expert."

In the final analysis, while there are many failures and problems in the world of "development work," there are many wonderful things that happen all the time. The young boy Wambua, who despite his physical handicap, shows courage, determination and a zest for life. Professor Nimrod Bwibo, who accomplished in his lifetime what it took three generations to achieve in some developed countries. And the elderly people near Vihiga who show us that life does truly get better after eighty. And one can only consider himself fortunate for having been a first hand witness to everything described in these pages – the good and the bad, the successes and the failures, the funny moments and the human failings on a large scale. All of this guaranteed a life that saw few dull moments.

CHAPTER 46

POSTSCRIPT

"I'm Ina Gerber."

"No you are not."

"Yes I am."

"Prove it!"

After considering a number of countries for the next stage of our lives – the golden years – we eventually decided on moving to southern Portugal. Other places had been contemplated (South Africa, New Zealand) but this beautiful country on the Iberian Peninsula was our final choice. The key factors leading to our decision were two – a mild Mediterranean climate and a somewhat "central location" in relation to family members who were scattered from California to Florida, from New York to Sevenoaks in the UK. We made a good choice. This is a beautiful country with wonderful people, tasty food, and good football, actually very good football.

Still, our introduction to Portugal was somewhat memorable; but it also made us feel right at home, given our adventures in other countries. The cause of this unforgettable introduction was the fact that my wife Ina, according to Portuguese bureaucracy, did not know who she was.

Moving from Kenya at the end of September 1998, our household furniture and other items had to be packed, inventoried, and shipped to Portugal. A professional moving company was contracted to undertake this. The movers came to our Nairobi house and accomplished the packing in one day. Before leaving, they went over the inventoried items with Ina, checked to ensure everything was listed, and issued a formal inventory document, which was necessary for clearing the goods through customs at the Portugal end. Being non-European Union citizens, there were many regulations we had to comply with before we were able to become permanent residents of Portugal. Ina confirmed everything was O.K. and signed the document "Ina Gerber." Now the fun began.

We were told that shipping goods by sea from Kenya to Portugal would take between thirty to forty-five days. That timetable would have allowed us to receive the container sometime during the first two weeks of November.

The container did arrive as scheduled. However, in November 1998, there was a major strike by workers in the Port of Lisbon where our goods would be cleared before being sent by road to our new home in Portimao. The container could not be offloaded from the ship and approved by Portuguese Customs until the strike was settled. That settlement came at the end of November.

At the beginning of December, the telephone at home rang.

"Is this Senhor Michael S Gerber?"

"Yes, I am Michael Gerber."

"This is Portuguese Customs in Lisbon. There is a container here with an inventory list of household goods for Michael S Gerber."

"Finally it has arrived. Can you please quickly clear it so we can have our furniture?"

"Sorry, you cannot have this container."

"Why not?"

"The clearance document lists the owner of the goods as Michael S Gerber."

"Yes, that is me so what is the problem?"

"The paper is signed by Ina Gerber. That is a different person. We will have to impound the container."

"But Ina Gerber is my wife! We have been married for thirty-six years and we are still together. We own everything jointly. She is right here. Do you want to speak with her?"

"Sorry, there are two different people involved here. We cannot clear the goods."

Welcome to Portugal. Every country has its bureaucracy and red tape. Having spent so much time in different places, we were well aware of that and prepared for unexpected eventualities. But how do we now convince the Portuguese authorities that we were married and everything we owned belonged to both of us?

Through simple analysis, the situation seemed clear. The customs document listed me as the owner of the goods. Unfortunately, I didn't sign the document. Ina did. Now all we had to prove was we were husband and wife. Or so we thought. Actually, proving we were married was the easy part. Proving Ina was Ina turned out to be much more complicated.

After a number of inquiries, we were told we would have to go to Portimao's Registry Office and provide documents that showed we were married. We found our marriage certificate issued by the State of New York. To be on the safe side, we also brought along our birth certificates, passports, and a copy of the inventory list given to us by the shipping company. Ina was born in the Ukraine and became a naturalized American citizen after moving to the United States. Therefore, we also took along her citizenship papers. What else could be missing?

The woman in the Registry Office was sympathetic and listened carefully to our problem. We needed a notarized certification that we were married for the customs people in Lisbon. She looked carefully at our marriage license and then asked to see all the other documents as well. Finally, she said:

"You have a problem. I cannot give you what you need."

"Why not?"

"I can accept that you are married. But that is not the problem. I don't know who your wife is."

"What?"

"Look at the customs inventory list. It is signed by Ina Gerber."

"Yes."

"Now look at her passport. The passport lists her as Ina O Gerber. And look at the marriage license and the citizenship papers. It lists her as Ina Olynyk. If Ina Olynyk married Michael S Gerber, she should be Ina Olynyk Gerber. I do not know who she is – is she Ina Gerber, Ina O Gerber, or Ina Olynyk Gerber? Her signature on the inventory paper doesn't match the names on the other documents."

No amount of explaining and pleading was going to convince the woman that Ina was actually all three. And unless we could convince her, we would be sleeping on the floor in retirement while our furniture would be rotting in Lisbon.

"Alright, what do we have to do to prove Ina is actually all three people combined into one?"

"Firstly, you will need to come back to this office with two Portuguese witnesses who are legal residents of Portimao and who have voted in the last election. The two witnesses must then swear an oath before the President of the City Council that in effect, Ina Gerber, Ina O Gerber, and Ina Olynyk Gerber are one and the same person. Then Mrs. Gerber must swear the same oath before the President. After everyone swears to that fact, I will issue you with the proper document that will allow you to have your goods cleared by customs."

"But we just moved here from Kenya. We do not yet know two Portuguese residents of Portimao to have them attest to the fact that Mrs. Gerber is Mrs. Gerber."

"Sorry, but that is the rule."

Outside we went and standing on a street corner in the middle of Portimao, our various options were examined. We could hold up a sign that would read "1000 Escudos (about £3) to anyone willing to come with us to the Registry Office and serve as a witness." I figured we would have no trouble having people sign up quickly. Ina nixed that idea. She was one step ahead of me.

"Why not go the estate agent's office that arranged for us to buy our house? The Portuguese staff there at least knows us because of the house sale. Perhaps they can give us some idea as to what we could do."

This proved to be the answer to our prayers. After explaining our predicament and everyone having a good laugh, the Portuguese lawyer working in that office, along with one of the secretaries told us they would come to the Registry Office and serve as our witnesses. We didn't even have to offer them the £3. Bless them. And that is exactly what happened. In the end, the Portuguese authorities accepted the fact that Ina and I were really husband and wife and that Ina Gerber, Ina O Gerber, and Ina Olynyk Gerber were one and the same person. Yes, we had our furniture for Christmas. And we felt right at home in Portugal.